SOCIALIST INVESTMENT CYCLES

International Studies in Economics and Econometrics

VOLUME 27

The titles published in this series are listed at the end of this volume.

Socialist Investment Cycles

Analysis in Retrospect

Peter Mihályi

United Nations Economic Commission for Europe, Geneva
and Institute of Economics of
The Hungarian Academy of Sciences, Budapest

SPRINGER-SCIENCE+BUSINESS MEDIA, B.V.

Library of Congress Cataloging-in-Publication Data

Mihályi, Peter.
Socialist investment cycles : analysis in retrospect / by Peter Mihályi.
p. cm. -- (International studies in economics and econometrics ; v. 27)
Includes bibliographical references and index.
ISBN 978-0-7923-1973-3 ISBN 978-94-011-2676-2 (eBook)
DOI 10.1007/978-94-011-2676-2
1. Communist countries--Economic policy. 2. Capital investments--Communist countries. 3. Central planning--Communist countries.
I. Title. II. Series.
HC704.M464 1992
338.947--dc20 92-31351

ISBN 978-0-7923-1973-3

Originally published by Kluwer Academic Publishers in 1992

To Judit, Eszter and Dávid

Table of contents

List of tables

List of charts

List of Abbreviations and Symbols

For countries

Bul	Bulgaria
CSSR	Czechoslovakia
GDR	German Democratic Republic
Hun	Hungary
Pol	Poland
Rom	Romania
EE6	Six east European countries (Bulgaria, CSSR, GDR, Hungary, Poland, Romania)
USSR	Soviet Union
EE7	Six east European countries plus the USSR
EE8	EE7 plus Yugoslavia

For publications and data sources

ASR	*Anuarul Statistic al României* (Romanian statistical yearbook)
BÉ	*Beruházási Évkönyv* (Hungarian investment yearbook)
ECE/DEAP	United Nations Economic Commission for Europe, Division for Economic Analysis and Projections
HSR	*Historická statistická rocenka* (CSSR, Historical statistics)
KS	*Kapitalnoye stroitel' stvo* (Soviet data compendium on investments)
Nkh	*Narodnoe khozyaistvo SSSR* (Soviet statistical yearbook)
RS	*Rocznik Statystyczny* (Polish statistical yearbook)
RSI	*Rocznik Statystyczny Inwestyczji* (Polish investment yearbook)
SG	*Statisticki Godisnjak* (Yugoslav statistical yearbook)
SÉ	*Statisztikai Évkönyv* (Hungarian statistical yearbook)
SR	*Statistická rocenka* (Czechoslovak statistical yearbook)
SYA	*Statistical Yearbook of Albania* (Albania, bilingual edition)
UN BUL	United Nations Economic Commission for Europe, *Economic Bulletin for Europe* (annual series)
UN ESA	United Nations Economic Commission for Asia and the Far East, *Economic Survey of Asia* (annual series)
UN ESE	United Nations Economic Commission for Europe, *Economic Survey of Europe* (annual series)

For economic variables

A	Amplitude
AGRC	Gross output of the arable (crop) sector of agriculture
AGRL	Gross output of the livestock sector of agriculture
AGRT	Gross agricultural output
b	Capital intensity
CGINV	Volume of investment completions
di	Logarithmic growth rate of GINV (lnginv - lnginv<1>)
D(t)	Total volume of unsatisfied (delayed) demand arising from ongoing investment projects
EMPC	Number of employees in construction
EMPI	Number of employees in industry
GDP	Gross domestic product (SNA)
GFCF	Gross fixed capital formation (SNA)
GINV	Gross fixed capital formation (MPS)
GSP	Gross social product (MPS)
INDT	Gross industrial output
IND (A)	Output of Group "A" in industry
IND (B)	Output of Group "B" in industry
i(t)	Annual investment outlays (=GINV)
IR	Investment ratio (GINV/NMP or GFCF/NMP)
NMP	Net material product produced (= national income in MPS)
NMPUT	Net material product used
NYUA	Accumulation from NMPUT
NYUAF	Fixed capital formation from NMPUT
NYUAI	Inventory formation from NMPUT
NYUCC	Collective consumption from NMPUT
s	Savings rate
S(t)	Total planned costs of all contemporaneous investment starts
t, T	Time
UGINV	Changes in the stock of uncompleted investments
ΣUGINV	Stock of uncompleted investments
y	Total incomes generated in a given year
ß	Realisation coefficient
σ	Coefficient of variation
Θ	Phase
∩	Frequency

MISCELLANEOUS

BR	Bureaucratic rationality
CMEA	Council for Mutual Economic Assistance
CPE	Centrally planned economy
CPSU	Communist Party of the Soviet Union
FYP	Five-year plan
ICM	Investment commitment model
ICP	International Comparison Project
KSH	Central Statistical Office (Hungary)
MPS	Material Product System of National Accounts (CMEA)
NBER	National Bureau of Economic Research (USA)
NEM	New Economic Mechanism (in Hungary)
OECD	Organisation for Economic Co-operation and Development
SEP	Shortage economy paradigm
SITC	Standard International Trade Classification (UN)
SNA	System of National Accounts (UN)
SOE	State-owned enterprise
UN/ECE	United Nations Economic Commission for Europe

SYMBOLS

...	Not available
.	Not applicable
-	Magnitude not zero, but less than half of the unit employed
0	Magnitude zero

Preface

by *Peter J. D. Wiles*
Professor Emeritus
University of London

There are two sorts of writers of prefaces: the obliging and the disobliging. Surely Peter Mihályi knows where to place me in this taxonomy. For the most part I write my own irrelevant opinions, but there was one act of gross interference: my insistence on a point he had already quietly made, the greater stability of the production of consumer goods under Communism even of food, if we exclude bad harvests. The many Marxist and some other scholars who wrote about Dr. Mihályi's subject discarded consumption *a priori*. They looked at investment only because they displayed marked fluctuations and so were grossly misleading, because they underplayed the greater stability of Communism at GNP level.

It seems that this neglect is ideological, or at least due to a quirk of Karl Marx's own assumptions and attitudes. This quirk was shared by Albert Aftalion who was one of the first economists to state a theory of investment fluctuations: a version of the accelerator. He was not a Marxist but had clearly read him, and his accelerator smacked of engineering and the supply side. Naturally the theory contained and was meant to contain no multiplier; so it left consumption stable. It also omitted that great third force, stock exchanges and international finance. Happily for us we leave that force alone, because Communism had not the institutions that allow it to exist.

But even Communists consume, so how lucky they were not have a multiplier! If only the Western world today (March 1992) had none, so that an investment downturn (or was it a consumption downturn? it hardly matters) had not propagated itself to produce a general international slump! True, the system reigning in Eastern Europe and the USSR until 1990 hardly had, and managers did not understand, any macro-economics. Nor did they need to, except in some cases of hyper-inflation. Micro-markets are excellent, and we have done right to give this concept the hard sell in the East. But 'market forces' are macro, and very dangerous. Even the multiplier and the stock exchange are dangerous. We do not know how to control them ourselves.

Indeed these macro-market forces cause not merely "cycles", which are by definition at least a little predictable and comport less risk, but also "fluctuations", which Mihályi very justly defines as unpredictable in height and depths as well as length. There are scarcely any serious cycles in a Communist command economy, and it is difficult to understand how they ever became a serious subject of study. For their causes are always either external (the world slump of the 1930s) or "Politburogenic" (i.e. political decisions independent of the state machine and the way the economy normally functions, like rearmament during the Korean War, or agricultural collectivization, or the Bulgarian decision in 1961 to imitate China's Great Leap Forward); or natural (a bad harvest).

Both "cycles" and "fluctuations" characterize capitalism more. Eastern Europe has been plunged into these two, at the same time as having to learn to handle Adam Smith's great discovery, the micro-market. Perhaps at macro-level it has something to teach us? If so, the history of its cycles and fluctuations will be valuable indeed. Retrospectively many aspects of the Communist economies will have to be re-examined, partly because we know the end of the story but partly because new materials are coming to the surface.

Acknowledgements

I should like to thank my Hungarian colleagues at the *Institute of Economics* - T. Bauer, I. Berend, A. Bródy, A. Halpern, M. Lackó, I. Major, Gy. Molnár, A. Simonovits and A. K. Soós for extensive and extremely helpful discussions around various drafts of this work. Comments and suggestions were also received from J. Arvay, Gy. Szilágyi working at the *Central Statistical Office* in Hungary, as well as from J. M. van Brabant, B. Cohen, P. Hanson, D. Hesse, M. C. Kaser, R. Nötel, J. Slater, M. Virén and C. Wittich (staff members and consultants of the *United Nations* in New York and Geneva). Whilst the forenamed are indeed responsible for the absence of various flaws from the following work, they bear no responsibility for those which remain.

I am presently associated with the *United Nations Economic Commission for Europe* in Geneva. Although this working environment has been invaluable in helping me to round off important portions of this study, it bears stressing that the views expressed in this book are my own and do not imply expression of any opinion on the part of the United Nations.

In several paragraphs scattered in Chapters 3 and 4 I have drawn, more or less freely, on my previously published works and I wish to thank the editors of *Economics of Planning* and *Soviet Studies* for permitting me to do so. Early drafts of these two articles provided the basis for papers presented at two conferences devoted to the issues discussed in this book.[1] Conversation and correspondence with the participants of these meetings (A. Bajt, Ch. Bettelheim, B. Chavance, C. Frateschi, I. Grossfeld, B. W. Ickes, G. Roland and J. Sapir) have greatly helped me in understanding the complexity of the problem.

Finally, I would like to express my gratitude to John Slater and David Williams for friendly help to turn my rugged, Hungaro-Germanic style of English into a more effective vehicle of communication with the English speaking academic community.

[1] *Régulation, cycles et crises dans les économies socialistes* (École des Hautes Études en Sciences Sociales, Paris, March 1986) and *Fluctuations and Cycles in Socialist Economies* (University of Padua, March 1987). The materials of both conferences are already available in book form (Chavance 1987a, Frateschi 1989a).

INTRODUCTION AND SUMMARY OF MAIN POINTS

THE BROADER FRAMEWORK

The entire world was taken by surprise when 1990 brought an end to Soviet-type communism in Europe and thus a genuine end to World War II. In the 45 years since 1945, temporary solutions which had been the result of a specific military situation, had ossified into political and economic structures. First, Germany was divided in two. Very soon communist regimes were imposed on eight countries in Europe and then later on many more countries on three other continents. As time passed by, everybody came to acquiesce in these arrangements. However, with the crumbling of the Berlin Wall, the fragility of this empire became obvious in the twinkling of an eye. Within a year the German Democratic Republic disappeared from the map and this development shook the entire post-Yalta system to its foundations.

This evolution was spontaneous, driven by complex interactions among the party leaders of the USSR, the GDR, Poland and Hungary. Communist rule was not overcome by a block of enemy states, nor by its own internal opposition. At the time of collapse - during the autumn of 1989 - the economic machinery of these countries was still working adequately.

The fact that these developments took not only the leaders and the people of the countries concerned but also scholars by surprise is an extraordinary challenge to the students of Soviet-type economies. In the academic world, where predictive force is one of the key indicators of a successful theory, this weak performance calls into question the validity of earlier findings and interpretations. Something was wrong in the general framework.

This book offers a tentative, and necessarily partial, explanation of this intellectual failure. From the first page to the very last, everything in this book revolves around the theory of socialist investment cycles - a laboriously built concept, which, as I believe, has also been proved wrong. The reader is kindly asked to keep always in mind (and occasionally the author will try to help him in doing so) that our deliberations on the investment cycle serve a more ambitious purpose: help to pave the way to a better understanding of the structure of socialist systems and the outcome of this 70 year long adventure. Retrospectively, it is clear that the causes of the collapse were more socio-political than economic. The theory of socialist investment cycles, as I see it, was misconceived precisely at this point. In explaining the fluctuations of investments, socio-political factors were deliberately discarded and non-recurring or country-specific factors were elevated at the level of theory.

In this book, an attempt is made to extend the frontier of analysis beyond Eastern Europe and the Soviet Union and to include those developing countries which at some point in their history had opted for Soviet-type communism. Undoubtedly, this is a debatable decision. Compared to Eastern Europe or the USSR, these countries had a much shorter history and they worked with ramshackle economic institutions. On the other hand, these countries shared three important characteristics of all Soviet type economies and this justifies their inclusion in our sample.

Firstly, these countries were all command economies in the narrowest sense of the word. By its very nature, this means that the most important economic decisions are placed in the hands of a few individuals (very often a *single* individual), in contrast to market economies, where developments are shaped by the interaction of a large number of economic agents. Secondly, all these countries committed themselves to the use of the medium and the long term plan, an instrument which in itself was often perceived as the main explanation of periodic fluctuations. Thirdly, the data problems we encounter are - in their essence - not very much different from those we experience in the study of the more developed socialist countries.

Although it would be an exaggeration to assert that there was not a single person in the academic world who foresaw this kind of collapse, I think it is not far from the truth to say that until 1988-1989 the majority of the economic profession rejected doomsday scenarios.[1] The consensus view was that the system worked. It operated in its own ways but it functioned. Through the help of traditional mechanisms of adaptation, it was surmised, the ruling elites would always be able to overcome temporary economic difficulties.

This assessment rested on three different, yet inseparable, motives or levels of argumentation usually followed by Eastern and Western economists alike: (i) the model approach, (ii) the adherence to a value-free vocabulary and the reliance almost exclusively on printed evidence, and (iii) the commitment to economic reforms.

(i) Economic models and universal theories are always based on abstraction. In this sense the distortion of reality of a complex, rapidly evolving world is intentional. It also flows almost inevitably from the logic of model building that in the process of discarding superfluous elements, the selection criteria are consistency and workability.[2] A model of a system contains no more and no less detail than is logically required to mimic the self-sustaining behaviour of the system. As was often said, the task of economic science was to explain how the socialist system worked and not to demonstrate - what was known anyway - that this system was full of deficiencies.

Economists, like scientists in general, do not like to intrude into the business of other professions. The shoemaker should stick to his last. But, as Wiles (1982) persistently argued, economic events in general - and economic turns in the socialist countries in particular - need not have economic causes, nor political events political causes. Endogenous reasoning is the product of the existence of separate university departments rather than a description of the real world.

(ii) The adherence to a value-free vocabulary was partly justified as an individual survival strategy for economists living in the socialist countries. It served also as an admission ticket for Easterners and Westerners alike to Western academic circles, where such behaviour was considered as a part of civilized manners. Indeed, to claim that the socialist system does not work - in the sense that it goes from bad to worse - was undoubtedly a highly normative statement, which was not even necessarily true when only one or a sample of issues were examined (e.g., economic growth, the state of agriculture, foreign competitiveness, etc.).

Moreover, research was seriously hampered by the secretiveness and dishonesty of the communist regimes. Irrevocable facts could not be documented at all or published documents stated the complete opposite of the truth. In this jungle world, the outright questioning of available documents, statistics and the scholarly work of hundreds of fellow economists required a certain degree of Don Quixotism.

[1] Perhaps Birman's (1989) article came the closest to what actually happened: "I am not saying that the [Soviet - P.M.] economy will collapse next Thursday morning, but it is a possibility in the relatively close future, during this millennium." (p. 46)

[2] This caveat is needed, if allowance is made for the existence of such new directions of research as chaos and catastrophe models. These models, however, were not used for the interpretation of socialist economies.

(iii) The majority of theoretical economists were - in one way or another - involved in and emotionally committed to the idea of economic reforms. This applied to economists working on both sides of the Iron Curtain. Reform, by definition, means the amendment of what is defective, vicious, corrupt or depraved in an otherwise feasible and alluring system. Reform thinking did not exclude criticism of the existing setup but it was hardly compatible with a downright rejectionist stand concerning the viability of an entire system.

ISSUES INVOLVED IN THIS BOOK

While it would not be appropriate to set out the relevant issues in detail at this point - for that is precisely the function of this book - they may be summarized in twelve points. The various qualifications and explanations will be considered later on. Sacrificing elegance, I give a sharp statement of the principal propositions, hoping that this will help to convey my ideas.

1. Together with the "shortage economy paradigm" (SEP), the theory of socialist investment cycles is one of the most popular, elaborated and formalized frameworks for understanding what happens in a socialist economy. Both of them are the product of a theoretical effort to pinpoint the "invisible hand" operating within that system.

The theory of socialist investment cycles is inseparable from a particular perception of socialism. In many versions of the model, the concepts of planning and shortages are the main theoretical building blocks. Investment planning is claimed to mean physical planning. On the surface, it might appear that planners distribute monetary funds among alternative utilization possibilities but as understood in this perception of socialism, physical quantities of raw materials, equipment and labour power are allocated. Planning and the SEP are strongly interdependent concepts. On the one hand, a bureaucratic distribution system, based on physical allocation of resources continuously regenerates shortages. This is inevitable and occurs largely because plans which appeared to be balanced on paper, are - in reality - replete with internal inconsistencies from the very outset.

In general, discussions of cyclical fluctuations mean a critique of the existing economic mechanism. Nonetheless, when partisans of the investment cycle theory insisted that there was a certain type of regularity, a deterministic rule behind these investment fluctuations, indirectly they acquitted economic policy makers of their responsibility. In the light of their model, policy makers were not responsible for the fluctuations, since they were only cogs in their own perpetuum mobile.

The debate over investment cycles was important from a practical point of view, too. If the socialist economy has a built-in tendency to generate investment cycles, then a carefully calibrated anti-cyclical policy might help to stabilize it. By contrast, if the investment cycle theory is faulty or unfounded, the pursuit of an anti-cyclical policy is not only pointless but may even be harmful.

2. Various models describing the same phenomenon but based on different lines of thought and yielding different numerical results, cannot be simultaneously correct.

According to the protagonists of the investment cycle theory, the observed or estimated length of the investment cycle varies between 2 and 12 years. This is not plausible. It is difficult to believe that any economist's behavioural formulation is as good as any other's, and that it is simply an empirical question of which fits the data best. A more acceptable conclusion is to say that these models taken individually do explain a part of the truth but this portion is rather small.

3. *There are three rival approaches to explain the fluctuations of gross fixed investments (GINV) experienced by the socialist countries.*

One can express the essence of the three schools by the following equations:

(1) *Control theory model*:

$GINV = f_1 (Q_1, \dots Q_n)$,
where $Q_1, \dots Q_n$ are system-invariant economic factors and **n** is a relatively small number.

(2) *Endogenous cycle theory model*

$GINV = f_2 (Q_1, \dots Q_n)$,
where $Q_1, \dots Q_n$ are system-specific economic factors and **n** is a relatively small number.

(3) *Theory of exogenous fluctuations*

$GINV = f_3 (Q_1, \dots Q_n)$,
where $Q_1, \dots Q_n$ denotes economic, political and other factors and **n** is a relatively large number.

The essential flaw in the first two frameworks is the deterministic explanation of investment fluctuations. In addition, the endogenous cycle theory does not differentiate between regularities in cross-country comparison and regularities in time, although this would be crucial from a systemic point of view. The endogenous theory is strong in providing explanation and evidence for the first type of regularities but it is less convincing in its attempt to demonstrate that the subsequent investment waves in a given country are all explicable in a common endogenous framework.

The main objective of this book is to deliver strong arguments in favour of the third approach, which focuses on the exogenous elements of the entire story, by making a clear distinction between cycles and fluctuations.

4. *The term "cycle" is justified if and when a time series exhibits the three Rs: recurrence, reinforcement and regularity.*

In the context of fighting against Marxist dogmatism, an accurate distinction between "fluctuations" and "cycles" had little importance. For many decades the term used was a question of formulation and not of substance. For most authors speaking of "cycle", "quasi-cycle", "non-uniform growth", "fluctuation", or "uneven development" all meant very much the same. Serious analysis, however, cannot live without a clear distinction between cycles on the one hand and fluctuations or its synonyms on the other. Cycles are predictable but fluctuations are not.

5. *Once we proceed from the assumption that investment fluctuations must have somehow originated in the planning process, it is not easy to find purposeful starting and end-years for empirical investigations.*

Thinking about the starting point of analysis, many authors have thought that the investment cycle could be meaningfully analyzed only in the post-1960 period, as the impact of politics had been too strong in the years before. When these analysts looked for a meaningful cut-off date, they made a case for distinguishing "planning" in a reformed socialist economy from "direct planning", which was abolished in some countries at a later stage of communist rule. Retrospectively, it is clear that the various reform attempts to overhaul the planning system had not brought about fundamental changes. It is more appropriate to consider the post-war period in its entirety and to put less emphasis on elements of discontinuity.

This argument holds not only in time but in a regional context as well. Yugoslavia and a dozen other socialist countries cannot be excluded from the investigation just because central planning has played a minor role in their development.

6. *The size of observed investment variations in the socialist countries is not significantly different from Western standards.*

This result was achieved by a very simple calculation (coefficient of variation) for a sample of socialist and market economy countries. The results did not reveal any standard pattern for explaining country specific differences. By contrast, the Soviet Union exhibited much smaller variation than any Western country, or most countries of Eastern Europe.

7. *The seemingly fluctuation-free Soviet investment behaviour is largely a statistical artefact.*

Investment fluctuations were seldomly regarded by scholars of the Soviet economy as a portentous subject. There was a general belief that this kind of instability was a typical East European "disease". After a closer examination of the underlying investment series, however, it can be shown that the relatively good Soviet performance was chiefly due to two types of data distortion: the impact of hidden military expenditures and the use of improper price deflators.

8. *Contrary to widespread beliefs there is no strong relationship between fluctuations in investment demand on the one hand and labour market developments on the other.*

Socialism is a system without the Keynesian multiplier. The absence of regular spill-over from changes in investments to changes in the demand for labour can be well demonstrated by the facts, and it is likely that the propagation hypothesis is not tenable for other suspected cycle relevant macro-variables (foreign trade, consumption, etc.), either. The centralized political and monetary system had extremely powerful instruments to stop spill-over effects from one production sector into the other, from the sphere of investments to the sphere of employment and consumption.

9. *It is erroneous to believe that large investment projects were the main culprits of investment fluctuations.*

Many economists are inclined to attach central importance to a subset of total investments, notably the total volume of centrally-financed large investment projects. They assume that the amount of resources tied up in them has a decisive impact on the short-term equilibrium situation.

Empirically, however, it can be demonstrated that at the macro-level, the gestation period (lead time) of the average investment project is between 1 and 2 years. This is too short to explain a phenomenon which recurs in every 3-4 years. On the other hand, the lead time of truly large projects is somewhere between 8 and 12 years.

It is true, however, that in the minds of central planners macro-economic policy was equated with control over a few dozen large investment projects, while real macro issues, such as global fiscal and monetary control, were almost totally neglected. Unfortunately this wholly mistaken judgement concerning the importance of large investment projects was even corroborated by the proponents of the investment cycle theory.

10. *A non-trivial part of investment fluctuations is the result of deliberate policy synchronization.*

In the 1950s and 1960s, and again in the late 1980s, U-turns in domestic investment strategies were politically initiated. The regional synchronization effect was indirect (and therefore somewhat approximate only) since these political changes were the echoes of shifts in Soviet domestic policies. Intra-CMEA trade played only a minor role in the transmission process.

In the second half of the 1970s, the impact of Western trade developments became much more important in all socialist countries. First, by using borrowed Western money, an otherwise unsustainable investment boom had been created. Later, the conduct of domestic investment policy was constrained in the opposite direction as the countries proved to be unable to service their accumulated debt from the yields of these debt-financed investment projects. In most cases the reduction in the volume of annual investments was the only remedy to reduce the need for larger cuts in current consumption.

11. *There is no single way to remove the trend effect from the investment time series.*

Econometrically based cycle analysis cannot live without trend fitting and a strict interpretation of periodicity. Experience has shown that several types of trends can be fitted to the original data but due to the presence of autocorrelation, the estimated coefficients are not reliable. In addition, it can be shown that such detrended time series have very different statistical properties, depending on the way they were generated.

There are several methods to test time series for the presence of cyclical factors. The more sophisticated ones (periodogram, spectral analysis) however, require rather large samples ($n > 50$ at least). If this requirement is not fulfilled, mechanically applying the tests suggests that the time series contain nothing else but a random walk. A simple method based on the analysis of turning points in the time series of annual growth rates yields similar results, though not for all countries.

12. *The measurement errors in our investment data are endogenous and cannot be considered as random.*

It is very odd that the traditional analysis of socialist investment cycles, which aimed to shed light on systemic differences, never examined the underlying data for systemic errors. These are intrinsic problems, deeply rooted in the socio-economic texture of the socialist countries.

i) In the absence of reliable data sources, the role of variables which are potentially relevant to explaining cycles (budgetary deficit, money supply, balance-of-payments, defence expenditures, harvest) cannot be properly analyzed.

ii) In many relevant series the absence of quarterly or monthly data - as distinct from annual - is another serious data problem.

iii) The precision of investment related data, such as gross and net investments, the value of completed and uncompleted construction, investment commitment and investment scattering, varies enormously. This problem is particularly relevant in such investigations, where an attempt is made to explain changes in relatively "hard" data by reference to reported movements in "soft" variables.

iv) Mishandling of the basic investment data is widespread. This problem manifests itself most sharply in Soviet statistics, where a good part of defence expenditures appears to have been hidden among the investment figures. Hence, it is very likely that the independent dynamics of such expenditures neutralized the impact of "true" investment fluctuations.

v) Issues which are seemingly methodological represent another source of problems. The treatment of capital repairs is a good example. In socialist countries, statistics have subserviently followed the constantly changing internal rules of planning and taxation. Hence the statistical separation of these categories was far from consistent. In addition, the underlying instability of planning and accounting rules opened the way for abuse and misreporting at the micro level.

vi) Many difficulties of quantitative analysis originate in biased price indices. Here the problem is that the magnitude of hidden price changes may tend to change simultaneously with the "true" volume fluctuations.

vii) Finally, it is important to note that in cases where alternative investment series are available from independent statistical sources, the cyclical properties of these series are very different from those of the so-called "official" data.

1. GENERAL FRAMEWORK

1.1 THREE SCHOOLS

There are three rival approaches explaining the fluctuations of fixed investments experienced by the socialist countries. In describing these theories, I shall first give a brief overview, followed by a more detailed exposition later in Chapter 2.

The first family of models does not attempt to build a causal relationship between wave-type movements in investments and the intrinsic features of the socialist order or of the particular type of economic management system within this order. The fluctuations are interpreted within the framework of *control theory*, which claims a general applicability in all societies. In the final analysis, the theory holds, investment fluctuations stem from technical progress. Due to the complexity of the modern world in general and the time required to create a large investment project in particular, it is theoretically impossible to operate an economic control mechanism free from frictions or fluctuations. In every economy there is a latent possibility that fluctuations may turn into cycles. Whether this metamorphosis occurs or not is a question of macro-economic proportions. Only these proportions, and not some country- or system-specific features, are responsible for the emerging cycles.

The second school looks at investment fluctuations as a necessary outcome of certain intrinsic features of the socialist economies. The explanation is deduced from the internal logic of the investment regime. This justifies the appellation of "cycle". Tensions and imbalances emerge within the investment sphere, which later make the slowdown of capital formation unavoidable. Tensions do not disappear in the deceleration phase either but simply weaken. This temporary improvement, however, gives enough ground for the decision makers to accelerate the process once again. Hence, according to this approach, investment fluctuations are essentially *endogenous*.

In fact, the theory claims more than this. The investment regime is regarded as the "heart" or "engine" of the socialist economy. The theory implies that fluctuations in investments are usually transmitted to other macro-economic variables, such as industrial output and productivity, construction and foreign trade, as well as to the markets for consumer goods and labour.[1] At first sight, it may seem that this alleged multiplier effect is identical with the observed properties of capitalist business cycles. But this is not true. The theory of endogenous socialist investment cycles holds investment fluctuations responsible for all kinds of other fluctuations. Consequently, this theory embodies a different concept of the cycle in comparison with conventional western business cycle analysis, where - apart from the highly theoretical works of Keynes and his followers - fixed capital formation does not have such a preeminent, all-determining role. While I share in many respects the views of the authors belonging to the second school, I do not agree with their final results or the implications thereof.

A third approach puts forward what I believe to be a more realistic, logically and empirically more defensible story. First, it states that there is not enough solid evidence to call investment fluctuations "cycles". Second, it holds that the fluctuations are generated by various external shocks, meaning that these shocks have little or nothing to do with the regularities of the investment regime itself. The shocks have many reasons. They may originate, for instance, in random changes of weather having an influence on fixed investments either through harvest

[1] See Kornai (1982, p. 38), Bauer (1988, p. 3), Lissowska (1987).

fluctuations or changes in the number of working days suitable for open-air construction work. World market changes or political events may also trigger these shocks. In the approach this school favours, it is not the investment process which determines developments in the rest of the economy. Just the contrary - investment activity adapts itself to changes in other macro-economic variables. The annual changes in the volume of investments are explained in terms of the buffer role of fixed capital formation. In sum, this approach perceives investment fluctuations as *exogenous* developments and in this sense contests the theory of socialist investment cycles.

1.2 Cycles or fluctuations ?

The terms most often used in this book, and in the title itself, require precise and unambiguous definitions, although they are commonly used in everyday language. This poses a first question which must be answered: why is it important to make a distinction between cycles and fluctuations? Why does it make sense to differentiate the three approaches discussed in accordance with the interpretation of these two words?

The Three Rs. Every cycle is some sort of fluctuation, a sign of instability. However, not all fluctuations satisfy the definitions of cycles. But where and how can we draw a line between the two phenomena? A succinct definition was given in a survey article on the subject (Ickes 1986). The term "cycle" is justified if and when a time series exhibits what Ickes calls, the three Rs - *recurrence*, *reinforcement* and *regularity*: "Merely to note that the current cycle grows out of past events is inane. It is always true that a current economic situation is the product of the past. This is not evidence of a cycle." (p. 43)

Beyond its brevity, the advantage of this definition is that it is sufficiently general to be accepted by the representatives of the above-mentioned three schools of thought without further reservations. What is more, it fits well into the theory of western business cycles (Burns and Mitchell 1946, Gordon 1961), as well as into the theoretical framework of mainstream Marxism.

Although the words used in the three Rs definition have a strong explanatory power, a short detour is required to see the full implications of the "second R", the least self-explanatory of the three.

Reinforcement means that the cycle models are deterministic by their nature. They must contain - in a logical sense at least - as many equations as there are unknowns. Otherwise, as was pointed out in a seminal paper of Ragnar Frisch (1933), no explanation of how one situation grows out of a preceding one can be given. Keynes (1936) also stressed the deterministic nature of business cycles:

> By a cyclical movement we mean that as the system progresses in, e.g., the upward direction, the forces propelling it upwards at first gather force and have a cumulative effect on one another but gradually lose their strength until at a certain point they tend to be replaced by forces operating in the opposite direction; which in turn gather force for a time and accentuate one another, until they too, having reached their maximum development, wane and give place to their opposite. (Keynes [1973] pp. 313-314.)

Reinforcement and regularity are intimately interlinked concepts. In Keynes's presentation, for example, the paragraph cited above ends like this:

> We do not however, merely mean by a cyclical movement that upward and downward tendencies, once started, do not persist for ever in the same direction but are ultimately reversed. We mean also that there is some recognisable degree of regularity in the time-sequence and the duration of the upward and downward movements. (*ibid.*)

The idea behind the term reinforcement is often used in the context of socialist investment cycles. This is the so-called positive feed-back. There is agreement that no cycle occurs without it. Positive feed-back means a self-reinforcing digression from the equilibrium position, which must appear during both the acceleration and the deceleration phase. Without damping, positive feed-backs are a source of disturbances in any system and can endanger the existence of the system itself.

By contrast, negative feed-back is not a sufficient cause of a cycle. Regulatory mechanisms, based on this effect can help to keep an economic process close to the equilibrium path. However, as a Hungarian specialist on the subject - Attila Károly Soós (1986, p. 25) - rightly stressed, throughout many decades textbook economics in the socialist countries had resolutely denied the existence of any kind of feed-back control. In the fight against this dogmatic approach, therefore, the clear distinction between positive and negative feed-back remained blurred (if it was theoretically raised at all). Textbook writers, economic commentators and politicians themselves alleged that in a socialist economy growth was always smooth, predetermined (planned) and proportional. Using a Soviet textbook's formulation, "the internal, essential connection between public property and public regulation of the whole economy from a single centre, their mutual interdependence, and the conscious establishment and maintenance of proportionality are expressed in the law of planned, balanced development of the socialist economy." (Khudokormov 1967, p. 87).

Hence, ex post macro-economic control (i.e. feed-back mechanisms) have no or only a small role to play. There are no fluctuations that resemble even to the smallest degree the periodical cycles of capitalism. Economic development in socialism knows no setbacks or recessions. As the Soviet author sums it up:

> In practical economic organisation under socialism certain disproportions may arise at different periods. They may be the result of objective circumstances (for example, the result of natural calamities, especially in agriculture), and also of subjective factors (insufficient guidance of production, errors and miscalculation in planning). The economic disproportions of socialism are not conditioned by the socio-economic system and are not, therefore, antagonistic; they are partial and not universal in character and do not develop into recessions and crises as they do under capitalism. Such individual proportions in socialist economy are corrected in a planned way. In this field the creation of state reserves is of great importance; with their aid socialist society is able to overcome disproportions that arise, e.g., in cases of harvest failure or the lagging of some branch's production behind the general rate of economic development. (*op. cit.* pp. 90-91.)

It is more than understandable that eastern and western economists dissatisfied with this poor and evidently insincere argumentation chose the same obvious and elementary weapon. They looked at the numbers, put them on a chart and demonstrated that economic growth in the socialist countries had neither been predetermined, nor proportional - in fact the most important macro-economic variables displayed considerable fluctuations.

Chart 1.1 is reproduced here from the 1956 annual report of the United Nations Economic Commission for Europe (UN ECE 1957). It shows that in the east European centrally planned economies the envisaged smooth development path did not materialize in the period under review. This failure catches the eye, if one looks at investments. Two years later similar analysis was produced by the China-experts of the United Nations (UN ESCAP 1958, p. 107) and Chinese politicians themselves - e.g., Liu (1958) - also noted the instability of Chinese investment growths rates.

CHART 1.1 UN/ECE data on investment fluctuations, 1950-1955

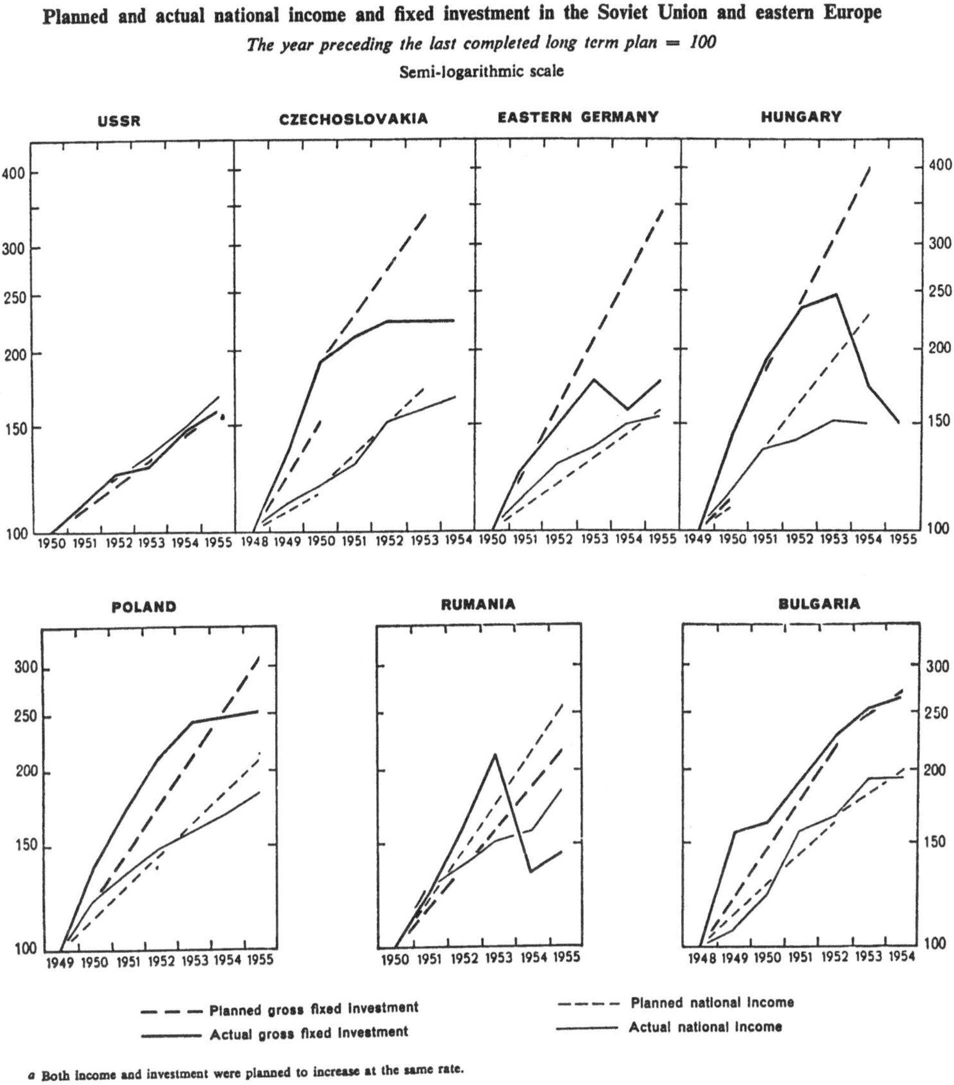

Source: Reproduced from UN ECE (1956) p. 227.

CHART 1.2 J. Goldmann's data on investment fluctuations, 1950-1964

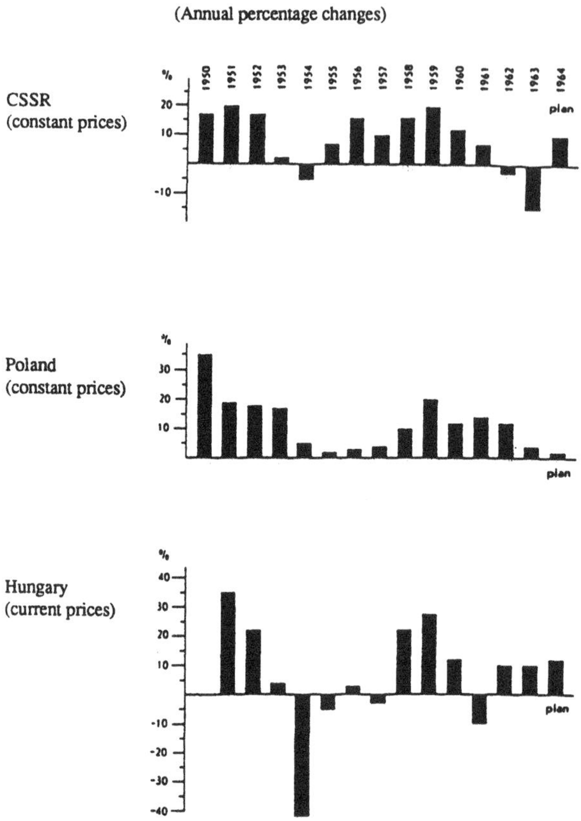

Source: Reproduced from Goldmann (1965)

Chart 1.2 portrays the state of the art evidence, available ten years later. Josef Goldmann (1965) was already concentrating on investments alone. Using longer time series, he had no doubts that instability of investments could not be considered an exceptional phenomenon in Eastern Europe. Evidence from three countries showed that there was something for a theory to explain. Goldmann's preoccupation with cyclical growth was more than understandable, since his country - Czechoslovakia - was the first where negative investment growth rates were coupled with an absolute dip in national income (NMP).

Comparisons with or allusions to the capitalist cycles were self-evident for economists trained in Marxist traditions. This spoke in favour of using the word "cycle" without any further explanation. For economists engaged in the fight against dogmatism the term used was also a question of formulation and not of substance. For these authors, *cycle* (Czechowski 1957, Kliszko 1967), *U-shaped development* (Liu 1958), *M-shaped development* (Bogár, 1986, 1989), *uneven development* (Notkin 1961), *non-uniform growth* (Minc, B. 1962), *quasi-cycle* (Goldmann 1964, Goldmann and Kouba 1970), *stagewise development* (Chelinski 1964), *unbalanced investments* (Dziewulski and Maciejewski 1980), *fluctuation* (Hoch *et al.* 1965) or *disharmonious growth* (Kupka 1983) all meant very much the same thing.

Although they used a language that seemed somewhat cryptic to Western ears, partly because the authors had good practical reasons to be cautious and partly due to their Hegelian-Marxist training, their main message was straightforward in economic terms and very unorthodox in a political sense. These observers, be they Czech, Hungarian or Polish, Soviet or Chinese, had realised the existence of a policy conflict, revolving around the inherent contradictions of a vision-induced pursuit of industrialisation: The industrialisation drive led to resource mobilisation at an unprecedented scale but also to input rises which were similarly unprecedented, unforeseen and unplanned. This created imbalances and disincentives in the utilisation of added inputs to such an extent that the economic rationale of the original goals became doubtful.

The consequences of this policy conflict were particularly dramatic in the less developed countries (China and the Soviet Union), where economic decision making was most of the time in the hands of fanatical, unscrupulous leaders.[2] The on-the-spot recognition of the problem by prominent economists was an important development. In those countries, where the political leadership was receptive to criticism (e.g., Czechoslovakia) and willing to learn, it helped to attenuate the conflict itself.

However, a conflict is a conflict and not a cycle. Little analytical advantage would be gained if the term "cycle" were used interchangeably for "conflict". Serious analysis cannot live without a clear distinction between fluctuations and cycles. Accordingly, throughout this book the term "cycle" will always be used in the way Ickes defined it (three Rs). If one of these conditions is not met, I will avoid "cycle" and instead speak of fluctuations or waves.

Regularity versus Periodicity. Genuine cycles can have various durations. Some of them are shorter than a year (quarterly, monthly and weekly fluctuations). Numerous authors are convinced that there are much longer cycles with a 6-12 year duration or even longer (Kuznets and Kondratieff cycles). No attempt is made in this book to analyze the very short or the very long cycles. Attention is focused on fluctuations whose peak-to-peak length is somewhere in the 2-5 year range.

Unfortunately, this simple categorization is not easily applicable in practice. In one of his first writings Goldmann (1964) formulated a model describing cycles with an 8-10 year duration. Cobeljic and Stojanovic (1969) also worked with 6-8 year cycles. Twenty years later, Bajt (1989) came to the conclusion - using Polish and Yugoslav data - that the cycles last 8 to 12 years. A Hungarian author - Major (1983) - has recently found traces of a 9-10 year periodicity in Hungarian data. Using the same Hungarian figures, other authors (Ungvárszki 1986, 1989, Bogár 1986, 1989) believe that cycles recur every 6-8 years.

Tamás Bauer (1981), another prominent Hungarian author, whose 600 page long monograph on socialist investment cycles will be frequently referred in this book, is convinced that his four-

[2] This aspect of the problem was strongly stressed in the seminal work of Eckstein (1968).

phase cycle model gives a full account of all sorts of investment cycles ranging in periodicity from 3-4 years up to 12 years.[3]

There is no *a priori* reason to exclude the possibility that both the short cycles, with a duration of less than 12 months, and the secular cycles are detectable in socialist economies. In fact, we can make a further step in this direction. On purely theoretical grounds it can be assumed - as it is by Bródy (1983b) - that various types of short, medium and long cycles co-exist. However, the separation of these different types of cycles may prove impossible in practical terms. While econometric theory provides adequate tools to carry out this exercise, the shortness of time series means that the investment data cannot be analyzed with a conventional degree of confidence.

The definition of the cycle, as used by most Eastern scholars, does not require that recurring fluctuations must follow each other with a strictly determined time lag. In other words, strict periodicity, as understood in mathematics, is not a necessary condition for investment fluctuations to qualify as cycles. In a more generous sense, however, regularity - the third of the three Rs - does imply some degree of uniformity of the fluctuations in time. It is assumed throughout this book that a true cyclical movement of an economic variable resembles a sine curve - i.e. the distance between successive peaks (or troughs) is more or less stable and the amplitude (and depths) of the waves also display some uniformity.[4]

It will be shown later that econometrics, a powerful weapon often deployed to obtain black-and-white answers to complicated questions, requires that periodicity be included in the definition. This may seem technically fully justified but if this is accepted a more intricate problem must be faced. The socialist investment cycle theory was born out of the analogy with capitalist business cycles. Therefore it does not seem justified to insist upon periodicity in the socialist theory if Western business cycle theory can live without it. There is wide agreement among western business cycle analysts that in a strict sense western data do not exhibit periodicity either. It is worth quoting at least one authority:

> Although business cycles represent recurring alterations of prosperity and depression, virtually all authorities are agreed that there is nothing periodic about these movements. There is no evidence that business cycles tend to recur over and over again in virtually the same form, with the same duration and the same amplitude of movement. Some cycles are mild and others severe; some last two or three or four years, and others eight or ten years. In some the upswing is longer than the downswing; in others the reverse is the case. (Gordon 1961, p. 250)

Intensity. Finally, in order to complete our definition of the cycle, we have to require that wave-type movements display a certain degree of intensity. From the point of empirical analysis, it makes little sense to speak of a cycle if fluctuations, expressed in the form of annual percentage change, remain within a very narrow band and therefore the distinction between real endogenous changes and measurement errors becomes impossible. We shall revert to this question in Chapter 3.

[3] This was explicitly confirmed by Mr. Bauer's letter to the author, dated 7 September 1989.

[4] In this matter, I am in full agreement with Soós (1989, p. 78), who thinks that "we can call «investment cycles» investment fluctuations with systematic successions of negative and positive feed-back processes and a minimal extent of regularity in time". For a similar view see Avramov (1990).

1.3 SOCIALISM

Endogenous investment cycle models grew out of a clearly defined theoretical perception of socialism. The discussion of these models, therefore, is not possible without describing this relationship in more detail.

Since the terms "socialism", "socialist" or "socialist countries" will be very frequently used in the text, they are used systematically here. The notion "socialist countries" will be used as a geopolitical term - meaning the group of about 30 countries that were or are generally considered as a geographical extension of Soviet political influence. The expressions "socialism", "real socialism", or "Soviet-type economies" will always be used as synonyms and they will refer to a particular theoretical construct. The starting point of this construct is, I believe, a justified assertion. It is claimed that these economies represent a duplication of the Soviet economic model, with many substantial similarities and a few less important individual specificities.

In the past, the socialist character of these countries was also reflected in the official names of the country which were enshrined in each country's constitution. Most of these countries called themselves "people's republics" or "people's democratic republics" (table 1.1). In the post-1945 setting this was the reflection of a then important theoretical concept, according to which the new countries of the socialist world order were not yet fully developed communist societies so that some elements of civil democracy (private property, multi-partism) were to survive for a while. A few years later, however, all this was largely forgotten. Nevertheless, the subject resurfaced when the communist parties lost their monopoly of power during 1989/1990. Most countries have now changed their names again and the adjectives "socialist" or "people's democracy" have been dropped.

Socialism = planning + shortages. Political and economic control in the socialist countries were based on centralized, non-market mechanisms. There is nothing new in this statement. The endogenous investment cycle theory, however, is based upon a more elaborate perception of real socialism. It asserts that within these non-market mechanisms, two interlinked sub-systems played the dominating roles: the institutions of planning and the logic of the *shortage economy paradigm* (SEP). These are the cornerstones of an institutionalist perception of socialism, which aims at identifying the rules of motion of an "invisible hand", in the same way as capitalism is perceived in the Smithian doctrine. And this is the point where my doubts have their origin.

Planning is seen as the main pillar of economic control. There is a long tradition behind this interpretation, which explicitly or tacitly identifies economic control with planning. Theoretical, ideological but also practical reasons speak for this approach. If an author discusses some particular aspects of the Soviet-type economies, having no direct relationship with planning as such, this approach simplifies the matter. The word planning is fairly neutral in comparison with such terms as "communism" or "totalitarianism". In fact, it is more neutral than "socialism" since this adjective is often used to characterize those western countries that follow some sort of social democratic orientation. This explains why international organisations such as the United Nations preferred to use the term "centrally planned economy", instead of any of the other labels mentioned. With time this practice has become widespread and commonly accepted in the literature, although in many cases the authors themselves do not really put any emphasis on the term "planning".

TABLE 1.1 List of socialist countries

Full name of the country as used in official documents around 1988	Communist/Marxist party rule
Europe (9 countries)	
Socialist People's Republic of Albania	1944-1992
People's Republic of Bulgaria	1945-1990
Czechoslovak Socialist Republic	1948-1989
German Democratic Republic	1949-1990 a/
Hungarian People's Republic	1945-1990
Polish People's Republic	1945-1989
Socialist Republic of Romania	1945-1989
Union of Soviet Socialist Republics	1917-1991 a/
Socialist Federal Republic of Yugoslavia	1945-1991 a/
Asia (9 countries)	
Democratic Republic of Afghanistan	1978-1992
Socialist Republic of the Union of Burma	1962-1988
People's Republic of China	1949-
Democratic Kampuchea	1975-1992
Democratic People's Republic of Korea	1945-
Lao People's Republic	1975-
Mongolian People's Republic	1921-1991
Socialist Republic of Viet Nam	1945-
People's Democratic Republic of Yemen	1969-1990 a/
Africa (14 countries)	
People's Republic of Angola	1975-
People's Republic of Benin	1972-1990
Burkina Faso	1983-1991
Republic of Cape Verde	1975-1991
People's Republic of the Congo	1963-
People's Democratic Republic of Ethiopia	1974-1991
Revolutionary People's Republic of Guinea	1958-1984
Republic of Guinea-Bissau	1974-1991
Democratic Republic of Madagascar	1975-
People's Republic of Mozambique	1975-
Democratic Republic of Sao Tomé and Príncipe	1975-1991
Somali Democratic Republic	1976-1991
United Republic of Tanzania	1964-1990
Republic of Zimbabwe	1980-
America (3 countries)	
Republic of Cuba	1959-
Republic of Guayana (Cooperative Republic)	1966-
Republic of Nicaragua	1979-1989

Note: a/ Ceased to exist as a country.

For those, however, who believe in the theory of socialist investment cycles, planning means much more than this. In the first two decades after World War II, when observers were first confronted with fluctuations seemingly similar to those produced in the market economies, planning meant roughly the same in all socialist countries. It is not surprising, therefore, that they tried to look for an explanation within the system of planning.

In this approach planning means macro-economic planning, in its long-, medium- and short-term aspects. Planning is always understood as a joint effort of more than one central institution. It is well known that these institutions were in permanent conflict with each other. The proponents of the endogenous cycle theory, however, usually portray these conflicting interests as a secondary issue. Since the pioneering study of the Argentine economist Julio Olivera (1960), several authors have proceeded from the assumption of one "Centre", representing a solid block of preferences and intentions vis-à-vis the other players in the game - the subordinated group of state owned enterprises (SOEs) and consumers at large.[5] This vision is well exemplified in the econometric modelling approach of Marrese (1981), which is based upon the assumption "that central decision-makers (members and staffs of the Central Committee, the Council of Ministers, the Planning Office, the National Bank, the Development Bank, and the State Planning Committee) exercise the constraining forces on the magnitude and distribution of investment funds". (p. 222)

Planning - and investment planning in particular - essentially means physical planning. On the surface, it might appear that planners distribute monetary funds between alternative utilisation possibilities but in reality, as understood in this perception of socialism, physical quantities of raw materials, equipment and labour power are allocated. According to an apposite formulation, "real investment is the primary factor and the availability of finance is a secondary phenomenon; the former is the cause and the latter the effect." (Kornai 1980, p. 526)

The other cornerstone of the model, implicitly used in the theory of investment cycles, is the SEP. Kornai's main thesis holds that shortages are an inevitable consequence of the institutional set-up of the socialist system. In other words, economic imbalances do not originate in mistaken or inconsistent macro-economic decisions but are inherent in the given socio-economic framework. Shortages are universal, chronic, self-generating and pervasive. This does not mean, however, that there is always a shortage of everything. Nevertheless, they appear everywhere: on the market for consumer goods and services, in production and trade, and, of course, within the investment process itself. Shortages are chronic; efforts to eliminate them never bring more than a temporary attenuation. Shortages are self-generating. Shortage breeds shortage. The phenomenon is intensive, meaning that it has forceful repercussions upon every single sector of the economy.

Planning and the SEP are strongly interlinked concepts. On the one hand, a bureaucratic distribution system based on physical allocation of resources continuously regenerates shortages. This is inevitable and occurs - so the theory holds - largely because plans which appeared to be balanced on paper were in reality full of internal inconsistencies. In this sense, the plan is always "wrong" in every segment of it but the investment chapter is believed to be worse than the others. This is so because investment decisions are unique, non-repeatable actions, implying more risks and uncertainties than routine-type allocation decisions required in the control of current production.

[5] In this respect Olivera faithfully followed the reasoning of the official textbooks, which - as in our citation above - also spoke of "public regulation of the whole economy from a single centre".

Looking at plans from the perspective of SEP, it is clear that economic control amidst constant shortages can never be based on serious planning. The Centre has no time or energy to work out fundamentally different, alternative scenarios or competing variants. Planners do not plan. Their time is spent on minimizing the waste arising from the extensive bottlenecks throughout the production system.

Alternative visions of socialism. In the world of politics and sociology, as well as in everyday life, other perceptions of socialism are frequently met that are fundamentally different from the one discussed above. In a sense, the alternative approaches are also built on a simple and unquestionable observation. They proceed from the fact that non-economic factors play an important role in Soviet-type economies. Depending on how much explanatory power we credit to the term "important", we can arrive at different concepts of socialism.

(i) Reliance on the concept of planning in describing the economic system of the socialist countries is essentially an Anglo-Saxon tradition. By contrast, the German literature is resistant to this approach and prefers to label the socialist countries as centrally managed economies (*Zentralverwaltungswirtschaft*). The German academic tradition feels that the term planning lends itself too easily to an all-embracing interpretation.

> Protective tariffs, public roads or state rail roads, hydraulic dams, city planning, and also the monetary and financial policy of governments, are based on some preconceived idea or "plan". If all these things are "planning", the term becomes absolutely meaningless. (Röpke 1936, p. 336)

Terms like planning or bureaucratic control sound similar at first hearing. Nonetheless, they generate distinctly different connotations in the mind of the reader. This is not accidental. Authors using these terms deliberately commit themselves to these concepts and know the consequences of their choice. The word "planning" can be used with positive or pejorative connotations. In both cases it implies the vision of scientific foresight, based on a reliable set of macro-economic data, with some degree of control over the details. By contrast, the term "bureaucratic control" clearly has a negative connotation. Within this framework, it is almost trivial to assume that in such an economy, decision-making is arbitrary (in the sense that commands coming from the offices of a governmental department are replacing the mechanisms of the competitive market), and public information is likely to be inaccurate or simply false.

Proponents of the socialist investment cycle theory depict central planners as powerful, dominating creatures in the game called "socialist economy". Huge resources are at their disposal and they have little inhibition to implement their will against the manifest interest of society in general and SOE managers in particular. Although a certain discrepancy between real and formal rules of planning is taken into account, most versions of the investment cycle theory assume that by and large the game is played according the publicized rules.

This interpretation came under renewed criticism as economists from Czechoslovakia and the GDR were given the opportunity to join the theoretical discussion on the true nature of the socialist economies.[6] In their presentation, these two countries had exhausted their growth potential within the framework of the existing set-up some time in the late 1960s and the entire system underwent serious modifications. After the first decade of radical structural rearrangements, planners had nothing to restructure any more. Their room for manoeuvre was considerably reduced. Central hierarchical decision-making was gradually replaced by a horizontal (more or less) cooperative game, where the partners were merely "playing at planning". This process was based on a "mutual understanding of the planning ritual and on the deep dichotomy between the plan's real and formal rules." (Klaus 1988, p. 8) According to Henschel (1990) the game in the GDR was of a less cooperative character. The centre's behaviour was rather autocratic, capricious and inconsistent. The important decisions were made not according to the plan, or in the framework of the plan, but "outside the plan".

(ii) A recurring line of thought in the literature is that the socialist system (at least in its early periods) was essentially a *war economy*. This view is held not only by historians (Castoriadis 1981) and Kremlinologists but also by economists - men of theory and practice alike.

Since the 1917 Russian Revolution, several scholars have applied the so-called Spartan analogy to the Soviet Union. The idea originates in Spenser (1914) and it was used to describe imperial Russia.[7] For a man of practice, like R. Gates, Deputy Director of the CIA, the analogy inspired the following words, when he testified before the Joint Economic Committee of the US Congress: "The Soviet Union is much like Sparta. Virtually the entire economy and society is organized in a way in which the military and its needs receive first priority. That doesn't mean they have exclusive priority. It doesn't mean that there is no competition for resources but by and large when hard choices come to be made, the military's interest will be protected." (quoted by Bernstein 1989, p. 2).

Lange (1943) and Baran (1952) were probably the first to conceptualize what Stalin's slogan - "socialism in one country" - really meant for economic theory. The institutions of war communism, which had, in the post-1917 years, been conceived as a set of provisional arrangements until the victory of the communist forces over the West, were later stabilized for ever. These scholars believed that not only the Stalinist terror but also the main body of practical devices applied, as well as the functioning of the economy itself, were all determined by political considerations. During the last days of Soviet-type communism, Soviet authors themselves became receptive to this reasoning. Academician Bogomolov, for example, was quoted by a Soviet newspaper as saying that for decades the Soviet people has been living in conditions of a wartime economy.[8]

[6] For reasons that do not require explanation, until 1989, the economists of these two countries were deprived from travelling and publishing for several decades. Consequently, the academic literature was heavily dominated by the work of their more fortunate colleagues from Hungary, Poland and Yugoslavia. It is certainly a loss for the whole academic community that the representatives of the two most developed east European economies were unable to make their voices heard in the international arena.

[7] For more references see Bernstein (1989).

[8] See the report on an international conference *Comparing the Soviet and American Economies: Overall Output, Levels of Consumption, Military Expenditures*, held near Washington, D. C. (*Moscow News*, No. 20. 1990.)

After a decade of east European experience, the already quoted Polish economist, O. Lange felt that militarization had shaped the fortune of the newly born socialist countries. Writing in the mid-1950s, he said in a somewhat apologetic manner: "Methods of highly centralized administrative planning and management widely using meta-economic coercion are not a characteristic feature of socialism but, rather, constitute a *sui generis* technique of the war economy." (quoted in Kaser and Radice 1985, p. 15). H. Minc, Vice-Premier responsible for economic affairs in Poland during the execution of the first six-year plan, held similar views: "The building-up of the defense industries, of armament production, and the armed forces skimmed the cream of output - alloy steel plate, roller-bearings, pipes, the most precise machinery etc. It took the best technicians and engineers and also contributed to the non-fulfilment of investment plans in a number of branches of industry. (...) This situation, it has to be said clearly, led to the creation of a half-war economy in 1951-53." (*Nowe Drogi*, No. 10, October 1956)

I. Friss, the *eminence grise* of the 1950s in Hungary, looked back at those years with the same feeling. "In those days the danger of war had to be reckoned with, hence, economic considerations had to be subordinated to this" (Friss 1966, p. 103). More recently, the distinguished Hungarian economist, András Bródy, whose various cycle models will be referred to on several occasions in this book, has expressed similar views, which openly contradict SEP. In a review article, commenting on Kornai (1990), he refers to his long-standing contention with the author of the *Economics of Shortage*. In Bródy's view, the main reason behind the shortages is not the soft budget constraint, as Kornai claims, but "that which this softness serves and hides: the unadmitted, unnecessary and unprofitable production of armaments, costing many times the budget of the Ministry of Defence." (Bródy 1990b, p. 14)

Independently from Bródy's proposition, I. Birman, a Soviet emigre specialist on national accounting and Soviet budgetary issues, came to very similar conclusions. According to Birman (1981, 1990) the defence burden of the Soviet economy was predominantly financed through inherently inflationary methods and this was one of the most important sources of excess demand at the macro-economic level. American defence analysts of the RAND Corporation - Hildebrandt and Staugaard (1991) - have also adopted a critical attitude toward Kornai and his followers for ignoring the role of the defence-oriented priority allocation system in generating disequilibria in the civilian part of the Soviet economy.

(iii) In many current works, notably those deriving from the work of I. Wallerstein and A. Gerschenkron, it is argued that national economic policies are shaped by a country's location within the *international division of labour*. In a way, this is a more generalized version of the war-economy hypothesis. Proponents of this view often suggest that everything which has occurred in the Soviet Union since 1917 - or since 1950 in the case of Eastern Europe - was essentially the continuation of a centuries' old effort on the part of the underdeveloped peripheral economies of Eastern Europe to catch up with the advanced market economies of the West by means of exclusive reliance on centralized state power. In this perspective, socialism meant little new in the history of the region.

(iv) In another version of this kind of historical approach, the sociology of state structure comes into the foreground. No one can deny that the economic strategy followed by the socialist countries was heavily dependent on the ambitions of the ruling elite. Leadership and the rules of succession are of critical importance in this respect.[9] In some countries an infatuated leader may have possessed enough power to determine the fate of his nation for decades and only his timely or untimely death could bring change. In other, more fortunate, circumstances, members of the elite mutually counterbalance each other; thus economic policy both in its conceptual form and in its implementation represented a certain kind of balanced synthesis of rival political interests and professional expertise, necessarily required by the process of consensus formation.[10]

It seems rather self-evident to me that one cannot build a system-specific cycle theory on these perceptions of real socialism. Once the emphasis is placed predominantly on the historical aspects of the story, it becomes impossible to justify any uniformity based on logical grounds. We arrive at the same conclusion if ideology and political campaigns are at the forefront of the argumentation. It would be difficult to deny the importance of the role played by these factors in Soviet-type economies. Nevertheless, building a counter-theory on these elements is also a risky venture. The task of the present work is to explain the fluctuation of investments. Once history, ideology and political campaigns are admitted into the story as protagonists, we have a *deus ex machina* which can be used to explain almost any behaviour.[11] Therefore a judicious analysis is required in every instance, if and when these elements are used in the argument.

Continuity and discontinuity. For the majority of socialist countries, investment time series are available from 1950 onwards. For several reasons, however, this date is unsuitable as a starting point for analysis if it is assumed that investment cycles are somehow related to planning itself.

(i) The planned economy as a system emerged in Eastern Europe during the first years of the 1950s. Its consequences, therefore, were not yet observable in its early years.

(ii) It is generally accepted that in this period military plan considerations overshadowed the economic ones. So, the lessons from these years were not appropriate to yield general conclusions. For a different reason, the second part of the 1950s was again atypical. Those were the years of the DIP (from the Russian acronym of "catch up and overtake") in the Soviet Union, and the years of the Great Leap Forward in China, when the entire block of socialist countries made a bold attempt to accelerate economic growth, to catch up and surpass the western world.[12]

[9] See e.g., Narkiewicz (1986) on leadership changes and the length of east European rulers' reigns. For a more theoretical approach along these lines see Comisso (1986).

[10] This seems to have happened, for instance, in the post-1968 Czechoslovakia. See Klaus and Jezek (1989) and Dyba and Jezek (1990) for a more articulate exposition of this view.

[11] This dilemma was mentioned in another context by Granick (1987, p. 124).

[12] After a detailed analysis of this period, Bauer (1981) came to a similar conclusion. "In the six (east European - P. M.) countries plan targets were revised upward. Although there were some differences in implementation, in substance this manoeuvre was a co-ordinated act. In its economic and foreign trade aspects, it was closely linked to the policy decisions of the Soviet Union and China - i.e. to the Seven-Year Plan and the policy of the Great Leap Forward." (p. 84)

(iii) After the rupture with the Soviet Union in June 1948, Yugoslavia did not consider itself a planned economy. To emphasise this distance, a unique national accounting system was created and the country remained outside the reach of the international statistical data collection centres (OECD, CMEA). With this simple ploy the Yugoslav authorities were successful in escaping from the horizon of comparative economic research.

(iv) Partly as a result of the three above-mentioned factors, statistical material for the 1950s is rather uneven in quality. Sometimes data for the first part of this decade are simply missing from the historical time series. The faultiness of some figures is apparent; it is difficult to believe, for example, that the volume of annual investments had increased by more than 50 % in Bulgaria in 1959, as official statistics continue to claim even today. The still valid 1959 figure for Hungary, indicating a 36 % annual rise, is also questionable on similar grounds.

Thus, it is understandable that many authors - including Bauer (1981), Marrese (1981), Winiecki (1982, 1986), Soós (1987b) and Ickes (1988) - concluded that in eastern Europe the investment cycle can be meaningfully analyzed for the post-1960 period only. So much for the starting points. Let us now look at the arguments pertaining to the cut-off date of the analysis.

Once we proceed from the assumption that the cycle must somehow originate in the planning process, it is not easy to find an appropriate closing year, either. Bauer (1981), for example, suggested that "direct planning" has to be distinguished from planning in a reformed economy. As a consequence, his cut-off date was 1968 in the case of Hungary, and 1979 for Bulgaria, Czechoslovakia, the GDR, Poland, Romania and the Soviet Union.

From a post-communist perspective, these cut-off dates are no longer tenable. Retrospectively, it is clear that the various reform attempts to overhaul the planning system had not brought about substantial changes by the end of the 1980s. In fact, such differences as there were between subsequent and earlier periods, or between countries, lay not so much in the methods and institutions of central economic control but rather in the quality and judiciousness of this guidance - including the amount of tolerance *vis-à-vis* the non-centrally administered part of the economy (legal and semi-legal private activities).[13]

In sum, it seems more appropriate for the purposes of this analysis to consider the 1950-1989 period in its entirety and to put less emphasis on elements of discontinuity.[14] This argument holds, I think, not only in time but in a regionwide context as well. Yugoslavia cannot be excluded from the investigation. Although central planning in that country played little role in the period under review, and the relevance of SEP is also questionable[15], there can be little doubt that for forty years Yugoslavia was a socialist country where economic control was essentially based on non-economic methods.

[13] See Mihályi (1983).

[14] With respect to Hungary, Marrese (1981) expressed similar views: "(...) bargaining over the nature of financial regulators (the post-reform situation) is not that different from bargaining over the nature of mandatory plan directives (the pre-reform situation)." (p. 225)

[15] Kornai (1980) also excludes Yugoslavia from his analysis. However, in defending his theory against Soós's (1984) criticism, Kornai (1985) underscored the relevance of his model to the Yugoslav economy as well.

TABLE 1.2 Empirical studies on investment fluctuations, 1956-1991

Author(s)	Year of publication	Analysed period	Analysed country(ies)	Main method applied	Observed or estimated periodicity in years	Data limitations
UN ECE	1956	1950-1955	EE6	T	.	CSSR, R: Net accumulation
Minc	1962	1950-1960	CSSR, P, USSR,China	T	.	Industry only
Goldmann	1964	1950-1964	CSSR, P, H	G	8--10	H: Current prices
UN Bulletin...	1966	1951-1965	EE7	T,G	.	GDR: Current prices, B, H: Soc. sector
Goldmann-Flek	1967	1950-1965	CSSR	...	6--8	
Kliszko	1967	1950-1965	Poland	G	.	Industry only
Eckstein	1968	1949-1965	China	T	.	State construction investments
Bajt	1969	1950-1965	EE7, YU	R	.	Industry (except GDR), GDR: Current prices
Bródy	1969	1924-1965	Hungary	T	.	
Cobeljic-Stojanovic	1969	1948-1963	CSSR,P, USSR,YU	T,G	6--8	CSSR, P: 1950-1963
Goldmann	1969	1950-1966	CSSR	G	8--9	Changes in inventories at current prices
Goldmann-Kouba	1969	1950-1967	CSSR	G	8--9	
Nove	1969	1930-1966	USSR	T	.	1930-57: Without private housing
Bajt	1971	1951-1965	EE7, YU	G	7--8	Industry (except GDR), GDR: Current prices
Berend	1974	1951-1970	EE7, Mongolia	G	.	5 year average growth rates
Neményi	1975	1961-1974	Hungary	T	3--4	
Tényi	1976	1960-1975	Hungary	G	4	
Green	1977	1961-1974	USSR	R	.	
Bauer	1978	1951-1978	CSSR, H, P	G	.	
Székffy	1978	1950-1974	Hungary	R	.	Net accumulation
Kyn-Schrettl-Sláma	1979	1948-1973	CSSR	R	.	
Shapkarev	1979	1960-1978	Bulgaria	R	8	
Dziewulski-Maciejewski	1980	1950-1976	Poland	G, T		Material sector
Bauer	1981	1960-1979	EE7	T	3--12	
Marrese	1981	1961-1975	Hungary	R	.	
Simon	1981	1970-1979	Hungary	R	5.2	SOEs only
Wiles	1982	1950-1980	EE7, Mongolia	T	.	
Winiecki	1982	1961-1977	EE7	R	5	
Major	1983	1950-1981	Hungary	I-O	9--10	

(continued)

Boot	1984	1955-1981	GDR	R	.	Material sectors
UN ECE	1985	1950-1980	EE7	R	.	
Bogár	1986	1950-1986	Hungary	G	6--8	Net accumulation
Soós	1986	1955-1980	H, YU	T	.	H:1968-1980
Subáné	1986	1950-1980	Hungary	G	4	
Winiecki	1986	1960-1983	EE7	R	5	
Bettelheim	1987	1962-1984	Cuba	T	.	Current prices
Chavance	1987	1950-1984	China	G	4.1	Current prices; SOEs only
Dimitrov	1987	1950-1985	Bulgaria	S	4.3	
Grosfeld	1987	1956-1981	Poland	R	.	
Lissowska	1987	1961-1980	H,P	T	.	H: Industry. P: Soc. industry
Roland	1987 a	1958-1982	USSR	R	.	Non-agric. soc. sector
Roland	1987 b	1958-1982	USSR	R	.	Non-agric. soc. sector
Szakolczai et al.	1987	1960-1981	Hungary	R	3.5	
Bauer	1988	1976-1985	EE6	T	.	
Bajt	1989	1947-1980	P,YU	R	8 and 12	Industry ; P:1949-1980
Bogár	1989	1945-1988	Hungary	T	6--8	Net accumulation
Frateschi	1989	1954-1985	CSSR	R	4.7	
Salvini	1989	1953-1982	China	...	4--7	
Soós	1989	1960-1979	Hungary	G	3--4	
Ungvárszki	1989	1948-1984	Hungary	T	6--8	Net accumulation
Ickes	1990	1960-1984	EE7	R	8 or 3-4	Depending on the method of detrending
Lackó	1990	1966-1980	Hungary	R	.	State sector, data for 1976-80 heuristically estimated
Summers	1990	1960-1982	USSR	R		Non-agricultural soc. sector
Christin-Short	1991	1963-1984	Poland	R	.	
Summers	1991 a	1962-1982	USSR	R	.	Industry only
Stankiewicz	1991 b	1950-1982	Poland	T	6--12	Net fixed investments (NYUAF) only
Summers	1991 b	1960-1989	USSR	T	2--7	Net fixed investments (NYUAF) only

G= Graphs I-O = Input-output analysis S= Spectral analysis
T= Tables R= Regression analysis

Table 1.2 provides a summary list of the recent empirical works to be found in the literature. The list confirms the agreement of several authors with the position outlined above. Nove (1969), Goldmann (1969), Bajt (1969), Wiles (1982), Boot (1984), Major I. (1983), Chavance (1987b) and Dimitrov (1987) go back in time as far as their data constraint permits and push forward their cut-off date as close as technically possible to the time of writing.

Frontiers of the socialist sector. The view that the theoretical frontiers of the socialist economy coincide with the statistical border line of SOEs is not tenable, either. For practical purposes this view is a tempting simplification. Nevertheless, I strongly believe that this approach must be rejected. First, it should be noted that in at least three countries the weight of private fixed investments had already exceeded 20 % by the end of the 1980s (table 1.3).

TABLE 1.3 Private investments, 1989

	Percentage share in total investments at current prices
Bulgaria	4.7
CSSR	4.8 a/
GDR	...
Hungary	20.1
Poland	17.4 a/
Romania	1.9
USSR	1.9 a/
Yugoslavia	25.5 b/
China	21.0 c/

Notes: a/ At 1984 prices b/ 1988 c/ 1986

Source: Own calculations, based on national statistical yearbooks.

In most models of economic fluctuations, resource constraints play a very important role. It is assumed that under normal circumstances the economy is unable to generate enough resources to sustain an investment boom for several consecutive years. Shortages and bottlenecks emerge. The design bureaus of the Ministries cannot supply construction workers with blueprints on time, labour is scarce at the construction site, the raw-material supply keeps stalling, the authorities cannot provide convertible currency to install planned types of imported machinery, etc. At some point, the Centre has no alternative but to halt the boom.

Note, however, that the reference to this type of bottleneck makes sense only in a nationwide context. This is particularly true of the labour market. It applies also on the market for construction materials. Notwithstanding this simple fact, several models in the literature use the concept of investment in a limited sense, reflecting only a sub-set of the economy (the socialist sector, the state sector, SOEs, material branches, industry, raw material producing branches).[16] While the general assumption that a sudden rise in total investments can easily create extensive bottlenecks can be accepted, there is no reason to believe that a similar increase in industrial investments alone, for example, will have the same consequence. The last column in table 1.2 draws attention to the limitations which characterize the empirical works listed. Surprising as it may seem at first, such limitations appear even in such seminal works as Bajt (1969, 1971), Boot (1984) or Roland (1987a), and they were not commented upon by later students of investment cycles.

[16] Kornai's shortage model, for example, deliberately stops at the border of the socialist sector. In the Introduction to his *Economics of Shortage* he stressed that his interest had been focused on SOEs functioning in industry and services. The co-operatives and the legal and illegal private sector were not incorporated in his concept (Kornai, 1980 p. 14).

1.4 Statistical definition of investments

Throughout this book the term fixed investment is understood in a nationwide context in gross and real terms (i.e. without deduction of provision for depreciation and excluding movements due to price changes) and is abbreviated to GINV. To avoid confusion, the term gross fixed capital formation (GFCF), as defined in the United Nations' system of national accounts (SNA), will be reserved to denote investments by the Western market economies. For most countries under review, GINV is directly estimated from the expenditure side, and cannot necessarily be reconciled with the principles of MPS, the national accounting system applied in the CMEA member countries.[17] The fact that GINV is not a direct entry in MPS is a source of many misunderstandings. For this reason a short detour is necessary at this stage.

The difference in the concepts of capital formation flows employed in SNA and MPS are of a lesser magnitude as compared with the concepts of production and consumption. In both systems, the concept of capital formation is limited to the outlays of reproducible tangible assets and excludes outlays on intangible and financial assets and non-reproducible tangible assets (e.g., land). In another important aspect, there is also a concurrence between both types of national accounting systems: work put in place on structures, roads, dams, ports and other forms of construction is included in GINV. In other words, uncompleted investment projects are also taken into account.

Considering unfinished construction works as a part of GINV (and GFCF) results in the most useful data for analyzing the factors of demand for inputs (building materials, labour, etc.,) which contribute to fluctuations in economic conditions in general. However, with regard to other aspects of economic analysis (capital-output coefficients or factor productivity), it is desirable to exclude, where feasible, the value of uncompleted projects.

However, and this is the source of confusion, in the MPS, the principal category of capital formation, accumulation, is computed on a net basis, whereas in the SNA the opposite is true.[18] For the purpose of illustrating the above, table 1.4 displays a numerical example based on actual Hungarian data. The main aggregates of two national accounting systems are presented here, using both MPS and SNA terminology. The table also helps to understand the quantitative relationship between GINV on the one hand and the categories of the two accounting systems.

[17] The Material Product System (MPS) is the conventional name of the national accounting system of the CMEA member countries. Its function is analogous with the SNA. The official appellation, however, runs as *System of Statistical Balances of the National Economy*. For a full description of the MPS see UN (1989b).

[18] In order to convert the MPS concept of net fixed capital formation into gross fixed capital formation as defined in SNA, apart from capital consumption, the following additions to and subtractions from the MPS concept have to be made:

plus: (i) losses due to foreseeable as well as non-foreseeable damage to fixed assets;

plus: (ii) transfer cost with regard to purchases and sales of existing second-hand fixed assets, including land;

plus: (iii) work in progress on the construction of structures, roads, dams, etc. (UGINV);

plus: (iv) the difference between outlays on fixed capital formation by extraterritorial bodies representing the country in question abroad;

less similar outlays by extraterritorial bodies of other countries and international organizations located in the country in question.

TABLE 1.4 The place of GINV in MPS and SNA : A numerical example

		Acronym used in this book	In percentages (GDP = 100.0)			Acronym used in this book
	MATERIAL PRODUCT SYSTEM	MPS			**SYSTEM OF NATIONAL ACCOUNTS**	SNA
1	NEW FIXED ASSETS PUT INTO USE	CGINV	21.0	21.0	COMPLETED INVESTMENTS	CGINV
2	CONSTRUCTION IN PROGRESS	UGINV	1.5	1.5	UNCOMPLETED INVESTMENTS	UGINV
3	Gross investments (1+2)	GINV	22.5	22.5	GROSS FIXED CAPITAL FORMATION (1+2)	GFCF
	Investments in buildings, etc.	GINV-C	...	...	CONSTRUCTION	
	Machinery and equipment investments	GINV-M	...	...	LAND IMPROVEMENT, ETC.	
	Domestic machinery	GINV- DM	...	...	PRODUCER DURABLE GOODS	
	Imported machinery	GINV-IMP	...	...	BREEDING STOCK, ETC.	
4	Changes in inventories	NYUAI	0.8	0.8	INCREASE IN STOCKS	NYUAI
5	Gross accumulation		23.4	23.4	GROSS CAPITAL FORMATION (3+4)	
6	Amortisation		16.2	...	...	
7	INCREASE IN STOCKS (2+4)	NYUAS	2.4	...		
8	NET ACCUMULATION (5-6)	NYUA	7.1	...	...	
9	Net investments in fixed assets (8-7)	NYUAF	4.8	...		
10	PRIVATE MATERIAL CONSUMPTION	NYUCP	53.5	58.7	PRIVATE FINAL CONS. EXPENDITURE	
11	COLLECTIVE MATERIAL CONSUMPTION	NYUCC	9.3	10.9	GOVERNMENT FINAL CONS. EXPENDITURE	
12	TOTAL MATERIAL CONSUMPTION (10+11)	NYUC	62.8	...	...	
13	TOTAL DOMESTIC UTILISATION (8+12)	NMPUT	70.0			
14				48.1	EXPORTS OF GOODS AND SERVICES	
15				41.1	IMPORTS OF GOODS AND SERVICES	
16	EXTERNAL BALANCE		7.1			
17	Statistical discrepancy		...	..	...	
18	**NET MATERIAL PRODUCT** (13+16+17)	NMP	77.0	100.0	**GROSS DOMESTIC PRODUCT** (5+10+11+14-15)	**GDP**

Note: Only those entries which are printed in block letters refer to categories used in MPS or in SNA.
The proportions used in this example correspond to actual Hungarian figures in 1988 at constant prices.

Source: KSH (1990, p. 22,25), UN (1986a, p. 3), UN (1989b, pp. 48-49)

As noted, GINV is a gross concept. By contrast, accumulation (NYUA), a term which is seldom used in the context of Western economies, refers to an accumulated (non-consumed) part of national income (NMPUT), which is measured net of provision for depreciation. In fact, the word "measured" is not fully appropriate. Depreciation was not measured but only estimated. Since the estimation was based on capital stock data, which were again only estimated and not measured, this "netting out" exercise brought a great deal of imprecision into the final results.[19]

As seen from the table, accumulation (NYUA) was required to be calculated from three components: New fixed assets put into use (CGINV), changes in inventories (NYUAI) and changes in the stock of construction in progress (UGINV). Indeed, this was the practice in many CMEA countries but not in all. The GDR, Poland and Romania never followed the MPS recommendations - they treated UGINV as a part of CGINV. Furthermore, it is worth mentioning that in most of the countries under review statistical discrepancies were not reported separately but included together with construction in progress (UGINV) and/or in changes in inventories (NYUAI). Hence, these categories became residuals in order to reconcile unexplained discrepancies between NMP and NMPUT.

Several authors, nevertheless, use the terms "investment" and "accumulation" as if they were synonyms or accept net investment series as a proxy for lacking gross series.[20] This approach is methodologically incorrect and misleading in practice. While it is true that a certain degree of correlation can be detected between annual growth rates of GINV and NYUA, there is strong evidence that the latter exhibits much greater instability than the former (table 1.5). If changes in stocks (NYUAS) are excluded from the accumulation time series - thus enabling NYUAF to be used to approximate GINV - the results are essentially the same. There is some correlation but standard deviations and coefficients of variation are significantly higher for net as against gross investment. Thus, any model using (net) accumulation indicators as proxies for GINV significantly overstates the actual degree of instability.

Data availability problems have forced some authors to make other kinds of unfortunate compromises. Boot (1984), for example, built his model on data covering the productive (or material) sectors only. In a similar manner, Bajt (1969, 1971) confined his analysis to industrial investments.[21] In Goldmann's first model, the fluctuation of investment in raw material sectors was placed at the centre of his story.

Table 1.6 is included here to indicate the magnitude of simplification tacitly accepted in these works. In most countries, investments in the material (productive) sectors represent 65-85 % of GINV, the weight of industry is below 50 % and the raw material producing branches have a total share of about 15 % only. Thus, empirical results based on such limited data sets have to be interpreted with a great deal of caution.

[19] Further, this was not always and everywhere the case. During the 1950s, accumulation in the Soviet Union, Czechoslovakia, Poland and Romania covered *new* investment (that is, gross investment *less* equipment actually retired from use) rather than *net* investment (gross investment LESS current provision for amortization). (UN ECE, 1956, pp. 199-200)

[20] In fact, the list of such works is surprisingly long: Kliszko (1967), Dahlstedt (1979), Székffy (1978), Ungvárszki (1989); Bogár (1989), Stankiewicz (1990), Summers (1991b).

[21] Surprisingly, neither Bauer (1981) nor Soós (1986) commented on this fact despite the considerable amount of space in their respective books devoted to the analysis of Bajt's writings.

TABLE 1.5 Net investment as a proxy for GINV, 1951-1989

	GINV	Net accumulation total (NYUA)	Net accumulation fixed assets (NYUAF)
Bulgaria (1956-1989)			
Correlation with GINV	1.00	0.68	...
Standard deviation	10.22	23.84	...
Coefficient of variation	1.18	2.57	...
CSSR			
Correlation with GINV	1.00	0.65	-0.25
Standard deviation	6.55	26.22	67.52
Coefficient of variation	1.12	2.88	5.30
GDR (1966-1989) a/			
Correlation with GINV	1.00	0.63	0.97
Standard deviation	4.55	8.09	6.76
Coefficient of variation	1.02	2.27	1.74
Hungary			
Correlation with GINV	1.00	-0.10	0.62
Standard deviation	11.20	76.52	24.48
Coefficient of variation	2.10	5.50	3.58
Poland a/			
Correlation with GINV	1.00	0.80	0.97
Standard deviation	9.20	12.91	11.99
Coefficient of variation	1.40	2.29	1.89

Note: Figures are calculated from volume series, expressed in annual percentage change form
a/ NYUAF includes changes in uncompleted construction.

Source: Own calculations, based on ECE/DEAP Common Data Base.

To draw conclusions for total investments is particularly dangerous. Again, in several countries there was a correlation between the growth rates of total GINV on the one hand, and the growth rates of productive or industrial investments on the other (table 1.7). No such relationship, however, exists between the growth rates of GINV and those of the raw material branches. More importantly, the data show that using series with limited coverage as proxy variables for GINV seriously overstates the underlying instability of the GINV series.

TABLE 1.6 Structure of investments, 1983-1987

	Material sphere	Industry total		Raw material producing branches in industry a/	
	Five-year averages at constant prices (GINV = 100.0)				
Bulgaria	72.3	47.9	b/	17.7	
CSSR	68.4	35.2		14.5	
GDR	78.0	55.6		15.0	c/
Hungary	68.1	31.8		16.0	
Poland	64.8	28.8		13.0	
Romania	84.3	49.4		28.1	
USSR	72.8	36.2		15.1	c/
Yugoslavia c/ d/ e/	83.1	47.7		26.3	
Albania e/ f/	83.0	43.8		..	

Notes: a/ Energy + metallurgy + construction materials
b/ Together with forestry
c/ 1978-1982
d/ Current prices
e/ Socialist sector
f/ 1981-1985

Source: Own calculations, based on ECE/DEAP Common Data base and SG (various years), SYA/88 p. 104, 106.

Authors sometimes have a tendency to forget their own data compromises. Bajt (1969) is a good example. The study was published first in a Yugoslav journal, with ample references to data sources. It was not difficult for the reader to establish that industrial investment data for the GDR at constant prices were substituted by total investment figures, expressed at current prices. (For several other countries, the references given were not enough to identify the exact source.) Two years later, essentially the same data set was used in the author's famous *JEL* article but all page references to sources were omitted.

TABLE 1.7 Investments in the sub-sectors of the economy as a proxy for GINV, 1971-1989

	Annual percentage changes of investments			
	total economy	material sphere	industry	raw material producing branches of industry a/
Bulgaria (1971-1988) b/				
Correlation with total economy	1.00	0.96	0.81	0.36
Standard deviation	5.15	5.99	6.08	11.61
Coefficient of variation	0.88	0.99	0.93	1.60
Czechoslovakia				
Correlation with total economy	1.00	0.93	0.77	0.67
Standard deviation	4.05	4.22	5.00	7.50
Coefficient of variation	1.19	1.04	1.22	1.76
German Dem. Republic				
Correlation with total economy	1.00	0.98	0.80	0.44
Standard deviation	3.77	4.04	4.45	9.41
Coefficient of variation	1.22	1.33	1.11	2.28
Hungary (1971-1987)				
Correlation with total economy	1.00	0.96	0.77	0.37
Standard deviation	6.15	6.99	8.18	8.46
Coefficient of variation	2.20	3.36	3.53	3.00
Poland				
Correlation with total economy	1.00	0.99	0.95	0.84
Standard deviation	12.12	13.34	14.91	14.54
Coefficient of variation	2.76	3.05	3.09	5.71
Romania				
Correlation with total economy	1.00	0.98	0.88	0.77
Standard deviation	6.51	7.00	8.93	8.00
Coefficient of variation	1.28	1.37	1.74	1.33
Soviet Union (1971-1988)				
Correlation with total economy	1.00	0.95	0.90	0.11
Standard deviation	2.19	2.50	2.04	2.19
Coefficient of variation	0.44	0.49	0.38	0.35

Notes: a/ Energy + fuel + metallurgy + construction material
b/ Industry together with forestry.

Source: Own calculations, based on ECE/DEAP Common Data base

The role of large investment projects. Many economists are inclined to attach central importance to a sub-set of state investments, notably the total volume of large, centrally-financed investment projects. They assume that the amount of resources tied up in these projects has a decisive impact on the short-term equilibrium situation.

The Centre - the Politburo, the Planning Office, etc. - was of the same opinion. Thus the plight of these large projects was in the hands of the top political leadership. Simultaneously many organisations were charged with the task of scrutinizing these projects. The press and the statistical authorities were also obliged to report regularly on the state of the construction works. This extensive concern and attention were not altogether superfluous. These projects usually had far-reaching ramifications. As construction work proceeded new issues emerged that affected domestic and foreign policy interests, as well as foreign trade relations. It is logical to assume - and everyday practice confirmed this - that the Centre was unable and unwilling to coordinate several large projects at the same time.[22] The investment cycle school, however, failed to recognise that this constraint originated in the limitations of central administration and not in the exhaustion or overburdening of the economy in a physical sense. Analytically, this makes a great difference.

Goldmann was probably the first east European economist to assume that large investment projects should play an important role in the explanation of fluctuations in macro-economic aggregates.[23] On the basis of Czechoslovak experiences, he asserted that GINV fluctuations were closely related to the simultaneous launching of several large projects in the raw material branches (mines, power stations, steel mills) and the simultaneous commissioning of these very projects 7 or 8 years later.

> The disproportions and acute economic difficulties, ensuing from an above-optimum rate of growth, can only be overcome by slowing down the pace of economic development. This breathing period will continue until new investment projects, initiated in the preceding period, predominantly in the "basic industries", will successively mature and go into operation. As a result of both, the slow-down in growth and the contribution of new output facilities, the supply situation will gradually improve. Thus, conditions will be set up which - through a certain voluntarism inherent in the traditional system - will permit such a quasi-cycle to restart again. (Goldmann 1964, p. 92.)

To illustrate his point, Goldmann tabulated a list of production capacities in terms of physical units of production capacity commissioned in the period 1948-1955, and then for the years 1956-1963 annually in the basic industry of Czechoslovakia. This is clear evidence that large projects were indeed central to his line of reasoning.

[22] In this respect, the size of the economy does not count for very much. In a large economy like the Soviet Union, of course, the term "large investment project" has a different meaning than in a small country, such as Bulgaria.

[23] As will be shown in the next chapter, the pre-war business cycle literature had already taken up this point in the context of western market economies. It is very likely that Goldmann was familiar with this line of research.

Yet, observations collected about large investment projects cannot be generalized and considered valid for the totality of annual investments. It is simply not true that large investment projects are to blame for fluctuations in socialist countries. The average lead time of all simultaneously ongoing investment projects is much shorter than required to explain events recurring every 3-4 years.

In the Soviet Union, for example, it was found that the average lead time was only 15 months. This was shown by V. P. Krasovskii (1967 p. 49), a leading specialist in the field, who based his analysis on a sample of 200 thousand projects (including housing investments). He also showed that the relevant figure for industry was no more than 18 months.

TABLE 1.8 Hungary: Investment outlays by size, 1968, 1980, 1987-1989

(At current prices, percentages)

		1968	1980	1987	1988	1989
/1/	Households a/	11.3	11.1	17.4	20.2	20.7
/2/	Cooperatives	14.2	11.7	12.7	11.3	...
/3/	State sector	74.5	77.1	69.8	68.4	...
/4/=/2+3/	Socialist sector	88.6	88.9	82.6	79.7	79.3
/5/=/6+7+8/	Centralised investments	44.8	40.6	18.8	18	16.6
/6/	Large projects	17.1 b/ <95>	12.2 <20>	4.6 <8>	3.6 <6>	3.6 <6>
/7/	Group investments c/	20.1	19.7	9.1	9.2	7.9
/8/	Other investments	7.7 d/	8.6 d/	5.1	5.2	5.1
/9/=/1+4/	Total	100.0	100.0	100.0	100.0	100.0

Notes: Figures in < > indicate the number of ongoing projects.

a/ Includes self-employed
b/ Listed large projects
c/ E.g., housing estates, roads, etc.
d/ Other state investments

Source: Own calculations, based on SE (various years) and KSH (1973) pp. 42, 342.

As far as the 1970s are concerned, a study prepared by Hungarian statisticians (Jánosi *et al.*, 1980) confirmed the view, suggested above. It was found that the 30 largest industrial investment projects with a construction time of 4 years or more had accounted for no more than 13-15 per cent of total investment outlays (at current prices) between 1970-1977.

Table 1.8 displays the distribution of Hungarian investments by size. These figures, which are more recent, show that in 1989 six projects fell under the "large" category.[24] The total value of expenditures on these projects amounted to only 4 % of total investment expenditures. This was not merely a result of the recent heavy cuts in investment. The relative importance of

[24] "Large" investment projects are usually the most expensive ones. However costs are not the only factor which count for the purposes of statistical classification. The definition used by the Central Statistical Office of Hungary, for example, was flexible. The appellation "large investment project" was the prerogative of the Council of Ministers, which awarded this title on the basis of case-by-case decisions. (KSH 1983, p. 409)

"large" projects was not dramatically different in earlier years, either, although in those years the number of large projects was many times higher. No comparison with the pre-1968 period can be made, as the classification was different in those years.

Data for Poland during the Gierek years (i.e. in the period which produced the longest investment boom in the entire history of socialist eastern Europe) suggest similar conclusions. Adam (1989, p. 99) quoted a figure according to which in 1974 there had been 109 large, priority investments in that country, which had meant preferential claim on supplies and inclusion in the state plan by name. These 109 projects amounted to only 22 % of all the investment costs in the given year.

For Czechoslovakia, only indirect results are available. On the basis of econometric investigations, Kyn *et al.* (1979) concluded that the gestation period of the average investment project in the 1970s was less than 1 year. The authors estimated Almon's polynominally-distributed lag coefficients between investment and newly completed capital construction. This was done separately for GINV and investment in building and construction. The estimates of individual lag coefficients showed that 44-56 % of GINV was spent on projects which were finished in the same year, and 19-28 % were spent on projects finished within two years. For GINV, the share of investment completed in more than three years was 10-15 %.

Beyond the lack of statistical evidence, there are no logical reasons either to suggest that large projects were the real culprits responsible for GINV fluctuations.

We have already seen in section 1.3 that there was a genuine military build-up everywhere. This process, by nature, must have had a macro-economic impact different from that of the long-lasting raw material projects. According to Goldmann, the cyclical impact of raw material projects arises out of a simple technological fact. Construction of these concurrent projects is a heavy burden to the nation's economy over several years. From the moment they are commissioned, their output appears on the market and makes a contribution to easing shortages and accelerating the growth process. For obvious reasons this impact is non-existent in the case of military projects. They are expensive but yield no economic return. The macro-economic burden may lessen as such projects come on stream but there is no positive feed-back to the growth process.

As military expenditures have always been closely guarded secrets in the socialist countries, estimates of their size are few and far between. Nonetheless, some data in the literature can be used as rough indicators of the size of the military build-up.

In Poland of the early 1950s, for instance, 80 % of total engineering output was channelled directly into armaments (the manufacturing of weapons and military transport vehicles). Mining, energy, the chemical industry and agriculture had to share among themselves the remaining 20 % (Montias 1962, p. 64). During 1950-1952, 60 % of investments in the Hungarian engineering branch was used directly for military purposes. Nationwide, it was estimated (Bencze 1990) that between 1950-1954 military expenditures (including both current and capital outlays) amounted to more than 50 billion forints, which is extremely high compared with the 67 billion forints used for fixed investments in the economy as a whole. Of course, this was not the general case after the 1950s - or perhaps after the mid-1950s. The military burden on the economies of the non-Soviet Warsaw Pact countries was generally considered to have been quite modest. But this is not the point. What is argued here concerns the early part of the 1950s: then the East European economies were unquestionably overburdened by the military build-up, and this was mistakenly perceived by contemporary observers - such as Goldmann - as something originating in the industrialization drive and the simultaneous launching of several large projects in the energy and the raw material sectors.

Finally, it is worth noting that the equilibrium-minded economists' fear from mammoth projects had a funny side-effect on actual developments. The more was said about the harmful impact of large investment projects on macro-economic stability, the more likely it was that the Centre increased its control over them. Pushing this argument to the extreme can lead to ridiculous conclusions. According to Selyunin (1989), Khrushchev was once told that Gosplan was unable to say a firm "no" to investment demands. So, he wanted to take a bold initiative. "From tomorrow, not a single major construction work can be put into the plan without my personal authorization," he rumbled, with the usual self-confidence of autocratic rulers. He was obviously not aware that about 100 thousand large projects were under construction in the Soviet Union in those years.

1.5 THEORY AND STATISTICAL REALITY

As we have seen in table 1.1, the observed or estimated length of the investment cycle varies between 2 and 12 years. This fact alone gives food for thought. To decide which results are acceptable, we have to do more than look at goodness of fit. Various models describing the same phenomenon, but based on different lines of thought and yielding different results, cannot be simultaneously correct. It is difficult to believe that one economist's behavioural formulation is as good as any other's, and that it is simply an empirical question of which fits the data best.

The fact that the number of empirical works is increasing is not in itself evidence of the existence of the observed phenomenon, if their conclusions are contradictory. For some authors it is a natural phenomenon, suggesting merely that more research is required to arrive at a final conclusion.

> "As it could be seen from the (...) summary of empirical results, well-documented facts of cyclical fluctuations in the Bulgarian economy are not few in number. They, however, are fragmentary and sometimes lead to contradictory conclusions about the duration of the cycle. Such a state of things is not unexpected. The accumulated facts are sufficient to corroborate the existence of cyclical development in the Bulgarian economy. Its existence is proved. Some of the possible sources of the cyclical fluctuations are localized. The discrepancy of the results obtained reflects the contradictory nature of the phenomenon itself. In the Bulgarian economy, like in any other economy, the cycle is not an unidimensional process. It is a complex structure formed of many individual interactions of cycles of different periodicity. Apparently, the diversity of these cycles and their inter-linkages are still poorly studied." (Avramov 1990, p. 36)

However, if we accept this approach, we might as well believe in the existence of the Loch Ness Monster. Since the 6th century thousands of observers have reported seeing "something" 3 meters or 30 meters long in the lake and hundreds of scholarly articles were written on the subject. However, most scientists believe that there is no monster in Loch Ness, and that most reported sightings are the result of an overactive imagination plus misidentification of waves, well-known animals or other common objects.

In this introductory chapter, words such as "theory" and "reality" were used in a narrow sense. First, when discussing theories (models), it should be understood that reference is made only to a sub-set of the various theoretical attempts to explain GINV fluctuations. This sub-set consists only of *empirical* works. This does not necessarily imply that all of the studies contain an empirical verification of the theory outlined in them. It does mean, however, that the models which they present are directly suitable for such a test. Purely *mathematical* studies, such as Bródy (1980), Roland (1987), Kovács and Tarján (1988) or Simonovits (1987,1990, 1991), however, remain outside the scope of this book. In many cases, there is a trivial similarity between mathematical models, which are not, as noted, analyzed in this book, and empirical ones, which in turn will often be cited or discussed. Some readers may object that this differentiation is artificial. This may well be true but in order to limit the scope of the investigation, for reasons of space, and also lack of competence, the exclusion of purely mathematical models appears a straightforward solution.

The second term which requires some further explanation is "reality". Throughout this book, reality means *statistical reality*. Undoubtedly, this is once again a very narrow concept. There are many things that statistics do not and cannot describe. In addition, the figures and time series actually produced by the statisticians are not necessarily relevant or reliable. A great deal of caution is required in substituting missing or obviously incorrect data. The example of Bajt's difficulties with the GDR investment figures has already been mentioned, and the research effort for the present work had to face even more serious problems.

Chinese investment data, for example, are provided only at current prices, and even these are is limited to expenditures by the state sector. A thorough analysis of investment fluctuations in China would undoubtedly be of very great importance. China was the second largest socialist empire, covering 40 years of history. The Chinese experience could offer conclusive proof for or against the theory of socialist investment cycles. Unfortunately, the official data are unsuitable for carrying out such an analysis. Without detailed information about price developments[25] and the pattern of investments occurring outside the state sector, nothing can be done. In such cases, professional probity requires us to recall what the German sociologist, Max Weber, quoted from a lecture of a 19th century anatomist: "The spleen. We do not know anything about the spleen. Gentlemen, so much for the spleen."

In the period under review, the socialist countries numbered almost 40 (table 1.9) but only 13 published investment data on a regular basis. The number of countries where the statistical authorities reported investment time series at constant prices was even smaller. This was a consequence of the fact that many of these countries refused to cooperate with the multilateral organizations (IMF, World Bank and CMEA).

For sound analysis, of course, a single time series is inadequate. Other macro-economic data are needed to compare movements with changes in other economic activities, and to explain the different amplitudes and volatility of various series. In practice, however, the real bottleneck was the availability of investment time series (GINV or GFCF) at constant prices. Thus, the detailed analysis had ultimately to be limited to 8 socialist countries: Bulgaria, Czechoslovakia, the German Democratic Republic, Hungary, Poland, Romania, Yugoslavia and the Soviet Union. In Appendix II series are presented for Albania, China, Mongolia, Viet Nam and Cuba as well, but most of them are at current prices and in some cases incomplete.[26]

Having reduced data needs to an absolute minimum - gross investment at constant prices - we still have to confront numerous other problems. GINV data are incomplete for the early periods. In some cases, it is known that those early figures, if available, were compiled according to a vastly different methodology. For several countries and several periods, there is every reason to be extremely sceptical concerning the reliability of the published figures. This will be demonstrated later in more detail.

[25] The assumption of "no-change" in prices is logically straightforward, but almost certainly incorrect. According to some fragmented data collated by Japanese China experts, between the late 1950s and the late 1970s unit costs in construction investments increased by 50-70 per cent (Salvini 1989, p. 52).

[26] In order to characterize the paucity of statistics in these countries, it is enough to mention just one aspect. Between 1973 and 1992 Albania had no regular statistical reporting system at all, although a pocket-book size yearbook has been available since 1987. In Viet Nam the national statistical yearbook was published irregularly, one in 1978, then in 1985 and recently in 1989. The situation is similar or worse with respect to North Korea. During forty years of communist rule, nobody in the West has ever seen its statistical yearbook. China released its first yearbook only in 1981. For a systematic, though not up-to-date account on statistical publications, see Westfall (1986).

TABLE 1.9 Data availability in the socialist countries, 1989

Name or abbreviation	Membership in CMEA as of end-1989	Membership in IMF as of end-1989	Availability of investment data according to MPS current prices	MPS constant prices	SNA current prices	SNA constant prices
Europe						
Albania	1949- c/		1950,55,58-69	1954-64,70,80, 87-		
Bulgaria	1949-		1983-	1950-1983		
CSSR	1949-			1950-1989		
GDR	1950-			1950-1989	1980-89	1980-89
Hungary	1949-	1982-	1950-89	1950-1989	1960-89	1960-89
Poland	1949-	1986-	1950-89	1950-1989		
Romania	1949-	1972-	1983-89	1950-1989		
USSR	1949-			1950-1989		
Yugoslavia	Coop. agreement	1945-		1950-1989		
Asia						
Afghanistan	Observer	1955-				
Burma		1952-			1970-	1970-
China		1945-	1953-87			
Cambodia						
Dem. Rep. Korea						
Laos	Observer					
Mongolia	1962-		1950,55,58-			
Viet Nam	1978-			1972, 1980-89		
Dem. Yemen	Observer	1969-			1975-80	
Africa						
Angola	Observer					
Benin		1963-		1970-	1970-78	
Burkina Faso		1963-			1964-85	1970-84
Congo		1963-			1978-	
Ethiopia	Observer	1945-			1973-86	
Guinea						
Guinea-Bissau						
Madagascar		1963-			1977,80-82	1970,77
Mozambique	Observer			1980-85		
Sao Tomé ...		1977-				
Somalia		1962-			1970-81	1970-81
Tanzania		1962-				
Zimbabwe		1980-		1970-	1970-85	
America						
Cuba	1972-		1960,1962-89	1962-65		
Grenada		1975-			1980-86	
Guayana		1966-			1970-	1970-75
Nicaragua		1946-			1970-	

One of the main themes in this book is indeed the contention that the data problem is one of the central issues of empirical analysis with regard to the socialist economies. It is very tempting for an economist to make life easier by shifting responsibility to the statisticians. However, a sentence or a paragraph describing the poor state of statistics in the socialist countries can suggest no more than half the truth, or even less.

Statistics are never perfect. Students of western business cycles, using data for the United States, the United Kingdom or Germany, have good reason to sleep well. In general, such confidence would be misplaced in the analysis of socialist economies. Were the data only imprecise, one could hope that distortions would be randomly distributed. Unfortunately, this is surely not the case. Distortions are one-sided, although of varying intensity. As we shall see later, these are intrinsic problems deeply rooted in the socio-economic texture of socialist countries.

Narrowing our focus to the subject of this book, we can say that the measurement errors of GINV data are of endogenous origin. This explains why such a seemingly technical issue has been brought to the forefront of the arguments presented here. The questions and problems related to data reliability are so important that I have felt obliged to use a *double-argument method* throughout this book. Though this is a rather unusual way of presenting scholarly ideas, I am deeply convinced that either to set aside the data problem or to focus the analysis exclusively on the data problem would be equally misleading. The analysis of the investment regime and the critique of the underlying data are logically inseparable.

In the following chapters, therefore, one line of argument stresses the poor reliability of the data and points out that for this reason every theory explaining cycles or fluctuations is built on quicksand. This line of argument obviously weakens any contentions concerning the theory of cycles itself. Doubts concerning data reliability also have some deleterious impact upon the validity of the looser approach - made in respect of the theory of exogenous fluctuations - but it is smaller than in the first case.

The second line of argument follows the logic of supposition frequently used in everyday language: "Let us suppose..." In our case, the second part of the sentence runs: "... that all GINV data are faultless." Thus, all the arguments advanced concerning the unreliability of data are shelved, and all GINV figures are considered as 100 per cent accurate. Following this, the most important investment cycle models are scrutinized and tested on the basis of evidence collected from the GINV data of the eight countries mentioned. The treatment adopted is to test the hypotheses, so that comparison may be made with the exogenous fluctuation model. It will be suggested that the variants of the investment cycle model provide no unified system for explaining fluctuations in the majority of the socialist countries in most periods under review. Partly because of its greater breadth of explanatory power in time and cross-country comparisons it is concluded that the exogenous fluctuation models are more satisfactory than the two competing approaches.

1.6 THE RELEVANCE OF CYCLE MODELS

Once an agreement has been reached on terminology, what remains to be decided is a matter of fact. My reading of these facts is that socialist investment cycles never existed. Apart from a few arguments, which will become apparent in the discussion of broader issues, the bulk of the evidence is assembled in Chapter 3. Some readers, however, will object already at this stage. "The author may be right or wrong on these facts. But does it really matter whether we accept or refute the theory of investment cycles?"

This question, in my view, is legitimate, though some authors are reluctant to pose it themselves. By definition, "cycles" are more or less predictable, while "fluctuations" are obviously not. From a practical point of view, the result of the debate over investment cycles is important because if the answer is positive then something could have been done about it. If the socialist economy had a built-in tendency to generate investment cycles, then a carefully calibrated anti-cyclical policy could have helped to stabilize the economy. And indeed such propositions were often made by various authors (Krasovskii 1979, Bródy 1983a, Kolodko 1986, Tsygichko and Nikolaeva 1989, Avramov 1990a). By contrast, if the investment cycle theory was faulty or unfounded, the pursuance of an anti-cyclical policy would have been not only pointless but possibly even harmful.

Discussions of cyclical fluctuations have usually amounted to an implied criticism of the existing economic mechanism.[27] Nonetheless, when partisans of the investment cycle theory insist that there is a certain type of regularity, a deterministic rule behind investment fluctuations, they acquit economic policy makers of their responsibility. In the light of their model, it seems that policy makers are not responsible for the fluctuations since they are only cogs in a powerful, socio-economic machinery. The men and women of economic power portrayed here, as Podkaminer (1989) says tongue-in-cheek, are shortsighted, and behave in an automatic, almost instinctive way: "they can (...) do little harm. Even if they blunder into some dreadful situation (e.g., start an overextended investment expansion) they will be, sooner or later, forced into a "normal" path characterized by much inertia, slow growth and even stagnation in almost every aspect of the economy - including the level and composition of the shortages" (p. 24).

The issue at stake is even greater, if viewed from a theoretical point of view. The investment cycle theory is not only one of the descriptive models of socialism. There is no exaggeration in saying, that after SEP, this is perhaps the most popular, most elaborated and formalised framework for understanding what happens in the Soviet-type economies.

As we saw, the endogenous cycle theory is inseparably related to a particular perception of real socialism in which planning and SEP are the main theoretical building blocks. Thus, the disapproval of this approach implies a direct challenge to the general perception of socialism described above.

For a very simple reason, the fate of the theory of socialist investment cycles has been closely linked to the process of reform thinking, too. At some stage of their professional life, the most prominent representatives of this school, such as Kalecki, Goldmann, Bajt, Bauer, were all closely involved in the preparation of reform blueprints. With the benefit of hindsight, it is not difficult to see this link today, and also its implications.

[27] Bauer made this point very explicit on the first pages of his *magnum opus*: "Throughout the book it is regarded as evident that dispersion of investments, their sluggishness and cyclical fluctuation have an unquestionably detrimental impact upon economic development". (Bauer 1981, p. 28)

Between the early 1950s and the fundamental political and constitutional changes in the autumn of 1989, reform proposals were necessarily self-limited everywhere in the region. First, there was a political constraint. It was assumed that the countries' constitutional set-up (including issues related to property rights, the role of the communist party), as well as the region's geopolitical structure could not and need not be changed. Thus, the predominance of state ownership was never questioned by the mainstream of reform thinking.

There was a second type of constraint, which was more pertinent from our point of view. The idea of reform presupposes that the subject of the exercise has a *definite* and *established* structure. Both adjectives are important. The structure was thought to be definite in the sense that reform economists assumed that the defectiveness of the system was in the domain of economics. Hence the conclusion: if economic performance is not satisfactory, it is the economists' job to identify the part of the economic machinery that has to be replaced. The system was believed to be established in the sense of feasibility. The economy was perceived in what I will call the *trend-oscillation* framework. The general trend of development was thought to be slowly rising (in terms of quantitative growth and qualitative improvements), while the occasionally surfacing imbalances and their subsequent attenuations were perceived as positive and negative oscillations around this trend. There were very few economists who questioned this framework.[28]

Retrospectively, it is easy to criticise this approach. Economic reform is unthinkable, if the system is believed to be in the process of continuous disintegration and the countervailing forces, which nonetheless keep the machinery running, are thought to be essentially outside the reach of economic decision making.

[28] Once again, the Birman (1989) article is the only one that springs to mind. In this seminal paper, the Soviet emigre economist explicitly states on two occasions that "Soviet-type economies do not work in cycles" (pp. 145-146). Instead, he argues, the Soviet economy was characterized by a process of cumulative disequilibrium which is bound to result in eventual collapse.

1.7 Formalised summary

To recapitulate, the quintessence of the three schools' attempts to explain investment fluctuations can be expressed in the following equations:

(1.1) Control theory model

GINV = f_1 (Q_1, ... Q_n),
where Q_1, ... Q_n are system-invariant economic factors and
n is a relatively small number.

(1.2) Endogenous cyclical theory model

GINV = f_2 (Q_1, ... Q_n),
where Q_1, ... Q_n are system specific economic factors and
n is a relatively small number.

(1.3) Theory of exogenous fluctuations

GINV = f_3 (Q_1, ... Q_n),
where Q_1, ... Q_n denotes economic, political and other factors and
n is a relatively large number.

What is not always clear in a verbal analysis of a subject may emerge as a triviality in the formal presentation. The essential flaw in the first two frameworks is the deterministic explanation of investment fluctuations. The assumption, which sometimes remains implicit in the verbal argumentation, is that factors Q_1, ... Q_n play more or less the same role in every socialist country, and in every period of economic history. This point is even more accentuated in the formalised econometric models, where Q_1, ... Q_n factors are presented with fixed β_1, β_2,... β_n weights. This is difficult to accept.

2. THREE SCHOOLS OF THOUGHT

> It is easy to obtain confirmations, or verifications, for nearly every theory - if we look for confirmations. (...) Every genuine test of theory is an attempt to falsify it, or to refute it. Testability is falsifiability; but there are degrees of testability: some theories are more testable, more exposed to refutation, than others; they take, as it were, greater risks.
>
> Popper (1968, p. 36)

The issues concerning the existence and origin of socialist investment cycles have been widely studied for decades. It is not the objective of the present work to survey this literature *in extenso*. This is not even necessary, since in the second half of the 1980s several studies were published which, taken together, leave very little more to be still discovered.[1] However, a bird eye's view summary of the literature is felt to be needed, since the position proposed in this book cannot be interpreted in a vacuum. It is also noteworthy that during the last two-three years the proliferation of cheap, user-friendly econometric packages together with improved access to Eastern statistical data has led to an unprecedented upsurge in the empirical research. Thus, it is essential to take stock of the latest findings.

Relying on the terminology introduced in Section 1.1, the views of three schools will be summarized in this chapter:

1. Control theory models
2. Endogenous models
3. Exogenous models.

As with all classifications, the above is not free from a certain element of arbitrariness. The studies which will be referred to are usually long and comprehensive. The models presented or the arguments marshalled are carefully built and worded. It was inevitable to some extent that the classification of an author or his model in one of the three groups would be based on a somewhat simplistic interpretation of the authors's position. The labels attached to the first two groups do not require any further explanation but the third one does.

There are two common characteristics in the studies grouped together under the label of "exogenous". First, they take account of stochastic, as opposed to deterministic, processes. Second, the authors go beyond the traditional model of socialism (as described in section 1.3).

[1] The pioneering work of Cobeljic and Stojanovic (1969) is still the best survey of the early east European and Soviet discussions available in English. Two dissertations written in German - Sabov (1983) and Paraskewopoulos (1985) - were also devoted to the subject, heavy emphasis being given to a survey of the literature in German. For a more recent summary see Dallago (1987), whose review article was published only in French. There is a growing Bulgarian literature on the subject, for which the best English summary is Avramov (1990).

In the perception of the authors concerned, the economy of the socialist countries is not a *sui generis* entity, where economic processes are determined by the intrinsic logic of the economic system itself. There are two important building blocks of the socialist system which prevent this:

(i) Despite their "official" claim to the contrary, socialist economies have permanently adjusted themselves to world market conditions, where essentially the rules of the market economies prevail. Undoubtedly, this adjustment was tardy and imperfect but it occurred.

(ii) Historically, socialist regimes were built on capitalist and pre-capitalist foundations. These traditions, which had shaped the mentality of consumers and managers alike, have survived. If not in other forms, these traditions continued to exert influence on the present, as the new regime was forced to wage a constant war against them.

2.1 Control theory models

As already noted more than once, several authors explain fluctuations in socialist countries in terms which are neither system-specific, nor necessarily economic. Most of these attempts are purely theoretical but they nonetheless represent a thought-provoking and influential body of literature.

2.1.1 The Complexity Argument. In its simplest form, it is argued that every economy is a sophisticated machinery, and that therefore its functioning cannot be free from unevenness. This is claimed to be true always and everywhere. Such a conclusion can of course be reached on purely speculative grounds, without any empirical work. Well before World War II, in an essay on socialism, planning and the business cycle, the German economist W. Röpke concluded that:

> the ultimate origin of the economic disturbances of the present economic system lies in facts which distinguish capitalism from pre-capitalism, not capitalism from socialism. The economic system has become so complicated that to attain a continuous and perfect co-ordination is a problem which capitalism and socialism have equally to face. It can be hardly emphasized too much that every economic system, no matter how organized, which is based on a very extended scale of the division of labour and on technique and structure of production as complicated as the present one, is bound to be exposed to all sorts of dynamic disturbances. (Röpke 1936, p. 324)

A dynamic version of the very same idea emerged three decades later, in the seminal works of two Yugoslav economists, Cobeljic and Stojanovic (1961, 1969). In their view, socialist investment cycles are the result of technical developments. It is a fact which is nearly forgotten, and therefore worthy of mention, that their 1961 paper, which appeared in Serbo-Croat, was the first theoretical attempt in the socialist countries to come to grips with the problem of investment fluctuations.

Since the most important innovations always come as a surprise, the argument says, and their impact on the productive branches is unforeseeable, overall economic development is bound to take place through a sequence of imbalances. In this perspective the investment cycle is nothing else but a reflection of this process. This framework, as we can see, owes a lot to Schumpeter, although the authors do not explicitly refer to him in their 170 page study.

Paradoxically, though not exceptionally, the weakness of this line of thought originates in the very strength of the concept. This model is truly deterministic in that there is no exogenous force needed to initiate oscillatory movements. However, as Soós (1976, 1986) rightly pointed out, the authors present planners as if they were powerless prisoners of technological developments. First, if their logic is accepted, then all ups and downs in economic activity appear to be fully justified and necessary - a conclusion which is difficult to accept and which is, probably, not in agreement with the authors's own intentions either. Second, the concept of a shock-like development of technology is not supported by the facts. Investment policies in the socialist countries were mainly characterized not by the utilization of unexpected new technologies but rather by a planned adoption of widely known technological achievements.

Another refinement in following up the complexity idea is that, in countries with similar development levels, not only are causal relationships identical but also the periodicity of the cycle as well. Among authors in the socialist countries, this proposition had first been advocated by the Hungarian economist András Bródy (1972), in a paper which was followed by a host of others from his pen.

> It is a widely accepted view of economists that large systems with a high degree of freedom are more or less unstable. In mathematical terms this means that they have a given system-immanent frequency which, once incited, can turn into wave-like fluctuations. The social division of labour in a modern economy can also be viewed as such a large system. It is thus little wonder that under capitalism and socialism the same or similar periodicity - i.e. system-immanent frequency - comes to the surface. Since the technical proportions of the division of labour are not very much different, one can reasonably expect similar wave-lengths.[2]

2.1.2 Election Cycles in Soviet-type Economies. Another body of literature, still within the group of control theory models, takes the similarity of social structures as its starting point. The argument advanced by authors such as Mieczkowski (1978) and Bunce (1980) is that socio-economic fluctuations observed in the socialist countries are essentially analogous to the "election cycles" of the Western market economies. Of course, one difference is noted: the recurring replacement of political leaders is not a reflection of the people's democratically expressed will but the result of eruptive fluctuations in the popular mood.

Politicians passing the torch to one another start the race to consolidate their power by popular moves in the area of living standards. This period, the theory holds, is usually followed by an acceleration phase, whereby consumers' interest is sacrificed on the altar of higher accumulation. After a few years, the population's open or concealed discontent triggers a backlash: top economic figures are replaced and a new team takes over the torch from the previous one.

The idea of a more complex mechanism, though similar to that described above, was elaborated independently in the empirical works of Brainard (1974), Lafay (1981), Shimakura (1982), McFarlane (1984) and Ungvárszki (1986, 1989). Ambitious investment effort, these authors argue, is always a potential source of danger. As the investment boom unfolds, important social groups or fractions of the ruling party may question the political and professional competence of the top economic leaders.[3] The boom, the subsequent slow down and the usual hugger-mugger accompanying both of them are bound to provoke various types of economic imbalance (foreign indebtedness, government deficit, shortages, etc.). As these issues inevitably surface, the political legitimacy of the ruling elite may also be questioned. There are two things that can happen in such situations. First, important social strata (e.g., industrial workers or the

[2] My translation from the original German manuscript (pp.1-2). I am grateful to Mr. T. Tarján (*Institute of Economics*, Budapest), for drawing my attention to this manuscript. Unfortunately, this truly seminal paper has hitherto remained unpublished, though its contents have long been known among Hungarian students of investment cycles.

[3] This argument can already be found in Olivera's seminal article on the theoretical possibilities of cyclical growth. He was sure that "generalized social disapproval will subject the planning authority to increasing pressure, urging a change in its allocation criteria; and that such pressure, if disregarded, will finally become an element in the internal competition for social control" (Olivera 1960, p. 245).

peasantry) may enter into open conflict with the regime. Second, the unity of the ruling elite may also suffer a setback.

Against this background a political cycle mechanism can emerge, with opposing factions of the ruling party playing a role similar to the inter-party battles in western democracies. The cycle takes the form of various institutional actions to bring about alternating centralisation and decentralisation of economic control. The result is that when the economy is centralized, it becomes rigid; when it is decentralized, it is thrown into confusion. This brings a return to centralized control, which in turn produces a greater rigidity.

2.1.3 Replacement Cycles and the Role of Large Investment Projects. For those generations of economists raised on Marxist traditions, it goes without saying that if investment cycles exist, they must one way or another be connected with the service life and/or the gestation period of investment goods themselves. From this basis, there are at least two possible branching offs.

(i) A tradition based on the most influential expression of this view - Lange (1969) - works with a conventional hypothesis. It is claimed that investment goods put into operation simultaneously would reach the end of their service life more or less simultaneously as well. If the actual replacement of this vintage of the capital stock is closely synchronized with the physical and technical depreciation process, then this breeds a *replacement (reinwestycnyni) cycle.*[4]

Since neither Lange, nor others who followed his footsteps did in fact attempt to verify their models in a direct, empirical manner, a very simple question remained unanswered. Assuming the relevance of the replacement cycle, what kind of periodicity might arise from this process at the macro-economic level? Five years, ten years, twenty years? Marxist textbooks - e.g., Lange (1978, p. 351) - used to work with a guess-figure of 10 years in their illustrative calculations. In reality, however, the average service life of the capital stock varies between 15-20 years. Several studies arrive at this common figure, based on statistical and econometric estimation procedures carried out both for western market and socialist economies.[5] Therefore, the idea of the replacement cycle as a proper vehicle for explaining GINV fluctuations cannot be seriously taken into consideration.

(ii) The unpublished paper of Bródy (1972), already mentioned in Section 2.1, worked with an expanded version of the Harrod-Domar growth model. The point he made was that uneven investment starts of *large investment projects* may lead to spontaneous cycles due to the commitment which is inherent in the launchings. Again, this is a system-independent mechanism which is able to produce identical wave-like fluctuations in any country. Bródy assumed that in a one-commodity world, investment projects always required two years for completion.

[4] For more recent studies along these lines, see Kovács and Tarján (1988) and Tarján (1988).

[5] In the United States and Germany the average service life of machinery in the manufacturing sector is estimated at between 15-20 years (UN ESE 1987, pp. 86-88). For the EE7 similar estimates are produced on a regular basis by the UN/ECE (see e.g., UN ESE 1985, pp. 137-138). Fink and Sláma (1976) and Kyn and Schrettl (1979) have published estimates of the service life of machinery and equipment in Czechoslovakia, the GDR, Poland and the Soviet Union and arrived at a figure of 15-20 years. Green (1978) looked at the service life of total Soviet capital stock (i.e. including buildings) and got a similar result.

The ß realization coefficient expresses what proportion of a given project's cost appears in the first year. In this two-year model, the value of the second-year realization coefficient is (1-ß). The time distribution of costs of the investment process - ß and (1-ß) - is a technically determined fact, dictated by the development level of the economy in question.

In the traditional Harrod-Domar model

(2.1) $$b(y_{t+1} - y_t) = sy_t,$$

where y_t is the income generated in year t, b is capital intensity, s is the savings rate. In the two-year model the basic equation is

(2.2) $$\beta\, b(y_{t+2} - y_{t+1}) + (1-\beta)\, b(y_{t+1} - y_t) = sy_t.$$

This means that in every year, total investment outlays consist of two parts. The first part - $\beta\, b(y_{t+2} - y_{t+1})$ - is used for new investments, as a result of which income will be generated only in two years time, and the second part - $(1-\beta)\, b(y_{t+1} - y_t)$ - is used for the completion of projects started in the previous year.

Using this simple two-year model, Bródy showed that if ß < 0.5 the investment process - and therefore the whole economy - may have a tendency to move toward a cyclical growth path.

Put simply, the cyclical pattern stems from the fact that if ß is small, several projects can be simultaneously launched in year t from a given investment budget, which in turn calls for much greater investment in year t+1. Perhaps the planned investment budget will allow the necessary completions to be financed in year t+1, and leave some finance for new launchings. Sooner or later, however, the total volume of investment commitments arising from the proliferation of launchings in the third, fourth, etc. years, will surpass the planned investment budget and nothing will remain for new launchings. A simple numerical example helps to make this clear (table 2.1).

Let us assume that the volume of annual investments is 100 and remains constant over the period. The value of the ß coefficient is 1/3 (Example 1) or 2/3 (Example 2), meaning that in the first year only 1/3 (or 2/3) of the total investment costs are spent on the simultaneously launched two-year investment projects. In Examples 1 and 2 we start in year t, with initial values which are different from the equilibrium values (66.667: 33.333).

In the first case (Example 1 and 4), when the economy is moving away from the equilibrium path, there are two alternatives. Either the launching of new projects will have to be sacrificed, or some ongoing projects will have to be frozen. Both solutions are likely to be the sources of new tensions in later years.

The idea that the cost distribution of investment projects is generally not uniform over time is a logical and defendable assumption, especially if the world of a simple two-year model is abandoned.

Now, consider a model with an average gestation period of 6 years.[6] In theory, four cases can be distinguished (Table 2.2 Panel A). The less likely possibilities are the uniform (linear) and symmetrical (normal) distributions. Following a terminology introduced by Tényi (1976), the distribution is "stem-heavy" if the bulk of the total cost are falling due in the initial phase of

[6] This is still a very far-fetched assumption. As we have seen, in reality the average gestation time is typically below 2 years. Nevertheless, we have to go along with this assumption for the sake of understanding the contention of this group of theories.

TABLE 2.1 Investment commitment in a two-year model

Total volume of annual investments = 100 units

	Example 1 $\beta = 1/3$		Example 2 $\beta = 2/3$		Example 3 $\beta = 1/3$		Example 4 $\beta = 1/3$		Example 5 $\beta = 2/3$	
Inherited state	Ongoing projects	New projects	Ongoing projects	New projects	Ongoing projects	New projects	Ongoing projects	New projects	Ongoing projects	New projects
	65	35	35	65	66.667	33.333	66.800	33.200	66.667	33.333
1. year	70	30	33	68	66.667	33.333	66.400	33.600	16.667	83.333
2. year	60	40	34	66	66.667	33.333	67.200	32.800	41.667	58.333
3. year	80	20	33	67	66.667	33.333	65.600	34.400	29.167	70.833
4, year	40	60	33	67	66.667	33.333	68.800	31.200	35.417	64.583
5. year	120	-20	33	67	66.667	33.333	62.400	37.600	32.292	67.708
5. year	-40	140	33	67	66.667	33.333	75.200	24.800	33.854	66.146
6. year	280	-180	33	67	66.667	33.333	49.600	50.400	33.073	66.927
7. year	-360	460	33	67	66.667	33.333	100.800	-0.800	33.464	66.536
8. year	920	-820	33	67	66.667	33.333	-1.600	101.600	33.268	66.732
9.year	-1640	1740	33	67	66.667	33.333	203.200	-103.200	33.366	66.634
10. year	3480	-3380	33	67	66.667	33.333	-206.400	306.400	33.317	66.683

Explanation: Example 1, 1. year: Investment needs for ongoing projects = 2*35 = 70. Free resources for new starts = 100-30 = 70

Source: Own calculations, based on an example in Tényi (1976) p.94.

TABLE 2.2 Hungary: Average coefficients of implementation of large investment projects

Author	1.	2.	3.	4.	5.	6.	Type of distribution
			year after start				
	Panel A: Theoretical distributions						
	16.7	16.7	16.7	16.7	16.7	16.7	Linear
	5	15	30	30	15	5	Normal
	5	10	20	20	20	25	Stern-heavy
	25	20	20	20	10	5	Stem-heavy
	Panel B: Expert's guestimates and empirical results for Hungary in the second part of the 1970s						
I. Berend (Planning Office)	25	10	10	18	25	12	Stern-heavy
I. Huszár (Planning Office)	7	15	27	23	17	11	Normal
Jánosi et al. (1980) (from investment surveys of the Central Statistical Office) 1970-1977: 30 state, large industrial investment projects	5	10	22	33	20	10	Stern-heavy
Jánosi and Pál (1983) (from investment surveys of the Central Statistical Office) 1970-1977: 70 state, large industrial investment projects	7	17	30	25	14	8	Slightly stem-heavy
1970-1977: 80 large industrial investment projects, financed by own funds of firms	14	17	20	21	18	9	Normal

(continued)

Panel C: Empirical results and econometrically tested models for Hungary in the second part of the 1970s

	1.	2.	3.	4.	.	.	
	year after start						
Jánosi et al. (1980) (from investment surveys of the Central Statistical Office) 1970-1977: 30 state, large industrial investment projects	9	28	45	18			Stem-heavy
Jánosi and Pál (1983) (from investment surveys of the Central Statistical Office) 1970-1977: 70 state, large industrial investment projects	13	40	33	14	.	.	Slightly stem-heavy
1970-1977: 80 large industrial investment projects, financed by own funds of firms	22	29	32	17	.	.	Normal
Lackó (1980) (experimental values)	19	29	33	19	.	.	Slightly stem-heavy

Source: Lackó (1980), Soós (1983b), Jánosi et al. (1980), Jánosi and Pál (1983)

the project (Years: 1,2,3). The distribution is "stern-heavy" if the lion's share of expenditures fall due in the completion phase of the projects (Years: 4,5,6).

As we can see, there are two implicit working hypotheses in Bródy's seminal paper. First, large investment projects are stern-heavy by nature. His second assumption was that as a result of numerous simultaneously launched high cost projects, the expenditure pattern of the aggregate investment process is also likely to be stern-heavy.[7] What he demonstrated mathematically in a two-year model appears to be valid in a more general sense too. Tarján (1988), again using mathematical tools, showed that if in a one commodity world stern-heavy projects dominate the total investment pattern, then the investment process is bound to move towards a cyclical path. On the basis of the stylized facts suggested by Bródy, another Hungarian economist (Lackó 1980) was able to demonstrate that with a hypothetical, slightly stern-heavy lag structure of total investment expenditures, an illustrative model based on Hungarian data for total investment outlays was capable of explaining a good part of the GINV fluctuations.

We should not forget, however, that this body of literature (i) offers an answer to a question which is different from ours; and (ii) has a starting hypothesis which is contrafactual. Let us consider these two objections in order.

(i) We have to acknowledge that these authors were successful in marshalling some evidence to illustrate a sufficient condition of a GINV cycle. By contrast, our investigation is focused upon actual developments. Even if we accept the demonstration of the sufficient conditions, we need convincing arguments or hard statistical facts to be convinced that in a given country and period (or ideally in all socialist countries in all periods), stern-heavy investment projects really dominate the aggregate GINV pattern.

(ii) None of the countries reviewed in this book possesses a statistical monitoring system which registers the cost distribution of all ongoing investment projects. On the basis of the evidence presented in the previous chapter, the explanation seems rather straightforward. Taking the national economy as a whole, the average gestation time of investments is certainly much lower than assumed in the control theory models. It is not 5 or 6 years, which would make the creation of such a monitoring system technically possible and economically meaningful, but much shorter, somewhere between 1 and 2 years.

Fragmentary data on large investment projects, however, are available from Hungary, which had in fact been compiled exactly for such a purpose: i.e. to monitor the cost distribution of investments. Note, however, that these investigations produced markedly different results from essentially the same data sample. This greatly detracts from the credibility of these estimates.

Soós (1983) and Lackó (1986) reported three sets of such figures. Two of them had been originally commissioned from specialists at the Planning Office (Mr. I. Berend and Mrs. J. Huszár) and were actually guestimates produced on the basis of intuition and experience. The third set of numbers came from the Hungarian Statistical Office. Jánosi *et al.* (1980) worked with a sample of 30 large investment projects of the period 1970-1977, which were entirely financed from the state budget. In a later study (Jánosi and Pál, 1983), the same author increased the sample from 30 to 70 and an additional 80 other projects, mostly or entirely financed from the enterprises' own funds, were incorporated.

[7] More recently the Harrod-Domar model, as a starting point for explaining the fluctuation of investment behaviour, was "re-discovered" by two Soviet authors (Tsygichko and Nikolaeva, 1989) as well.

These four independent estimates are tabulated below (Table 2.2 Panel B). They are uniform in suggesting that large investment projects were - in their aggregate effects - stern-heavy but the actual sizes of the lagged coefficients were rather different. The first thing to notice is that the experts from the National Planning Office assumed that a six year time horizon is typical. The studies produced by the Statistical Office contained estimates for all types of investment projects, varying between 4 to 10 years in duration. (For the sake of comparability, however, only the 4 and 6 year samples are reproduced in Table 2.2.)

Berend's estimates suggest that investments typically have a stern-heavy lag structure, while Huszár thought that the lag structure was evenly distributed. Jánosi's first study produced some evidence for a stern-heavy lag structure but her second paper took a more neutral position.

Now, let us return to the original idea launched by Bródy (1972). His tacit assumption, wrapped in a somewhat blurred reference to "similar technical proportions in the division of labour", was that the lag structure of investment outlays - i.e. the realization coefficients of investment projects - is more or less the same in countries at a similar development level. In other words, with a given level of technology, the construction of a cement factory or a power station requires a technically determined sequencing, which in turn translates into a strictly determined time pattern of monetary expenses. While this starting hypothesis sounds logical on paper, there are signs, that reality may greatly differ from this assumption.

Against the background of a market economy, it is reasonable to assume that investment projects with long gestation periods are usually the more expensive ones and vice versa: projects bearing a high price require more time to be implemented. In a socialist economy, however, the gestation time of individual projects depends strongly on changes in the priorities of the Centre and a host of other circumstances.

Soviet and Hungarian data clearly showed that there had been little correlation between size and gestation time within a given sample of large investment projects. Green (1978) compared data on investment outlays and commissionings for the Soviet Union. He succeeded in identifying econometrically those sectors of the economy and branches of industry where central intervention in a given year resulted in an unusually small or an unusually long gestation time.

In 1980, the Planning Office in Hungary carried out a full-scale investigation of large ongoing investment projects. This showed that projects falling in the same cost categories displayed a relative variance of over 40 % around the mean gestation period, characteristic of the same cost category. This explained that, in the regression analysis, the variable of total costs proved to be practically unrelated to gestation time (Barát and Gegesy 1981). Similar results were obtained by the two studies already quoted from the experts of the Statistical Office (Jánosi *et al.* 1980, Jánosi and Pál 1983).

2.2 Endogenous models

> I myself held with conviction for many years the theories which I now attack, and I am not, I think, ignorant of their strong points.
>
> J.M. Keynes ([1973] p. xxi)

If planning is regarded as the quintessence of socialist economics and if it is furthermore assumed that its main objective is to eliminate economic instability, then fluctuations which nonetheless emerge require an additional explanation. This can be sought in two directions. The first involves the assumption that the existence of fluctuations is a reflection of errors or flaws in planning. The alternative is to assert that zigzags are generated by the internal logic of planning and therefore cannot be expected to die away as planning techniques improve.

From the SEP alone, no theory of investment cycles can be inferred. In a strict interpretation of Kornai's SEP, the consequences of changes in the hardness of individual enterprises' budget constraint will not result in an unequivocal modification of the volume of investments at the macro-economic level. We may, as an additional hypothesis, assume the existence of such a relationship but Kemme (1989) was right in pointing out that within the logic of SEP the required third element of the cycle definition, reinforcement, does not necessarily assert itself. "Investment cycles may result if the budget constraint is not uniformly and consistently soft (e.g., there are temporal changes in the investment plan or its financing). Cyclical pressure may temporarily alleviate shortages but it does not eliminate them. Within the chronic shortage model, cyclical behaviour *per se* is of little consequence." (p. 351)

Up to this point, the cycle model advanced in the works of Tamás Bauer (1977, 1978, 1981, 1988) does not go beyond the logic of the SEP.

> The driving force of the cycle is the more or less constant upward pressure operating both from enterprises and (not necessarily but in many cases) from ambitious central planners wishing to invest more. (...) This upward pressure is controlled (and self-controlled) by the central planners but the strength of this control fluctuates in response to the state of tensions (i.e. of the distance from equilibrium) in the economy. (Bauer 1988, p. 3)

So far this does not imply anything concerning the question that we would like to answer here: are the fluctuations endogenous or exogenous? To take a stand on this matter, we have to understand the logic which explains the state of tensions in the economy.

The SEP approach alone does not justify any assumption concerning the recurrence of imbalances. This model furnishes no compelling argument that a drift away from or towards equilibrium is causally linked to the investment process. According to Kornai, shortage is universal, affecting every corner of the economy. Shortages emerging in one segment of the market are likely to spill over to other segments, thereby contributing to the generation of shortages there. Thus, the examination of one selected segment of the market - e.g., the market for investment goods[8] - will never disclose any temporal regularity in fluctuations of the intensity of shortages.

The logic of SEP is construed here as being true only for the economy as a whole. In my interpretation this is a comprehensive model which cannot be meaningfully applied to a segment of the economy for the purposes of time series analysis. Due to the spill-over effects, the investment process - or developments in any other segments of the economy - does not and cannot display regularity over time. The picture is different, of course, if the SEP approach is used for cross country analysis. In this respect, there is good reason to believe that the investment process has similar qualitative features among the countries - both the achievements and the occurring problems may very well be similar. This matter, however, does not belong to the subject of this book - the economics of socialist investment cycles.

2.2.1 The Periodic Nature of Planning. It was already noted that, besides the medium-term fluctuations with a duration of 2-5 years, short-term oscillations such as monthly or quarterly peaks and troughs also manifest themselves in the socialist countries. Thus, it would make sense to attempt to a find a common explanation for both short- and medium-term movements. If the short-term cycles are explained by the periodic nature of planning within the year, the system of five-year plans must also have a cycle generating an impact on the medium term. This line of thought was given credit by several authors - e.g., Hutchings (1971), Gleitze (1975), Dahlstedt (1980), Vincentz (1980), Frateschi (1989b) - while others - Jasny (1961), Nutter (1962), Berend (1974), Ickes (1989) - came to negative conclusions in this respect.

The first attempt to test this hypothesis systematically for more than one country was made by the Polish economist Jan Winiecki (1982, 1986). His two contributions to the ongoing discussion are particularly relevant for us, since he focused his investigation on the analysis of investment data.[9] Before commenting on his results, we must to pause for a brief digression. First, we shall review the findings of recent works concerning the short-term cycles. Against this background, it will be demonstrated that the assumed analogy between the mechanisms of short- and medium-term fluctuations is in fact problematic from the very beginning.

In the traditional system of planning, the periodic reporting system attached to a calendar year or some part of it was believed to be responsible for the recurring speeding up of work (or *shturmovshchina*, as it is called in Russian) at the end of the reporting period (year, quarter or month). This was the conclusion of the pioneering studies of Bródy (1956) and Berliner (1956). Later, it turned out that such short-term fluctuations in output, investments, construction, exports, etc. continued to exist after the dismantling of the traditional system of planning.

In Hungary, for example, it was found that the intensity of these periodic fluctuations was even greater in the post-1968 period than before. The phenomenon has evidently been present, albeit to a lesser extent, in the Yugoslav economy, where the system of central planning had been abolished as early as the 1950s. At the same time, several authors came to the conclusion, independently from each other, that in the GDR, where the traditional forms of planning

[8] In this context of course (here and later on several times), the word "market" is used in a figurative sense only.

[9] His views were also presented in a synthetic form in Winiecki (1988, pp. 16-24).

remained in force up to the very last moment, the intensity of short-term fluctuations was minimal.[10]

However, there is mounting statistical evidence that end-year rush in economic activities is to a large extent a pure *artefact*, resulting from manipulated book-keeping practices by SOEs and their supervising ministries. In his path-breaking work on seasonal fluctuations in Soviet industry, Hutchings (1971, pp. 166-169) referred to Soviet studies from the early 1930s, where the existence of end-year "write-ups" had already been noted. Paying tribute to one of the authors, Hutchings introduced the term "Lozovskiy effect" to identify this particular type of statistical distortion. Unfortunately, this line of thought has remained largely forgotten in the literature.[11]

As noted above, the GDR was generally believed to have overcome *shturmovhschina* during the 1960s. After the collapse of the communist regime, however, it was acknowledged that, in the past, monthly statistical data, which had been regularly published in the national press and subsequently reported to international organisations[12], had been compiled on the 25th day of the month. This meant that the central statistical monitoring system had lived an independent life from the system of production control and incentives exercised at the micro-economic level, which continued to operate within the proper calendar framework.[13] To some extent, this was probably true in the Soviet Union, as well. Soviet newspaper reports repeatedly complained that most ministerial requests for plan corrections came in after the twenty-fifth of the month. After that date, GOSKOMSTAT officials could scarcely step out of their offices because of the rush of requests for corrections. (Formally, it was the statistical office that received the plan correction requests.)[14]

Birman (1988) quotes a Soviet source which suggests a similar interpretation. The article referred to (*Izvestiya*, 3 May 1984) gives an account of the results of the 1983 "large scale experiment". In this (already long-forgotten) reform exercise[15], participating enterprises were

[10] See e.g., Rostowski and Auerbach (1986), Garamvölgyi (1988a, 1988b).

[11] However, another aspect of the same problem, the frequency of "plan corrections" and the relevance of "plan fulfilment", were discussed in Gregory (1990, pp. 92-94).

[12] See e.g., the monthly editions of *Statistical indicators of short-term economic changes in ECE countries*, produced by the UN/ECE. This publication was heavily used by Rostowski-Auerbach (1986).

[13] See the interview with Mr. A. Donda, the long-time head of the Central Statistical Office of the GDR), in *Neues Deutschland* (16 November 1989). Interestingly, the President of the Hungarian Statistical Office had suggested earlier that such practices had been followed in the GDR, which made these monthly data useless for the analysis of short term fluctuations (Nyitrai 1988, p. 26). In a private conversation with the author, Mrs. Nyitrai confirmed this hypothesis and added that in the past Bulgaria and Romania were also thought to have followed such a practice, though there was insufficient evidence to support this assumption.

[14] See Gregory, *loc. cit.*

[15] This experiment was based on a decree adopted by the Central Committee of the CPSU and the Council of Ministers in July 1983, that was cautiously named "Decree about complementary measures to widen the rights of production associations (enterprises) in industry, in planning and economic activity through the reinforcement of their responsibility for the results of their work" (*Ekonomicheskaya Gazeta*,

better supplied than others and the objective was to test the impact of increased decision-making autonomy. The main story in the quoted article was that, despite the privileged treatment, *shturmovshchina* did not disappear. The firm, mentioned by name in the article, continued to produce half of its output during the last 10 days of the month. Birman's explanation of this is not very convincing. "Materials and parts needed were lacking at the beginning of the month but by the end were somehow found and supplied." (p. 215)

This explanation might be valid in general but it is probably not so in the given case. This particular enterprise was better supplied than before and better than the others. If we believe that the experiment was taken seriously by the planning authorities, in the sense that the privileged treatment meant not a recurring, preferential "quick fix" at the end of the month but rather an ex ante priority, then it is probable that there was no real need at the end of the month to "find" raw materials. They were there all the time, production was continuous and only book-keeping, statistical reporting and actual shipments to customers occurred in a panicky way at the end of the month.

A different type of problem existed with regard to Hungarian data. It turned out that fluctuations in labour inputs (measured in working hours) on the one hand, and output at constant prices on the other, were totally unrelated to each other. In the last two decades, output typically peaked in December, when labour inputs were always at their lowest monthly level due to the Christmas holidays. By contrast, output and the indices of capacity utilization were at minimum in January, while the volume of labour input was at the second or third highest level in the year. Thus, in December the biggest output is produced by the smallest amount of labour input, while in the following month minimum production is achieved with near maximum labour input. This paradoxical finding suggested to several Hungarian authors[16] that the end-year rush does not really take place in the sphere of production but rather in the back offices of the accounting and statistical departments.

As far as investment activity is concerned, our own conclusion based on the inspection of Bulgarian, Czechoslovak and Hungarian data[17], is very similar. The reporting system, which is based on payment transactions and not on registration of the volume of actual investment works, shows that in these countries the figure for December is 3-4 times higher than the monthly average. In comparison with the annual minimum (January or February) the December figure is often 8-10 times higher. At the end of the second quarter, in June, the reported investment figure is twice as high as in May, the September figure exceeds the August figure by 50 %, etc. It is almost certain that these monthly figures based on payment statistics are to all intents and purposes unrelated to actual developments in terms of real physical magnitudes.

The mechanism behind this false reporting is rather simple. The client firm and the contractor are both strongly motivated to terminate financially ongoing projects by the end of the reporting calendar period (month, quarter, year). The contractor is eager to be paid in order to meet his own revenue plan figure. The client wants to report to the supervising authority the timely commissioning of his project. Thus very often actual financial transactions occur on the basis of fictitious commissioning reports. On the side of the client, this temporarily appears as a defective or sub-standard asset. In reality, however, the shortcomings will duly be made good

No. 31. July 1983).

[16] See e.g., Barancsi and Gyulavári (1983) and Pálfi (1988).

[17] For the other socialist countries, monthly investment data are not available.

by the contractor on the basis of compulsory guarantee schemes or by the client itself at the beginning of the subsequent reporting period.[18]

* * *

Three conclusions can be drawn from these findings:

(i) The periodic nature of the planning and reporting system does not always and everywhere result in periodic short-term fluctuations in economic activities, as earlier students of socialist economic cycles assumed.

(ii) However, SOEs are strongly motivated to doctor their figures in order to get the best fit with the calendar schedule. Therefore monthly and quarterly figures, based on financial and banking accounts, cannot precisely reflect the underlying physical processes.

(iii) The biassed nature of December or fourth quarter figures may cast some doubt on the reliability of annual data as well. At first glance, a priori reasoning and the available anecdotal evidences support the opposite. It can be argued (Gregory 1990, pp. 92-94) that such manipulations whittle away at the margin. Truly large deceptions are not possible under normal circumstances. Authorities tolerate small deceptions but they are unwilling to accept large ones. If a reported annual figure is x, indeed there is no reason to believe, that the "true" figure is x/2. The other side of the coin is that the literature on socialist investment cycles focuses precisely on the first derivative of the investment variable. Our data problem starts when it can be suspected that "true" figure is not a 5 % growth over last year's performance, as x would imply but rather a 5 % decline.

In fact, it is the doctoring of the monthly figures that opens up the possibility for top managers to calibrate the "final" annual figure according to the best interest of the firm. In a world where the December figure is always 2-3 times higher than the November one, practically any December figure is credible. By contrast, in a world where firms produce honest reports through 11 months of the year, little doctoring can be done on the December figure that will not immediately catch the eye.

Five-Year Plans - Five Year Cycles ? Let us return now to the main course of the argument. Winiecki claims that GINV fluctuations originate in the practice of five-year planning. His starting point is well known from the literature of the 1950s and 1960s. In the preparatory phase

[18] It appears that the Chernobyl accident can only be understood as an example of such behaviour. The safety test planned for that tragic day was one that should have been carried out before the reactor was certified. An authority on the subject, Z. Medvedev, quotes one of the day-shift operators at Chernobyl: "Can it really be that the Government Commission that accepted Block 4 as ready for operation did not know that it was accepting it incomplete? Of course they knew. If you look more deeply, then the accident started not (...) on 26 April 1986, but in December 1983, when the director of the AES (abbreviation of the words nuclear power station in Russian - P. M.), Bryukhanov, put his signature on the document of the Government Commission (...) without seeing the necessity of insisting that the run-down unit of the turbo-generator was tested. (...) And our Moscow comrades needed that run-down unit even less. They said, «The fourth block has been put into operation and will go into the report for this year. That's good.»" (quoted from *The New York Review of Books*, 19 July 1990)

of the plan, firms make the maximum effort to get their own projects written into the nationwide investment plan. To improve their chances, costs and the expected construction time are deliberately understated. Experienced managers know that the most important issue is to start the construction work. Cost overruns and missed deadlines are hardly ever punished. In the Polish and Czechoslovak literature of the epoch, this tactic was known as "hooking into the plan".

In this world, argues Winiecki, the Five-Year Plan (FYP) targets are inconsistent from the very outset. The planned volume of resources lags behind the true requirements of the volume of planned investments. These tensions manifest themselves very soon. Emerging shortages and bottlenecks hamper the timely unfolding of the investment process. Planned capacities cannot be commissioned on time, although their output has been already counted on in the consumption plans. As tensions mount during the first two years of the quinquennium, central planners are obliged to curb the investment process. Somewhere in the middle of the FYP, the Centre has to face economic realities and take measures to restore macro-economic equilibrium. Since by this time it has become evident that no effort can guarantee that all planned projects will be completed within the plan period, the Centre, albeit with a bleeding heart, calls for a moderation of investment growth. In the remaining part of the plan period, bottlenecks ease somewhat and the level of overall macro-economic tensions decline. Then planners start the preparation of the next FYP and tensions reassert themselves when it goes into effect.

Quantitatively speaking, Winiecki assumes that, within a FYP period, investment growth rates resemble a flattened bell-shape curve. The annual growth rates of GINV are always higher in years 2 and 3 than in years 4 and 5:

$$(2.3) \qquad (GINV_{t2}/GINV_{t1} + GINV_{t3}/GINV_{t2}) > (GINV_{t4}/GINV_{t3} + GINV_{t5}/GINV_{t4}).$$

Analyzing developments in seven countries over four quinquennia (1961-1980), Winiecki found that in 60 % of the cases, his hypothesis was justified by the data. However, he was fully aware of the fact that these two decades had not coincided with four regular FYPs in all seven countries. There were three types of difficulties for which he made allowance.

The Soviet Union offered a good example of the first type of problem. The Seven-Year Plan for 1959-1965 was abandoned after Khrushchev's fall and a two year plan had to be elaborated for the period 1964-1965. (It is noteworthy that official Soviet statistical yearbooks still carry annualized average figures for the period 1961-1965, as if it were a regular FYP period, comparable with any other quinquennium.[19])

Furthermore, Winiecki referred to institutional changes which occurred in Eastern Europe in the period under investigation. They were considered important enough to counteract the impact of the planning cycle. The reform initiatives in the GDR (1963), in Czechoslovakia (1967) and Hungary (1968) all fell in the middle of a FYP.

The third type of disturbance factor was purely external. For Poland, he excluded the 1971-1975 period from his sample, arguing that high rates of investment growth in the latter part of this FYP were sustained only by means of massive foreign borrowing.

Making allowance for these types of difficulty, which reduced his sample from 28 to 19, enabled him to come out with better results. The rate of coincidence between hypothesised and actual figures rose from 60 to 84 per cent.

[19] See e.g., KS/1989 pp. 8-9.

Although Winiecki's hypothesis appears to be logical and his testing procedure is compelling in its simplicity, I have some doubts concerning the logic of the model, the methods applied and the results of the test procedure.

First, on the basis of the findings reported in the previous section on short-term fluctuations, I have reservations about the simple comparison of GINV growth rates of successive years. In such an analysis, as the formula shows, the number of coinciding cases is calculated in a very crude form: is the average growth rate of the second and third year of the FYP higher or lower than in the fourth and the fifth year? This calculation method is obviously very sensitive to small errors, since the method boils down to a simple "true" or "false" type of comparison, in which small and large differences have an equal weight in the procedure.

The number of periods left out from Winiecki's sample is also a reason for concern. It is either too high (relative to the possible maximum size of the sample), or too low (once we look more thoroughly at the history of socialist FYPs).

With respect to the pre-1945 Soviet developments, the whole issue was the subject of a very detailed analysis by Jasny (1961). His conclusion was rather negative. "The FYPs are largely facade, not playing the role in the economy ascribed to them but serving principally as propaganda." (*op. cit.* p. 12). This statement is perhaps too strong to claim general validity for it as a proper assessment of the post-1945 development as well but there is an element of truth in it. The results of a more extensive investigation, based on a much larger number of observations, is presented in Table 2.3, where an attempt has been made to summarize the history of medium-term or perspective plans implemented in 22 socialist countries. There are a number of interesting conclusions, which partly confirm Jasny's hard words but point beyond them in the sense of being more specific.

(i) Perhaps the most important fact is that very often not five but two, three, six or seven years were considered to be the appropriate time horizon for a medium-term plan. In addition, some countries occasionally embarked upon the elaboration and implementation of ten, fifteen or twenty year plans, which make the picture even more complicated. In other words, it is an exaggeration to claim that the FYP has been the main instrument of planning.

(ii) On several occasions, plans were approved only in the second year of the quinquennium (or even later). In fact, the practice of adopting an FYP at the very end of the first year was more typical than exceptional. Investments in the first and, as noted, sometimes the second year are carried out without any formal plan decisions.

(iii) Apart from the unpublished and hence untraceable minor revisions of the FYPs, planners often drastically intervened in the middle of the plan. Sometimes attempts were made to accelerate economic growth through across-the-board upward modification of plan targets, or through a cut in the time originally foreseen for implementation. On other occasions, prompt deceleration was the objective of the planners' intervention. Shortening or prolonging the plan period by one year was also not unknown in practice. This was equivalent to a tautening or slackening of the plan itself.

TABLE 2.3 Regularities and irregularities of medium- and long term plans, 1945-1990

Panel A : Medium- and long term plans other than FYPs

2 year plan	3 year plan	4 year plan	6 year plan	7 year plan	10 year plan	15 year plan	20 year plan
Albania	Hungary	Burma	Poland	Bulgaria	Romania	Hungary	Bulgaria
(1949-50)	(1958-60)	(1966-69)	(1950-55)	(1964-70) NS	(1971-80)	(1971-85)	(1963-83)
		(1972-75)				(1976-90)	
Bulgaria	Poland		Romania	CSSR	Cuba		USSR
(1947-48)	(1947-49)	Cape Verde	(1960-65)	(1964-70) NS	(1971-80)		(1961-80)
(1979-80)	(1981-83) NS	(1982-85)					
			N. Korea	GDR	China		Burma
CSSR	Romania		(1971-76) S	(1959-65) S	(1976-85)		(1971-90)
(1947-48)	(1973-75)						
(1954-55)			Guinea	USSR	Mozambique		Cuba
(1964-65)	Viet Nam		(1965-71)	(1959-65)	(1981-90) NP		(1980-2000)
	(1958-60)						
GDR				N. Korea	Ethiopia		
(1949-50)	Yemen			(1961-67) P	(1985-95) NS		
	(1971/72-			(1978-84) S			
Hungary	1973/74)			(1984-91) NS			
(1947/48-				(1987-93)			
1950/51) S	N. Korea						
	(1951-53) NS						
	(1954-56)						
N. Korea							
(1949-50)	Mongolia						
	(1958-60)						
	Laos						
	(1978-80)						
	Congo P						
	(1975-77)						
	Ethiopia						
	(1986-89)						
	Somalia						
	(1979-81)						
	Zimbabwe						
	(1982/83-84/85)						
	Madagascar						
	1978-80						
	Tanzania						
	(1986-88)						

(continued)

Panel B: Irreguliarities within "regular" FYPs

Prepared but not started	Never published	Adopted with considerable delay	Shortened, suspended, prolonged	Internationally coordinated revision of tautness	
Albania	China	China	Albania	Bulgaria	
(1947-51)	(1958-62)	(1953-57)	(1956-60) S	CSSR	Tautness increased
	(1966-70)			<1950>	
CSSR	(1971-75)	GDR	Bulgaria	Hungary	
(1966-70)		(1966-70)	(1949-53) S	<1951>	
			(1976-80) S	Albania	
Hungary		Poland	GDR	Bulgaria	
(1956-60)		(1971-75)	(1956-60) S	CSSR	Tautness reduced
		(1976-80)		GDR	
Poland		(1986-90)	Romania	Hungary	
(1981-85)			(1951-55) S	Poland	
		USSR		Romania	
Ethiopia		(1951-55)	Yugoslavia	<1953>	
(1990-94)			(1947-51) P		
		Viet Nam			
		(1976-80)	Yugoslavia		
		(1981-85)	(1957-61) S		
			(1961-65) S		
		Laos	(1981-85) S		
		(1981-85)			
		(1986-90)	USSR		
			(1956-60) S		
		Tanzania			
		(1975-79)	China		
			(1953-57) S		
		Yemen			
		(1986-90)	N. Korea		
			(1957-61) S		
		Cape Verde			
		(1986-90)	Mongolia		
			(1931-35) S		
			Yemen		
			(1979-83) S		
			(1986-90) S		
			(1989-92) S		
			Congo		
			(1964-68) P		
			Somalia		
			(1974-78) S		
			Burma		
			(1971-75) S		
			Tanzania		
			(1964-68) S		

(continued)

Panel C: Major internal changes in the middle of an ongoing FYP

Major economic reform	Collectivisation in agriculture	Currency reform	Major stabilisation programme	Riots, uprising, revolution
USSR <1957>	Albania (1965-66)	Bulgaria <1952>	Hungary (1988-90)	Poland <1956,1980>
GDR <1958>	Bulgaria (1956-57)	CSSR <1953>	Yugoslavia <1990>	Romania <1990>
Bulgaria <1957>	CSSR <1959>	GDR <1957,1990>	Poland <1990>	
CSSR <1967>		Yugoslavia <1966, 1990>		
Hungary <1968>		USSR <1947>		
Yugoslavia <1961,1965>		Romania <1952>		
Poland <1973>		China <1955>		
Laos <1986/1987>		Viet Nam <1985>		

Panel D: Major external shocks in the middle of an ongoing FYP

Military conflict	Territorial change		Rift with a major ally	
Viet Nam (1961-75)	Viet Nam <1976>	Unification with the South	Albania <1961> <1978>	 with USSR with China
Afghanistan (1979-89)	GDR <1990>	Unification with FRG	Yugoslavia <1948>	with USSR
	Yemen <1990>	Unification with North	CSSR <1962>	with China
			Viet Nam <1979>	with China
			China <1960>	with USSR

S=Shortened or suspended NS= Not started P=Prolonged NP= Never published

2.4 The Winiecki hypothesis: Five-year plans and the planning cycles in six East European countries and the USSR, 1951-1985

Hypothesis: The growth rate of GINV is higher in the second and third years of the quinquennium than in the fourth and fifth years.

1951-1955	1956-1960	1961-1965	1966-1970	1971-1975	1976-1980	1981-1985
YES	NO	YES	YES	NO	YES	NO
YES	NO	NO	NO	YES	YES	NO
YES	NO	NO	NO	YES	YES	NO
YES	NO	YES	NO	NO	YES	YES
YES	NO	NO	YES	YES	YES	NO
YES	NO	YES	YES	NO	YES	NO
NO	YES	NO	YES	NO	YES	YES

Test result: The hypothesis holds if all periods are taken into account : 26 cases out of 49 (53%)

The hypothesis holds if only "undisturbed" periods are taken into account : 15 cases out of 26 (58 %)

[dotted box] Undisturbed FYP, announced on time and not revised substantially or abandoned during the plan period.

Source: Table SA.1

(iv) The history of the FYPs also shows that a number of essential political and economic policy decisions such as the collectivisation or de-collectivisation of agriculture, sweeping changes in the currency system, the rupture of an alliance with an important trading partner, the rescheduling of Western debts, etc. - happened to fall in the middle of a FYP period. It is difficult to imagine that these events had no impact on investment.

(v) Economic reforms have been a central issue on the political agenda in most socialist countries since the death of Stalin. Yet, whatever steps were taken in this direction, no attempt was ever made to time them with the beginning of an FYP. This is not merely a defect that mars the beauty of the theory, as Winiecki says. It is indirect evidence showing how little importance was attached to the whole idea of five-year planning by the central decision makers themselves.

Aside from these arguments about the relevance of the FYPs as such, Winiecki's position can also be criticized from an other angle. It is easy to argue for an alternative working hypothesis which suggests a conclusion directly opposed to that of Winiecki. Using the formulation introduced in section 2.1 and setting it in a somewhat different context, the model of a FYP cycle can be based on the assumption that five-year investment plans are stem-heavy. *A priori*, however, the opposite position can be defended - namely that FYPs are typically stern-heavy. If the mechanism of "hooking into the plan" works, this implies the simultaneous launching of several investment projects - which then means an increased investment need in the latter part of the FYP - i.e. a stern-heavy investment pattern.

In fact, Green (1978) tried to test exactly this hypothesis on Soviet GINV data. Using regression analysis for the period 1959-1974, he found significant concordance with this model for total industry, for some branches of industry (coal mining, oil extraction, chemicals), and also in the construction sector. Hungarian data were tested for the same hypothesis using a similar technique in Berend (1974) and Marrese (1981) but these authors were unable to confirm this conjecture.

Leaving aside these reservations, Winiecki's procedure for the entire 1951-1985 period was tested by the present author (table 2.4). If all 49 cases are taken into account, Winiecki's hypothesis holds in half of them. If all those periods when the FYP was not publicized in advance, or was abandoned ahead of time, are excluded, the sample has to be reduced to 26. Again, only 60 % of these FYPs met the criteria developed by Winiecki.[20]

[20] After closer inspection of Winiecki's figures, it was reassuring to see that for the overlapping periods these results were no different from his. In the final assessment, the divergence in our results stems from the fact that his observation period was significantly shorter than the one used here. The countries in the sample were identical: Bulgaria, Czechoslovakia, the GDR, Hungary, Poland, Romania and the USSR.

2.2.2 The Investment Commitment Model. In the previous section it was shown that oscillations in GINV growth rates do not exhibit a strong causal relationship with the periodic nature of planning as claimed by Winiecki. However, it should be mentioned that the Polish author considered his model as an enhanced version of those developed by Bauer (1978, 1981) and Lackó (1980). It is now time for the ideas of these authors, already mentioned several times in previous sections of this book, to be examined more closely.

The characteristic feature of these models was the incorporation of such elements as investment starts, investment commitments and the dispersion of investment resources. While acknowledging the relevance of these building blocks, Winiecki (1986, p. 210*n.*) felt that the measurement difficulties involved in including these factors were unsurmountable and he thus preferred to jettison them.

I venture to propose the name "investment commitment model" (ICM) to label the ideas developed by Bauer, Lackó, Kornai and other Hungarian authors. The term "vintage approach" is also known in the literature[21] in reference to this same school of thought but for reasons that will become clear later, the new name proposed may be considered more illuminating.

There have been several spiritual forefathers of ICM (see Chart 2.1) but there is little doubt that a 1933 essay by the Norwegian economist Ragnar Frisch and the already quoted 1972 manuscript of András Bródy were the most influential ones.

Within a dynamic framework, different types of lags can be taken into account in model building. The one which is most frequently considered is the time span elapsing between investment inputs and the commissioning of the investment project. ICMs, however, focus on another type of lag, namely the time difference between investment decisions and actual investment outlays.

Each project is assumed to have a construction period of a given length, and for every year in the construction period of an accepted project a given volume of deliveries is required. The timing of these "carry-on" deliveries for each individual project is regarded as a technical datum. This idea had led Frisch to make "a distinction between the quantity of capital goods whose production is started and the activity needed in order to carry to completion the production of those capital goods whose production was started at an earlier moment." (Frisch 1933, p. 181)[22]

Frisch's model worked with hypothetical numbers, of which the most important were: a) an assumed 3-year average lag required between the beginning of planning and the commissioning of a big unit; and b) a stem-heavy set of realization coefficients. The solution of the model's equation suggested the presence of a primary and a secondary cycle, with durations of 8.57 years and 3.50 years, respectively.

[21] Roland (1987) was one of those who coined this term first, generalizing the phrasing used by Kornai (1982).

[22] Frisch in his later writings on the OSLO CHANNEL investment model used a somewhat different terminology, when he distinguished between *investment starting* vs. *investment sinking* (meaning the carry-on deliveries). Interestingly, Frisch put a lot of emphasis in these works on modelling the cumulated impact of all simultaneous investment projects at the national level, but cyclicality as such receded from the foreground. (See Edvardsen (1965) and Frisch (1967)).

CHART 2.1 The family tree of investment commitment models

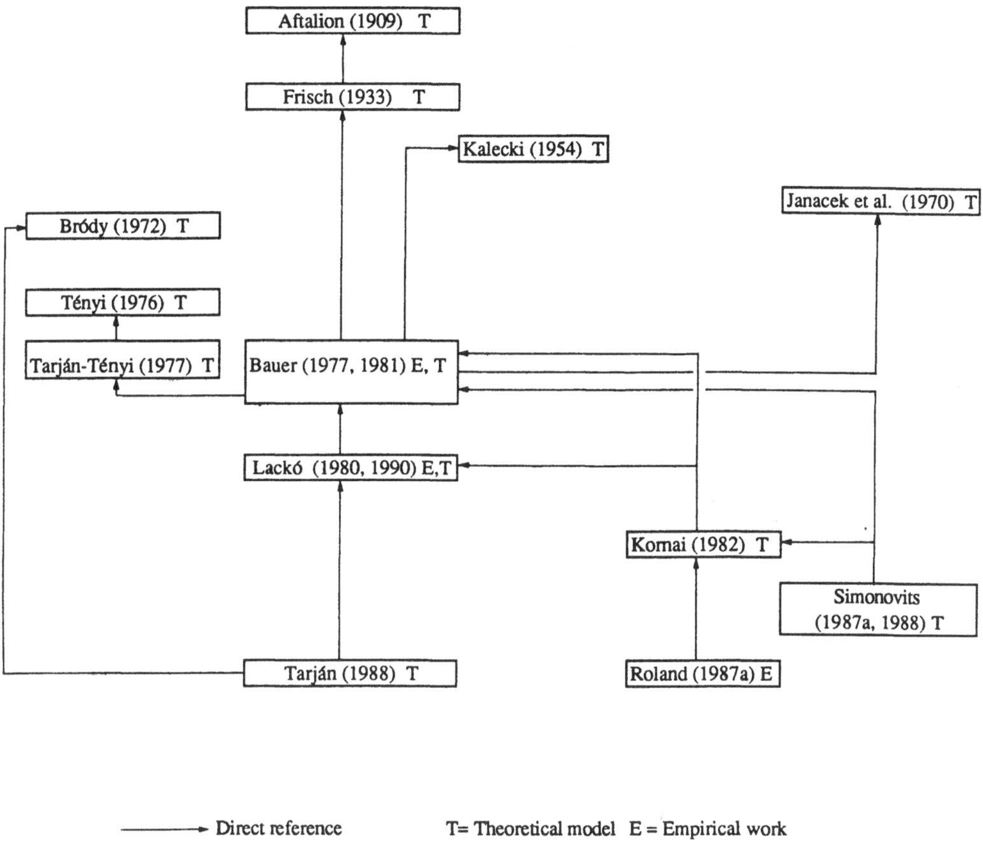

Such a Frisch-type model, adapted to the particularities of the socialist countries, is to be found in the Hungarian edition of Bauer's monumental work, which unfortunately remains inaccessible to the international research community as a whole due to the language barrier. It is a poor consolation but nonetheless worth noting that a short summary of the main logical building blocks was reproduced in a new study, available in English, from the same author. Here Bauer infers the successive course of events in the framework of his four-phase model:

> In the first phase new projects are started more frequently but the volume of investment outlays grows at a relatively low rate (*run-up*). The stock of investment projects in process increases considerably, the scattering of investments is growing and planners come under pressure to allow the growth of investment outlays to accelerate. Since the growth of outlays is still relatively slow in this phase, the economy remains in a more or less balanced state and planners do not see any reason not to give in to pressures for more investment.
>
> The starting of many new investment projects continues in the second phase, called *rush*. This is accompanied by an expansion of investment outlays. "Old" and "new" projects compete for the quotas of investment outlays the growth rate of which is likely to exceed the plan. The shortage of investment goods and services grows and the rate of investment in national income rises. Either the growth of consumption is delayed or the balance of trade deteriorates.
>
> Growing scattering of investment and tightening shortage of investment goods prompt the planners to rein in new investment projects in the *halt* phase. While the number of investment proposals continues to grow, a smaller portion of them is approved than in the earlier phases. The advancement of investment projects started earlier is, however, not checked but prompted. Investment outlays are planned to continue to grow at a high rate but capacity shortage often prevents this plan from being fulfilled. Hence, the planned improvement concerning the scattering of investment is not achieved. Due to the further growth of investment outlays and to the rising rate of investment, tensions in the economy continue to grow.
>
> Thus the planners are forced to curb the growth of investment outlays. This leads to the slowdown, or *setback*. Restrictions relate not only to the starting of new projects but also to the advancement of projects already in process (Bauer 1988, p. 2).

Using our own symbols, the ICM asserts that

(2.4) $GINV = f_4 (Q_1, Q_2, \dots Q_n)$,
where GINV = the annual volume of investments and
$Q_1, Q_2, \dots Q_n$ denotes other economic factors of which investment commitments, investment starts, investment dispersion, consumption and the foreign trade balance are the most important.

As already noted, Winiecki did not try to marshall arguments against the inclusion of new elements - such as investment commitments, starts and dispersion - into the cyclical model: he simply omitted them with a reference to data availability problems. He felt, however, that his approach was superior as he was able to determine the length of the periodic waves.[23]

In the remaining part of this section, attention is focused on demonstrating that the economic and statistical interpretation of these new elements in the cycle theory, as suggested by ICM, come up against fundamental theoretical *and* practical obstacles. Note that, in the previous

[23] "Bauer's cycle is time un-related while our explanation refers to the planning cycle as a time span of the investment cycle, with the latter generally beginning and ending within the five-year plan period." (Winiecki 1982, p.155)

sentence, particular emphasis was placed on the conjunction "and". In the arguments advanced below, theoretical and practical (statistical) considerations are seemingly lumped together without any effort to treat them separately. However, behind the so-called "data availability" problem, which in the eyes of many authors is a practical question only, serious theoretical considerations can be discerned. These considerations give good reasons why the required figures are not and cannot be meaningfully produced by any statistical office of the world.

No model is perfect. All models are built on a series of simplifications, and thus their empirical testing is always a daunting task. However, it seems obvious that in evaluating models, a distinction must be made between those in which empirical testing is hampered by truly practical data availability problems (which can be cured) and those where theoretical constructions prevent empirical verification due to the inclusion of imprecise ideas and concepts.

The Concept of Investment Commitments. The idea of "investment commitments" was described in a remarkably condensed form in the Hungarian version of Kornai (1982). "The investment decision maker is - to a large extent - the prisoner of his own previous decisions." (p. 54) At the first hearing this is a short but captivating statement. It is not easy to realize that rather strict assumptions hide behind it.

Let us note that the words "earlier decisions" are exclusively used to denote decisions leading to past investment starts. It is a truism, of course, that present decisions are influenced by the consequences of past decisions. Of course, this surely applies to all kinds of macro-economic decisions in all countries. Contractual agreements have to be honoured, money on loan has to be repaid, the existing capital stock has to be maintained, etc.

In other words, there are in fact two starting assumptions in ICM and neither is explicit enough to make transparent the weak points of the whole argument. The first assumption is that current decisions concerning the volume of investments in the next period are determined by past decisions on investment starts. All the other circumstances (such as honouring trade agreements or the importance of proper maintenance of capital stock) are taken into account only in the form of constraints. Second, ICM asserts that investment decisions are in this respect fundamentally different from other types of macro-economic decisions.

There are two protagonists in ICM: the Centre and the state owned enterprises (SOEs). To explain the cyclicality, however, attention is focused on the behaviour of the Centre. SOEs always want the same thing: more and more investment resources. While in other areas of plan bargaining, firms' appetites are, to a certain degree, limited by financial considerations or by real constraints such as labour supply, storage capacities etc.; investment hunger is assumed not to be limited by anything similar. Since investment funds are provided free of charge and/or the financial plans of firms are adjusted to the actual payment burdens of the ongoing investment projects, efforts to bargain for more investment are not limited by real financial constraints.[24] This effort is accompanied by a particular bargaining strategy. Firms "feed" the Centre with deliberately distorted information, costs are underestimated, technologically indispensable related investments are "forgotten", promised time schedules are over-optimistic.

Bauer gave a very detailed analysis of these practices in his 800 page long study, which is based on Bulgarian, Czechoslovak, East German, Hungarian, Polish, Romania and Soviet newspaper accounts as well as published party and government documents. It is astounding to

[24] See Bauer (1978, p. 245) for the first formulation of this assertion.

read dozens of convincingly documented examples that witness the fundamental similarities in the behaviour of the SOEs, ministries and the central authorities.[25]

However, to the present author the main weakness of ICMs in general and Bauer's book in particular seems to be in the way the behaviour of the Centre is described. Here ICM paints with a broad brush. In order to illuminate this very important point, I will use a schematic presentation (Chart 2.2), reproduced from Lackó (1980), which faithfully follows the logic of the concept of "investment commitment".

Chart 2.2 suggests that the three key variables of the model are:

- annual investment outlays (GINV), here represented as i(t);
- total planned costs of all contemporaneous investment starts S(t); and
- the total volume of unsatisfied (delayed) investment demand arising from ongoing investment projects D(t).

These variables are assumed to be observable and measurable quantities.

CHART 2.2 The idea behind the ICM: Realization of investment processes started at various dates

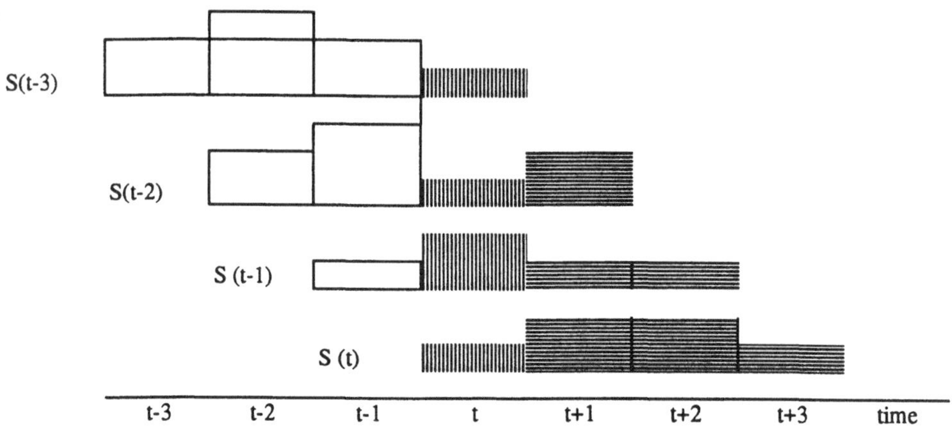

i(t)= sum of vertically striped fields D(t)= sum of horizontally striped fields

Source: Reproduced from Lackó (1980)

[25] Until the publication of Gregory (1990), which is based on interviews with former members of Soviet economic bureaucracy, Bauer's book was probably the most detailed account of how bureaucrats make the routine and extraordinary decisions that determine investments in Soviet-type economies.

Following a tradition begun by Czechoslovak, Polish and Hungarian economists, ICMs usually define investment commitments in the manner reflected in Chart 2.2.[26] The assumption is that if D(t) appears to be too high, judging from the mounting tensions on the investment goods and services market, planners curb new investment starts. Conversely, if the size of D(t) does not cause any particular headache, planners are less rigorous in authorizing more investment starts. Thus, the key variable of ICM is D(t).

In Bauer's formulation, what statisticians observe in GINV fluctuations is the impact of a positive feed-back mechanism built into the investment decision making system. His idea originates in Frisch (1933), a fact which he duly notes, where a so-called *advancement function* provides a link between fluctuations in starts and fluctuations in outlays.

In his four phase model the cycle is asymmetrical. Bauer is fully aware of this and offers an explanation which is very much in accordance with the facts but makes econometric formalisation very difficult indeed.[27] In his presentation, the cumulative processes assert themselves during the run-up and rush phases. In both these phases, he argues, rising GINV triggers a change in a determinate direction in output, employment, consumption and foreign trade. By contrast, movements in the opposite direction are never allowed to unfold during downward phases, mainly because stable employment and positive output growth are sacrosanct for planners. This argumentation is in accord with statistical observations: the two upward phases can stretch themselves into several years but the halt and the setback phases always occur within one or two years.

* * *

Though it is not easy to recognize at first sight, in macro-economic and statistical terms the message conveyed by Chart 2.2 is a fiction. In reality, the volume of true investment commitments, an undoubtedly real factor in the resource allocation process, bears little relationship with the magnitudes shown by the chart.

It is a commonplace in the economic literature of socialist planning that once an investment project has been started, it will sooner or later be finished regardless of profitability considerations. A factory in a half-ready state is certainly a loss from the point of view of the Centre. Once it is finished, the commissioning of the entire project justifies the initial expenditures.

In theoretical terms, the problem is often presented as a consequence of the indivisibility of investment decisions. Note, however, that this truism holds only at the micro-economic level. In aggregate terms (at the macro-economic level) what is true for individual investment projects is not necessarily valid for i(t) - i.e. total annual investments. All the ICM approach provides is a theory of the demand for investment goods at the individual firm level. (In fact, Lackó's symbolism, designating the total volume of investment commitments as D(t), reflects precisely this logic.)

[26] The term "investment commitment" is equivalent to the following expressions used for analytical and statistical purposes: *zustatek rozpoctovych nákladu rozestavenych staveb* (Czech), *zaangazowanie inwestycyjne* (Polish), *beruházási elkötelezettség* (Hungarian).

[27] Bauer's reservation concerning econometric methods is partly explained by this factor. Simple methods based on linear regression procedures cannot handle asymmetrical relationships.

Chart 2.2 attempts to aggregate micro-economic magnitudes at the macro-level, as if it were a simple arithmetic exercise. But for several reasons this is incorrect. In the view of the present author, the relevance of ICM stands or falls on this point.

(i) First of all, it should be noted that neither investment commitments nor the problem of indivisibility are applicable in cases where no - or only minimal - construction work is envisaged in the investment project. Undoubtedly, it is difficult to establish how much money is spent annually on investment projects where only the instalment of a single piece of equipment is required - i.e. in processes with an infinitely short time dimension. Nonetheless, some estimates indicate that what we are talking about is certainly not a negligible quantity.

According to Soviet estimates relating to productive investments (i.e. investments in the material sectors of the economy), the combined share of reconstruction, retooling and maintenance work, together with investments where installation of capital equipment was not accompanied by construction work at all, reached 42 % in the 1971-1975 period. During the next FYP this share went up to 46 and later to 50 %.[28] Czechoslovak data for the first half of the 1960s and the mid-1970s, showed that "simple machinery investments" represented about 20 and 30 % respectively of GINV (Bauer 1981, p. 33). In Poland, the corresponding figure was about 30 % of the total investment outlay of the socialist sector during 1971-1975 (*ibid.*). On the basis of a Hungarian source - Havas (1975) - my estimate for "simple machinery investment" in the state sector of that country, gives a 13-15 % share for the year 1974.

Nevertheless, even in those cases where the project does involve a certain amount of construction work, the hands of the planners are not really tied to the extent that ICM suggests. Housebuilding or civil engineering works are, at the macro-economic level, perfectly divisible. There is no physical constraint which determines whether 30 or 50 thousand dwellings can be built in year t. The construction of 10 miles or 100 miles of highway, as well as any figure between these extremes, is equally feasible in a technical sense.[29]

It is also misleading to believe that the hands of planners are tied by a few large investment projects, where indivisibility can rightly be regarded as a hard fact of life. On the basis of empirical findings presented in Section 1.4.1, the total volume of investment commitments arising from these construction-intensive projects cannot be regarded as a decisive magnitude at the macro-economic level. As noted before, Soviet, Czechoslovak and Hungarian data suggest that the average nationwide gestation period of all simultaneously ongoing investment projects is certainly below three years - and perhaps only one or two years.

(ii) Chart 2.2 disregards another important element, namely that the planned costs of ongoing projects are subject to change. The larger the project, the more likely it is that this will happen as changing circumstances require. Since these re-assessments and recalculations are bound to take place on an ad hoc basis, the concurrently existing S(t)s - i.e. S(t-3), S(t-2), S(t-1), S (t) - are (always) expressed at different price levels, and (often) reflect the use of different calculation methodologies.

Thus, the first erroneous step is to sum up the calculated volumes of investment commitments arising from individual projects. The second erroneous step occurs when a time series is built

[28] See Faltsman and Ozhegov (1983). For a more detailed presentation of the same phenomenon at the level of industrial branches, see Smystriliaeva (1983).

[29] This was already pointed out in Tarján and Tényi (1977).

for D(t)s. In fact, both the Polish and the Czechoslovak statistical offices were careful enough to warn users that the investment commitment data for successive years are not comparable with one another.[30] Unfortunately this warning has often fallen on deaf ears in the research community.

(iii) In practice, it is extremely difficult to identify the precise content of a large investment project or, therefore, the volume of commitments arising from it. Statisticians are right to define starts and the date of commissioning as a certain type of administrative action. A few examples can give a flavour of the inherent difficulties involved.

(•) In early November 1989, the Soviet media reported that a giant investment project, the Baikal-Amur Railway (BAM), frequently referred to previously as "the construction of the century", had finally been completed. However, more detailed reports suggested that not all the planned work had as yet been commissioned. A long tunnel, for instance, remained to be built and the planned social amenities were also lacking (BBC, *Summary of World Broadcasts* (Soviet Union), 15 November 1989).

If the day of commissioning of the BAM is not easy to pinpoint, this is even more true as regards the initiation of the project. Early in 1972, a brief news item in the Soviet press announced that work had begun on a new Siberian railroad, north of the existing Trans-Siberian mainline. Then in 1974, Brezhnev, in a speech in Alma-Ata, confirmed that the BAM project was being revived as one of the large undertakings of the 1976-1980 FYP. However, as far as the conception of the BAM is concerned, it is known (Shabad 1979) that it had first been contemplated in the 1930s and that during the early part of the 1950s the westernmost and easternmost segments of the BAM had actually been completed.

(•) In 1987, the fourth and last generating set of Hungary's first nuclear power station, with total planned costs of Ft 88 bn, was publicly inaugurated (*Népszabadság*, 31 October 1987). For the purposes of the investment statistics, however, the project remained unfinished until the end of 1990, because the full completion of the project counts and not the moment when the main production capacities were made operational. However, 1990 cannot be considered as a final deadline, as some important phases of the construction work (e.g., the building of waste storage capacities) will have to be implemented in subsequent years. From a statistical point of view, however, these works will not be treated as a part of the original project, because financing will come from the company itself, and not from budgetary sources (*Figyelö*, 21 March 1991).

On the other hand, it was also decided that after, or rather parallel with, the completion of the fourth 440 MW unit, an additional two units would be built at the same site, with a nominal capacity of 1000 MW each. For some reason this work was regarded as a new investment project, although in several respects the old and the new plant represent an indivisible whole.

[30] See e.g., RSI/1973 p. xxii; SR/1967 p. 167. It is a seemingly small detail, but worth mentioning to illustrate the process of information distortion, that there is a contradiction between the data presented in the annual Czechoslovak statistical yearbooks and HSR, the historical compendium of Czechoslovak statistical data. While the yearbooks precisely note that the investment commitment figures reflect only commitments occurring in state sector projects with construction work, this reference was omitted from the historical compendium (HSR/1985 p. 183).

If investment commitment means something for those who are responsible for planning investments, and I am convinced that it does, then this new project must have constituted such a commitment - at least since 1986, when the Hungarian-Soviet government agreement on cooperation in this matter was initialled. The whole issue is, however, viewed differently by the statisticians. While the Hungarian press put the cost estimates of these two units at Ft 93 billion[31], the project is still not indicated in the investment statistics, since it is considered as an "investment project under preparation".[32]

(•) Another large-scale Hungarian energy project, the Danube barrage power station, offers a different kind of example. This project, expected to cost Ft 53 bn[33], was first mentioned in the 1985 Investment Statistics Yearbook, with 1978 given as the starting date. Earlier editions of the same publication failed to list it under the heading of "major unfinished investment projects". It seems that there was a good reason for this. In the period 1978-1985, little work was done on the project, and thus financial outlays were also minimal.

(•) The last example is striking, not because of the amount of money involved in the project but rather because of its exceptionally long gestation period. For many years, Hungarian investment statistics have carried an entry for the reconstruction of Buda Castle on the hills of Budapest. Total costs were given as Ft 2.4bn, which is not a substantial sum. In spite of this, the work has reportedly been carried on since 1949 ! For those who have seen the area in question, where a number of buildings and institutions have been operational for several years, it is obvious that this Ft 2.4bn project could have been easily divided into 8-10 smaller parts, of which 5 or 6 projects could already have been classified under commissioned projects.

(iv) It has already been noted that, as a result of cost recalculations, S(t)-s are expressed at mixed price levels. Furthermore, S(t)-s, at time t, represent a mixture of actual (i.e. past) and planned (i.e. future) costs. The former is always a "hard" figure, which can be documented with settled payment accounts, while the second remains what it is - namely, a planned, future expenditure item, which is a relatively soft figure.

It is not by chance, or as a consequence of laziness, that the statistical offices of the socialist countries refuse to publish investment commitment estimates at constant prices. Model builders are sometimes inclined to reprimand the statistical offices for the lack of such estimates but these authors demand the impossible. The effort to bridge this gap by way of a simple deflation of

[31] This reported figure was expressed at 1985 constant prices. In 1988, the current price estimate surpassed Ft 140 bn. (*Világgazdaság*, 19 October 1988).

[32] At the time of finalising the present manuscript (February 1992), the fate of this investment project is once again in the air.

[33] There have been conflicting reports concerning the price base applied in the cost estimation. In 1986, one official was quoted as saying that allowances had been made for all future price rises, but three years later the Prime Minister said that these calculations were made at constant 1986 prices (*Figyelö*, 5 June, 1986, *Magyar Nemzet*, 23 May 1989).

S(t)-s and D(t)-s with published investment price data, reflecting price changes in current outlays in year t, t-1, t-2, etc., is totally arbitrary and cannot be accepted.[34]

(v) On the macro-economic level, projects substitute and complement one another. If the plans for opening a new coal mine are shelved, there will be no need for a new power station. This relationship also holds at the margin. Modifications in the plans of one project will probably have implications for dozens of other ongoing projects. Chart 2.2 thus also fails to account for the complications arising from this factor.

* * *

In the preceding paragraphs an attempt was made to demonstrate why it is mistaken to aggregate investment commitments arising from individual investment projects. This is an extremely important point, because, as I believe, the protagonists of ICM failed to present this problem explicitly. In the pioneering study of Frisch (1933) it had already been emphasized that the whole idea of investment commitment was relevant only in the context of the completion of big units of fixed capital.[35] Unfortunately, this warning was somehow forgotten by those who later tried to exploit this very original idea.

As noted in an early work of Bauer himself:

> The annual investment outlays of even the largest projects do not exceed a few percentages of the amount of investment outlays in the national plan. It must be added that the length of the cycles is shorter than the time necessary for the completion of a large investment project and especially of an entire development program." (Bauer 1978, p. 255*n*.)

Hence, the "miracle" that generates the cycle must conceal itself, as the impact of contemporaneous projects cumulate. This has to be quantified, or modelled at least. It is at this point where ICM is not robust enough.

The Missing Components of Investment Commitment. The previous sub-section challenged the way in which certain aspects of investment commitment were taken into account in ICM. We now examine what was left out of the model.

From the point of view of central resource allocation, there are several other types of commitment of investment resources which are totally unrelated to the one already discussed and which are taken care of in the ICM.

(i) The "true" volume of commitment of investment resources is impossible to determine unless account is taken of the fact that the production of certain types of capital goods cannot

[34] This is done, for example, in Bauer (1988) and Lackó (1990) without due consideration of the possible outcomes. Some twenty years ago, two American economists proved by trial calculations for the Soviet economy that the stock of projects in progress at constant prices might vary by 10 % or more, depending on whether just one year's price index or a weighted average of the past two-three year's is applied (Moorsteen and Powell 1966, pp. 94-95).

[35] The examples mentioned by Frisch were: big industrial plants, water-power plants, railways, big steamers (*op. cit.* p. 185).

be meaningfully carried out without additional investments somewhere else. Such a situation occurs when investment goods producing capacities are already in place but export outlets cannot be easily found at short notice. In such cases domestic investment plans always have to be adjusted to the pulsation of production of these factories. Thus, in many countries state investments in housing were determined by the throughput capacity of factories manufacturing building panels. If you do not want to stop production in these factories, you need housing investment to absorb the output. Similarly, in the absence of export markets, investment in public urban transport is dependent on the production of the domestic transport equipment factories.

(ii) With regard to investment commitments stemming from foreign trade obligations, the situation is somewhat different on the import and the export sides. A rise in domestic investment may occur as a result of an unplanned trade surplus in bilateral trade among CMEA countries. In such situations machinery and equipment are imported on a large scale in order to get rid of the surplus.[36] On the export side, there is the well-known example reflecting the bargaining game between the Centre and firms. SOEs can accept export obligations without previous central approval. This is part of their blackmailing strategy, since the firms are fully aware that these delivery plans also require investment inputs.[37]

In these cases, which are by no means exceptional, investment commitment arises not from a micro-economic determination to finish something which has already been started but rather from the inherent rigidities of production and foreign trade plans.

(iii) Finally, there remains another type of investment commitment that is related to investment activities but which nevertheless does not appear in the investment statistics. Foreign investments constitute the most important example within this category. In the socialist countries, national accounting practices are based on "domestic" and not on "national" concepts. Thus, any investment which occurs outside the territory of the country (such as the east European participation in Soviet energy projects located in Siberia) is *ex post* classified as an export. *Ex ante*, however, planners must also take these projects into account in the investment allocation process, because they compete for the very same resources (labour, capital and imports) as domestic investments.

(iv) A new phenomenon worth mentioning is that socialist countries in the second half of the 1980s started to include leasing in their economic arsenal. This development, which had already posed intricate methodological questions to analysts of Western economies (UN ECE 1987, pp. 77-79), is again not reflected in the investment statistics, as the acquisition of the equipment in question is not financed from investment funds. Fragmentary information suggests that the share

[36] Soós (1986) considered what he called the "machinery trade cycle", arising from the recurring trade imbalances which planners wish to eliminate via forced imports, as a unique Hungarian development (p. 419).

[37] See e.g., Soós (1978, p. 231*n*.)

of leased capital goods is still marginal in most countries, with the possible exception of Hungary.[38]

(v) Finally, it is worth noting that military appropriations are generally not included in the investment statistics either.[39] For good economic reasons, and for the sake of compliance with UN practices, these expenditures - in some countries at least - are regarded as part of current government expenditures.

Investment Starts and Commissioning. Having examined the theoretical and practical difficulties of quantifying the actual size of investment commitments in any given year, other concepts frequently used in ICMs can also be questioned. It is clear that if the real content and the cost of future projects cannot be measured precisely at the macro-economic level, this applies to the number of project starts and completions, as well as to the total investment commitment arising from authorised starts in a given year.

Moreover, there is a certain trade-off between the size of permissible errors in measuring these concepts. If it is assumed that the original and officially authorized costs of investment projects is deliberately distorted (underplanned), and this will be one of the engines of the cyclical movements, the relevance of measuring investment starts (in terms of planned commitments) becomes questionable. If the opposite is assumed, namely that no such underplanning occurs, it is difficult to see why the Centre should be incapable of keeping the process under control.[40]

This is an important issue, not only as a line of criticism directed at ICM but from the perspective of short-term economic analysis as well. Official statistical reports often mention as a success (or failure) indicator that the number of accomplished investment projects in a given year was bigger (or smaller) than in the year before. In reality, however, no firm conclusion can be drawn from these statements due to the very same type of difficulties discussed above regarding investment commitment data.

There are two further indicators, seemingly similar to the much-criticised concept of "investment commitment". The first is the variable calculated from the stock of unfinished investments (ΣUGINV). Analysts of socialist economies are well acquainted with this indicator, since plans and plan fulfilment reports of several countries cover it. In contrast to the concept of "investment commitment", which is a future related variable, there is nothing inherently wrong with this. However, ΣUGINV is not really suitable for the analysis of short-term GINV fluctuations. For the reasons already explained above, there is no way to build a meaningful price index to deflate this time series of stock data. Therefore model builders have to assume little or no price inflation if they include this indicator.

To my knowledge, up to now only Roland (1987a) has tried to build ΣUGINV into a realistic simulation model of Soviet GINV fluctuations between 1959-1982. Since in this period, officially reported annual price rises in the investment sector were not particularly strong, from a technical point of view, this was not a dangerous compromise. However, not long ago, a

[38] According to a Hungarian official report, in 1987 the volume of leased equipment was nearly equal to the total volume of imported western machinery put in use. (KSH 1988, p. 34)

[39] This may not hold for the Soviet Union. In section 3.1 the problem will be discussed in more detail.

[40] I am grateful to Mr. A. Simonovits for his clear formulation of this contradiction.

technically faultless method was found - Kohn and Leggett (1986) - to calculate the stock of unfinished investments (ΣUGINV) at constant prices on the basis of published Soviet data. The procedure is based on the assumption that there is a certain accounting relationship among the various statistics on capital formation which should hold for both current and constant price series. This is a logical hypothesis but there is no independent evidence to support the contention that Soviet statisticians are actually using these equations to calculate (or cross-check) the published data. In addition, as the authors themselves noted, the fact that their result suggests a reduction in prices of investments calls into question the validity of the original constant price series.

As seen in Section 1.4, this problem is eliminated within the framework of national accounts, where flow data are used to show the change between two past consecutive years in the stock of unfinished investments ($UGINV = \Sigma UGINV_t - \Sigma UGINV_{t-1}$). Hence, with respect to value figures calculated in this manner, the application of "borrowed" price indices is permissible. The statistical offices assume that the overall investment price index in the given year is a good proxy for the price element of the annual change in the nominal value of ΣUGINV.

There are two additional problems, however, when ΣUGINV is used to estimate investment commitment for analyzing GINV fluctuations in the Soviet Union. First, the smaller one: the published Soviet numbers do not cover unfinished construction of cooperatives (*kolkhozy*) and private individuals. The second constraint is more important. As Birman (1981, p. 223) rightly pointed out, both Soviet and Western literature takes into account only unfinished construction itself, although unfinished construction production (*nezavershennoye stroitel' noye proizvodstvo*) which amounts to about 1/3 of ΣUGINV, has the same economic significance. A precise account of investment commitment arising from the existence of investment projects in progress must, therefore, include this magnitude as well.

Dispersion of Investment Resources. At micro-level the meaning of this concept is straightforward. Excessive dispersion of resources means that less money, material and manpower are allocated to a given investment project than would be required by technological considerations. The interpretation of the concept, however, is somewhat ambiguous. There is some empirical evidence - Barta (1980) - suggesting that in the middle of the 1970s the number of workers simultaneously engaged on statistically well-definable investment projects such as power stations, oil refineries, cement factories, etc., was not significantly lower in the East European countries than in market economies. The long lead times were essentially the consequence of the 2-5 fold differences in hourly productivity of the construction workers. In this perspective, the concept of dispersion of investment resources seems to miss the point. The problem is the low level of productivity, a phenomenon which, of course, is not limited to the sphere of investments.[41]

The issue becomes even more complicated when we look at it from the point of view of all simultaneously ongoing investment projects. What does excessive dispersion (or "scattering", as it is often called) mean at macro-economic level?

The ICM assumes that "dispersion" (*raspyleniye* in Russian) manifests itself strongly during the upward phase of the cycle. This forces planners to curb new investment starts and to apply various restrictions on projects already in progress in order to accelerate the completion of certain

[41] The Soviet situation was probably different. The average Soviet plant is much larger than the average Western one; therefore the average construction site must have been larger too. Whether this was matched by a similar difference in the number of construction workers remains to investigated.

other ones. During the last, fourth phase of the cycle (setback), dispersion is believed to lessen, and, hence, the efficiency of the entire investment process improves.

As Bauer (1981, pp. 38-45) himself acknowledges, there are a number of open questions regarding the measurement of dispersion. His conclusion is, however, that although dispersion itself cannot be measured, there are many ways to monitor the changes in it. Unfortunately, even this moderate claim is overambitious. It is true that planners and politicians often make public statements to the effect that investment dispersion has increased or declined in a given time period but, as I will try to show, these statements are not well founded.

In ICM dispersion is defined as the change in D(t)/i(t). In other words, the volume of total investment commitments is related the annual investment outlays. Since i(t) is the same as GINV, there is no problem with this indicator. Of course, D(t) is a very soft indicator which cannot be measured with any acceptable degree of precision.[42] In other words, my objection to the D(t)/i(t) ratio is its inapplicability in practice. If dispersion is measured with it, there is no way to state with any reasonable degree of credibility that this variable has risen or declined in the given period. Let us repeat, the ratio of a hard and a soft variable is bound to be a soft variable, on the basis of which decisions cannot - and should not - be made.

There is another approach, however, that could promise better results in measuring investment dispersion. Using more reliable statistical variables than D(t), four other indicators can be constructed. In fact, all of them are known in the literature of planning, and Bauer occasionally makes use of them, too.

<1> Annual investment outlays (GINV) can be meaningfully contrasted with the total volume of frozen, uncompleted investments (ΣUGINV). In Chart 2.2, this magnitude is shown by the empty rectangles.

<2> A rather conventional method is to calculate the ratio of annual investments to annual completion. (CGINV). On Chart 2.2. this magnitude is shown by empty triangles.

<3> A chain index can be built from the stock data of ΣUGINV.

<4> GINV can be compared with the annual increase of uncompleted investments and expressed as a percentage change. This ratio shows the percentage of annual investment outlays which remained frozen in a given year in the form of uncompleted projects.

Now, these four indicators were deliberately defined in order to show a rise (decline) in dispersion, when the indicator rises (falls). Before starting a detailed investigation, it is important to note that even these indicators are not above all criticism. The data presented in table 2.5 are technically expressed at current prices, since ΣUGINV is published in this and only this form. In fact, for the reason already explained above, ΣUGINV is expressed in a mix of price levels. Hence, those indicators where ΣUGINV figures appear in the denominator or in the numerator also reflect such a mixed price base. Consequently, annual changes in the four indicators

[42] Instead of dispersion Lackó (1980, 1990) and Simonovits (1988) prefer the term "internal tensions of the investment process". From the point of view of our criticism, however, this is not pertinent, since this variable is also measured with the help of D(t) - either as a magnitude relative to the trend value of D(t) or as a percentage of GDP.

CHART 2.3 Hungary: Two indicators of investment dispersion, 1950-1989

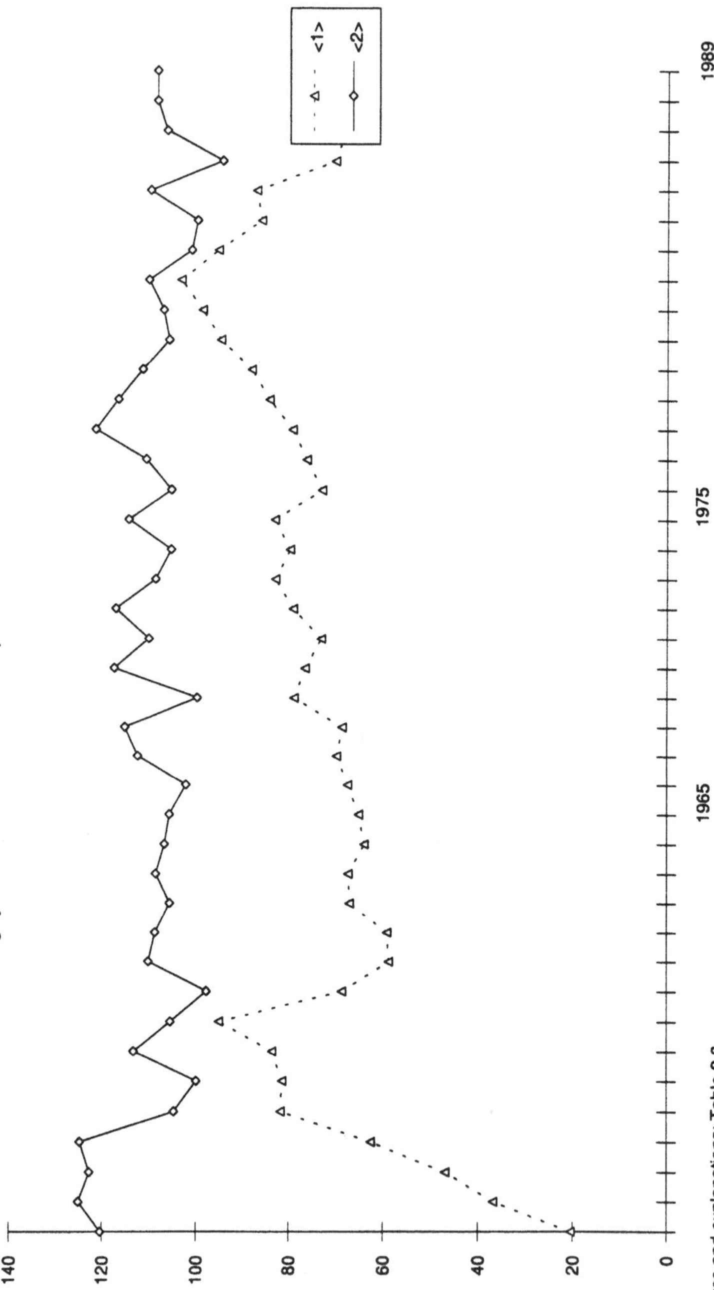

Source and explanations: Table 2.6

TABLE 2.5 Hungary: Investment dispersion (four indicators), 1950-1989

	ΣUGINV*100 / GINV <1>	GINV *100 / CGINV <2>	ΣUGINV(t) *100 / UGINV(t-1) <3>	(ΣUGINV(t)-ΣUGINV(t-1))*100 / GINV <4>
1950	20.4	120.3	.	.
1951	36.7	124.9	218.6	19.9
1952	46.7	122.5	155.1	16.6
1953	62.5	124.5	137.8	17.1
1954	81.6	104.5	99.6	-0.4
1955	81.2	99.8	96.8	-2.7
1956	83.4	113.1	111.0	8.2
1957	94.9	105.3	104.3	3.9
1958	68.6	97.5	93.5	-4.7
1959	58.6	109.9	190.5	27.8
1960	59.0	108.4	113.1	6.8
1961	67.0	105.3	106.4	4.0
1962	67.2	108.3	110.7	6.5
1963	63.8	106.4	108.1	4.8
1964	65.0	105.4	105.7	3.5
1965	67.3	101.9	98.8	-0.8
1966	69.7	112.0	114.3	8.7
1967	68.5	114.7	117.7	10.3
1968	78.6	99.4	113.5	9.4
1969	76.3	117.0	126.1	15.8
1970	72.9	109.7	114.7	9.3
1971	78.8	116.6	121.9	14.2
1972	82.6	108.2	108.5	6.5
1973	79.4	104.9	102.1	1.6
1974	82.7	113.9	115.5	11.1
1975	72.7	104.8	103.1	2.2
1976	75.9	110.2	109.0	6.3
1977	78.9	120.8	122.7	14.6
1978	83.8	116.0	115.2	11.1
1979	87.7	110.9	108.1	6.6
1980	94.2	105.2	101.6	1.4
1981	98.2	106.4	102.2	2.1
1982	102.7	109.5	107.7	7.4
1983	94.8	100.5	96.1	-3.9
1984	85.5	99.2	93.1	-6.3
1985	86.6	109.2	104.8	4.0
1986	69.9	93.9	87.3	-10.1
1987	67.8	105.7	110.3	6.3
1988	76.6	107.8	111.3	7.8
1989	73.4	107.8	112.2	8.0

GINV= Gross fixed investments (flow)
CGINV= Completed investments (flow)
ΣUGINV= Uncompleted investments (stock)

Source: Own calculations based on SE/89 p. 4.

amounting to a few percentage points only cannot be taken very seriously, as they also reflect the imprecision of such mixed price calculations.

For the sake of the argument, however, let us temporarily leave aside this objection. Unfortunately, other difficulties also appear. Even without a formal mathematical presentation, it is easy to see that movements in the four indicators do not necessarily result in parallel variations. Chart 2.3 was prepared on the basis of Hungarian data, using indicators <1> and <2> above. The first (ΣUGINV/GINV) signals a steady rise in investment dispersion in the 1950-1956 period. At the same time, the second indicator (GINV/CGINV) speaks of slight and inconclusive improvements. In a secular sense, indicator <2> therefore suggests that investment dispersion was essentially unchanged in the entire period, while indicator <1> points to a steady deterioration which includes two distinct waves of accelerated deterioration (1954-1957, 1975-1982). Which indicator should planners use?

It is interesting to examine the impact of three successive cuts in investment expenditures (1957, 1961 and 1965). Contemporary observers and high ranking officials made statements to the effect that investment dispersion had been reduced in 1961 and 1965, while in 1957 no improvement had occurred.[43] By contrast, for the year 1957 three indicators out of four in table 2.5 suggest that the investment situation did improve in this respect. For the years 1961 and 1965, three indicators support the official assessment, while the fourth (ΣUGINV/GINV) points in the opposite direction. This uncertainty, in fact, can be observed during the whole period under review. There are only 20 out of 37 cases where all four indicators signalled the same direction of change in the size of dispersion. Focusing on only the two most frequently used indicators - <1> and <2> - the situation is much the same: 21 clear answers out of 37 cases.

A similarly confusing picture arises when Soviet data taken from Bauer's book are scrutinized using the same method (table 2.6). During the first post-war investment slowdown, for which data permitted the Hungarian author to calculate at least three indicators, there is an alarming inconsistency in their movements.

[43] Such statements are quoted at length in Bauer (1981, pp. 106-107, 121, 138).

TABLE 2. 6 Soviet Union: Investment dispersion (three indicators), 1958-1963

(At current prices)

	GINV % change	Direction of change	Σ UGINV/GINV*100 (%) <1>	Direction of change	GINV/CGINV *100 (%) <2>	Direction of change	Σ UGINV(t)/ΣUGINV(t-1)*100 (Previous year = 100.0) <3>	Direction of change
1958	16.2		73.0		102.0		99.4	
1959	13.2	-	70.0	-	109.4	+	108.6	+
1960	8.5	-	69.0	-	109.9	+	112.6	+
1961	4.3	-	76.0	+	113.5	+	115.9	+
1962	4.9	+	76.0	0.0	106.4	-	105.2	-
1963	5.1	+	72.0	-	102.1	-	100.4	-

GINV= Gross fixed investments (flow)
CGINV= Completed investments (flow)
ΣUGINV= Uncompleted investments (stock)

Source: Recalculated from Bauer (1981, Table 16.6 p. 390)

Indirect Measurement of Tensions on the Investment Goods Markets. In the previous sections, the critique of ICM was introduced by a sweeping statement: the measurement of its key variables is a theoretical and statistical impossibility. In the preceding sections, I tried to present my arguments in a detailed manner. One question, however, remained open, even if the validity of my arguments was fully accepted. Irene Grosfeld, for example, in a survey of the ICMs, used a citation from Haavelmo to formulate the dilemma and position herself in this respect. "It may sometimes be more fruitful to develop a theory in terms of variables which we *should* like to measure, or which could be measured *in point of principle*. We may derive deeper understanding even by using abstract and auxiliary variables that could not conceivably be observed." (p. 50, italics in original)

Grosfeld claims that in the preliminary stage of research such an approach is acceptable. I am more critical in this respect, since most versions of ICM put empirical analysis before the public, and not preliminary models in the form of working hypotheses.

I can imagine two formulations of my criticism against ICM. The more rigorous one would claim that the key variables of this model, such as investment commitment, starts and dispersion cannot be measured with any degree of precision. A less radical formulation would assert that these key variables are to some extent measurable, though only with a great deal - say 20-40 % - of uncertainty. In the final analysis, however, this more moderate statement is just as devastating as the extreme one. Under normal circumstances, the fluctuation of GINV rates from year to year occurs within a range of ± 10 %. How can we possibly explain such a relatively small movement with explanatory variables whose measurement error is somewhere in the region of 20-40 %?

If this is so, let us try to be even less demanding with respect to our data needs. Instead of aiming at a hard figure on the size of dispersion, perhaps other sources of information can be exploited to form at least some vague ideas on the state of equilibrium on the investment goods markets. As a matter of fact, Bauer did make a heroic attempt to exploit the information content of public statements, speeches and articles delivered by national leaders or economic experts of the countries concerned. In his four-phase model, in addition to the available statistical information, he tried to use these materials for identifying the phases of the cycle.

There are two factors shedding some light on the applicability of these materials for such a purpose.

(i) As I have repeatedly argued, national economic leaders and their experts focus their attention on a few large investment projects. Their assessments of the state of the investment market is based on reports related to these projects and not on the state of the investment market in its entirety. This assertion is in fact supported by numerous quotations from Bauer's own research. For example, analyzing the GINV "cycle" of Czechoslovakia between 1958-1963, Bauer quotes at great length from party documents, government statements and speeches alike. Among these quotations, no less than 18 unambiguously related to the fate of the so-called centralized investment projects with an average gestation time of 7-10 years. In other words, relying on these policy statements, we are back to the problem discussed in section 1.4 - the confusion between the true state of the investment market and the fate of a half-dozen large investment projects.

In this case, there are literally a very small number of projects whose fate may unduly influence the hearts and minds of top decision makers. If the pace of construction is analyzed on a statistically significant sample of large projects, it may turn out that the length of the gestation period is invariant to the macro-fluctuations in GINV. Some empirical support for such a contention was already provided by a study of Hungarian state industrial investments (Jánosi and Pál, 1983).

How can we explain this phenomenon? An argument drawing on observations made in Soós (1987) and Podkaminer (1988 15*n*.) seems to bring us close to the answer. It is possible to accelerate the construction on one or two projects, if it is ordered from the "top". Such a benign concentration of resources, however, is not possible on a larger number of giant projects, since the scene is dominated by giant planning bureaus, construction firms and foreign trade organisations involved in all, or nearly all, contemporaneous big projects. Thus, the government has to make a choice. It has to select two or three out of fifty or a hundred large projects, and then see to it that the giant construction firms pool resources on these construction sites.

(ii) It borders on inexcusable naivety to believe that citations from public statements, newspaper articles or confidential documents of the planning organs can give an insight into the real motivations of the decision makers. Undoubtedly, the arguments and counter-arguments, wrapped in the terminology of macro-economics, have important messages which point far beyond their factual content. However, once we reject the simplifying approach in which the Centre represents a solid block of intentions vis-à-vis the SOEs (section 1.3), it becomes immediately evident that the seemingly professional discussion on accelerating or slowing down the investment process mainly reflects the state of internal interest conflicts within the apparatus.

There is always a good basis for members of the "equilibrium lobby" - the Ministry of Finance, the Planning Office and the National Bank - to complain about investment dispersion, the protraction of projects and the unsatisfactory quality performance of those commissioned. On the other hand, the branch ministry lobby has also some right on its side. *Ceteris paribus*, it is not difficult to prove that accelerated development of industry, agriculture or the infrastructural network would serve the general interest and that therefore some sacrifice in other areas would not be an inadmissible price to pay for it.

The public statements of government and party officials must be interpreted in this context. These statements do not directly reflect the true state of affairs in the real economy but rather the momentary outcome of fights between opposing lobbies. The two possible extremes concerning the evaluation of the state of the investment market have different value contents. If there is a consensus among the nation's economic leaders that the investment process can be accelerated, no one can feel any direct or implied criticism in statements to such an effect. In the Soviet-type economies nobody suffers if opportunities are missed. By contrast, if the general view is that there are too many investments and hence a slowdown is required, this position strongly implies criticism with regard to past economic policies.

* * *

Finally, a few more words on the concept of investment commitment. In the preceding pages I argued at length that, on the one hand, economic reality does know no such a thing as investment commitment, while at the same time I insisted that this phenomenon cannot be quantified by means of a single number. An analogy can, perhaps help to convince the reader that there is no contradiction between these two propositions.

The analogy I would like to recall is the division of gross industrial production (INDT) in the socialist countries into Group "A" and "B". In many but not all socialist countries, planners and statisticians used to operate with these categories - in Chapter 3 I will use them too - and there seems to be a consensus on their meaning. This separation distinguishes between the means of production ("A") and objects of consumption ("B"). For many decades politicians and economists were at daggers drawn when they argued that Group "A" must grow faster than Group "B" or *vice versa.*

At an abstract level, this made good sense, if for no other reason than because the distinction had it roots in Marxist theory. A closer inspection of the usage of these terms in economic analysis, everyday journalism and political thinking of the socialist countries reveals, however, that these pair of words were used interchangeably to mean "heavy" and "light industry", or "Department I" and "Department II". Some times "A" and "B" were even equated with "investment" and "consumption", which is a very different matter altogether.

However, the application of these categories in statistical practice, which in principle should have provided the basis for analytical and normative discussions, leads to total confusion. There are hosts of questions which cannot be meaningfully answered. For example, steel used for railways is classed under Group "A" and bicycles Group "B". But what is about the steel that goes straight to the bicycle factory? What about fuel, electricity, etc.?

So is it meaningless to look at the development of Groups "A" and "B" ? Is it a myth only? For me, the answer is a definite "yes", independently of the fact that, in conceptual terms, the division between the means of production and the objects of consumption does make sense. The point is, as Wiles (1962, pp. 272-288) lucidly brought out in a very detailed analysis of this question, that the doctrine that Group "A" must grow faster than Group "B" largely reflects a demand for a certain investment pattern and for a certain investment volume. Construction, for example, is not industry, and therefore is not in Group "A"; so a demand to accelerate Group "A" runs the danger of demanding steel and steel production plant but not the factories that house this plant. Diverse activities related to the military and armaments production - such as scientific research or the well-being of officers - were also meant to enjoy preferential treatment.

Hence, in terms of policy formulation, the division of Groups "A" and "B" is not a myth. They were simply shorthand expressions of certain ideas, which were quite well understood in the decision making circles. But this has nothing to do with the empirical categorisation of industrial output. So, in this sense, it is a myth.

2.3 COMMON ELEMENTS

Before embarking on the theme of exogenous models, it would perhaps be timely to make a few summary statements on both the control theory and the endogenous models.

In my view there is one common point of weakness in them, namely that they fail to give a sufficiently nuanced description of the role of the Centre. As I have already repeatedly stressed, it is a truism that no model is perfect. A complex problem like macro-economic fluctuations cannot be studied analytically without discarding a considerable amount of detail from the picture. The question is where to draw the line between detail and substance.

On the one hand, these models overestimate the role of economics under socialism. They disregard the fact that in Soviet-type economies politics dominate economic considerations. More specifically, macro-economic guidelines concerning the pace of growth, the tolerated level of inflation, foreign indebtedness, etc., are always set on the basis of political considerations. The seeds of a possible economic disaster - as Podkaminer (1989) says - are always sown at this level. In this case, managers and bureaucrats can do little to prevent chaos - even if they are endowed with the best will and a great deal of professional competence.

At the same time, both control theory and the various types of endogenous models underestimate the true level of sophistication of the planning process itself. First of all, it is assumed that investment decisions are made in real terms, being plans for a particular amount of extra physical capacities. Money does not appear in these models.

Under "normal" circumstances, when macro-economic policy decisions are not foolishly wrong from the very outset, it is mistaken to portray planners as impotent prisoners of technical developments, the periodic character of planning or their own past decisions. In all these respects there is considerable room for manoeuvre - partly because money never ceased to play a role in macro-economic control.[44]

If the volume of investments is considered relevant for modelling planners' behaviour, there is no reason to believe that other macro variables are not planned with equal persistence and stubbornness. In other words, the assumed direction of causation leading from GINV to all the other variables is questionable from the outset.

The two versions of the endogenous cycle model, discussed above, were relatively strong in providing a logically consistent account of the reinforcement mechanisms working during the upswing. This, however, cannot be said with equal confidence with regard to the downswing. After several decades of academic discussion, the issue remains as open as it was forty years ago.

As early as 1949, this deficiency was already pinpointed at a conference on cycles in planned economies. "In a planned economy the cumulative process of contraction will not be allowed to develop. (...) In the nationalized sectors it is not likely that investment will be quickly curtailed when prospects look a little less favourable." (Haberler 1951, p. 385) Indeed, if no allowance is made for external factors, the logic of the endogenous models (planning + SEP) points in the opposite direction. No matter how small, investment cuts were bound to lead to a lessening of imbalances. Thus room is created for immediate anti-depression policies.

[44] The role of money in the pre-reformed socialist economies was the subject of a heated debate between Kornai (1985) and Soós (1984, 1985). According to Soós, the author of *Economics of Shortage* underestimated the importance of monetary control even in the traditional planning system, and was *a fortiori* wrong in the assessment of the developments of the late 1980s.

In sum, there is a good deal of justice in the harsh sentence on the investment cycle models pronounced by a Polish economist (Podkaminer 1989, p. 31). For him these models are not true models but rather a malicious - although politically useful - caricature of socialist planning. Nevertheless, our final judgment should be more balanced. Reality is very complex and no useful theory can encompass it all. If a theory provides a good starting point for the analysis of real problems, it is already useful. If its main conclusions are approximately fulfilled in reality, it becomes a very good theory. I think that both types of investment cycle models failed on the second count but each was very successful on the first. This is already a considerable achievement.

2.4 Exogenous models

As already stated more than once, the term "exogenous" is used in this book for models in which investment fluctuations are not determined by system-specific mechanisms of Soviet-type economies. These models, therefore, go beyond the traditional vision of socialism outlined in Section 1.3 (planning + shortages). A salient weakness of the traditional theory of socialist planning and of certain models which attempt to quantify the actual process of planning is that they fail to take any account of stochastic, as opposed to deterministic, processes.

With the help of our standard formulation, the exogenous models can be described in the following way:

(2.5) $GINV = f_3 (Q_1, Q_2 \ldots Q_n)$,
where GINV denotes the annual volume of investments,
$Q_1, Q_2 \ldots Q_n$ signifies both economic and political factors and
n is a relatively large number.

2.4.1 The Role of Politics. Planners, like everyone else, are partially ignorant about the past, present and future. To a great extent they are defenceless against contingencies of their own environment. Ironically, flesh-and-blood planners are aware of these limitations - even if the textbook economics of socialist planning chastely say very little about it. The chronology of five-year plans, as presented in Section 2.2, seems to convey such a lesson.

I am not claiming originality in this matter. It is a historical fact that soon after the Bolshevik revolution the leaders of the Soviet Union assessed their situation in very much the same way. It is a different, and very far reaching question, to ask how it could have happened that the notion of external dependence was mixed with the notion of external threat even in the best minds of the country.[45] Stalin's famous slogan about "building socialism in one country" already contained both interpretations. More precisely, the slogan's function was to mobilize the Soviet people to rise above this humiliating position. It was only three decades later that the Soviet leadership invalidated this doctrine. To everybody's surprise, Cominform, a short-lived centre to control the world's communist parties, was called into being in 1947, and a new slogan was invented concerning "two world systems".[46]

External dependence is only one of many constraining factors. The survival of the institutions, habits and behavioural norms of the pre-capitalist past is also of great importance. In theory one

[45] In a brilliant historical essay Kennan (1962) describes the chain of events which led to such a colossal misinterpretation of history. After 1917, the ruling Soviet elite perceived the Western intervention as a capitalist attack against the proletarian revolution. The attacking forces of both Germany and the anti-German coalition were guided by the purely military considerations of the war against each other and hence were not greatly motivated by the threat of a communist revolution as such.

[46] There is some evidence to support the idea that during World War II the Soviet leaders contemplated the possibility of including a few east European countries in the Union (Hough 1985, p. 267). Immediately after the war, however, Soviet officials publicly argued for a transition period for the east European "people's democracies", before they became part of the socialist system. Had any of these two options materialized, it would have made little sense to talk about a socialist "world system" or a "socialist camp".

can think of an administratively controlled, rational and calculable economic system based on planning and the allocation of shortages. Such a pure system, however, is hardly viable in the real world. Side by side with the "rational" bureaucratic system, patrimonialism and collegiality continued to work in the Soviet-type economies. Thus, the elements of non-economic rationality regularly rise up to the surface.[47]

As Table 2.7 witnesses, socialist countries were typically ruled by patrimonial leaders, whose reigns often stretched over two decades.[48] Regardless of whether patrimonialism assumed its best or its degenerate face, the ruler always governed at his own discretion. The omission of this characteristic from the portrait of Soviet-type economies is perhaps one of the most salient shortcomings of the traditional interpretation of socialism in general, and of the endogenous school of investment cycles in particular.

In reality, specific policy objectives always reflected the ruler's individual programmatic commitments. This was particularly true with respect to large construction projects. Pretentious leaders' obsessions with canals, for example, had very little to do with meaningful economic objectives.

I am fully aware that the introduction of the concept of irrational megalomania is a dangerous *deus ex machina* from a purist point of view. In general terms this was already alluded to in Chapter 1 above. Nonetheless, David Dyker, the author of an excellent monograph on Soviet investment policy, was right when he warned us that "methodological messiness should not (...) be permitted to induce us to pigeon-hole this kind of thing as merely an «interesting aberration»". (Dyker 1983, p. 4)

This point is made simply to emphasize that in the socialist system certain very fundamental psychological tendencies exist, and some of these tendencies are particularly important in determining both the volume and the composition of total investments. In this context, of course, there is another factor which cannot be neglected. The limited applicability of law is a vital condition for the survival of patrimonialism and explains the affinity between this type of political process and the merciless drive for economic growth. Of course, it can be argued that in well-established socialist countries there was a tendency over time to move towards consensual rule, with the leader becoming a mediator between institutions over which he had much less control the earlier leader had. This argument, however, has a basic weakness. It fails to take into account that, in many cases, the socialist system as such is unable to survive this change. There was no institutionalized mechanism of succession: when the autocratic leader went, the system was immediately pushed at the verge of crisis, where anything could happen.

[47] For a more elaborate presentation of these issues see Comisso (1986).

[48] See Narkiewicz (1986, pp. 115-122) for a theoretical approach and an overview of East European leadership changes.

TABLE 2.7 Long-serving party leaders, 1924-1991

	40 years or more		30-40 years		20-30 years		10--20 years	
Europe								
Albania	Hoxha	1944-85						
Bulgaria			Zhivkov	1954-89				
CSSR							Novotny	1951-68
GDR					Ulbricht	1950-71	Honecker	1971-89
Hungary			Kádár	1956-89			Rákosi	1945-55
Poland							Bierut	1945-56
							Gomulka	1956-70
							Gierek	1970-80
Romania					Ceausescu	1965-89	Gheorghiu-Dej	1949-65
USSR					Stalin	1924-53	Khruschev	1953-64
							Brezhnev	1964-82
Yugoslavia			Tito	1945-80				
Asia								
China					Mao	1949-76	Teng	1980-
Cambodia							Heng	1979-
North Korea	Kim	1948-						
Laos							Kaysone	1975-
Mongolia			Tsedenbal	1952-84			Choybalsan	1936-52
Viet Nam					Ho	1945-69	Le Duan	1969-86
Africa								
Angola							dos Santos	1979-
Benin							Kérékou	1972-91
Burma			Ne Win	1958-				
Cape Verde							Pereira	1975-91
Congo							Sassou-Nguesso	1979-
Guinea					Touré	1958-84		
Ethiopia							Mengistu	1977-91
Madagascar							Ratsiraka	1975-
Mozambique							Machel	1975-86
Sao Tomé ...							Pinta da Costa	1975-91
Somalia					Siad Barre	1969-91		
Tanzania					Nyerere	1964-90		
Zimbabwe							Mugabe	1980-
Latin America								
Cuba			Castro	1959-				
Guayana							Burnham	1966-85
Nicaragua							Ortega	1979-90

2.4.2 Fluctuations Due to Planning Errors. As a first approach, it is perfectly legitimate to propose that investment fluctuations are caused by the inexperience of planners. This issue was touched briefly in Section 1.3 in regard to the delimitation of the time horizon of empirical investigations. However, planners presumably learn from their mistakes and the intensity of these fluctuations should therefore weaken.

Using the evidence from two decades of Soviet growth performance, A. Bergson (1951) came to exactly such a conclusion. His explanation was presented at the 1949 conference already mentioned, where a special session was devoted to the subject of cycles in planned economies. Commenting on Haberler's paper, he emphasized that the Soviet economy was much less centralized in reality than had been assumed from Soviet textbooks and public statements. Lower level managers and officials were able to learn from earlier mistakes. Since these experts had a certain degree of autonomy, in both the implementation and planning phases of economic decision-making, this had a dampening effect on fluctuations.

Some years later, a UN/ECE report noted that growth and investments in the newly emerging east European planned economies also displayed undulatory movements similar to those observed in Western market economies. As a preliminary explanation, the UN/ECE experts adopted the "inexperience hypothesis".[49]

Analyzing medium-term economic plans, the UN/ECE economists observed that the correlation between the fulfilment of output plans on the one hand and investment plans on the other was astonishingly weak. If investment was on target, then the planned output growth failed to materialize (Poland, Romania). By contrast, in Czechoslovakia, output figures were close to the planned levels but were achieved with much smaller investment efforts than envisaged. All this was attributed to technical miscalculations of several kinds:

(i) Planners were misled by the rapid rates of growth achieved in the years of the post-war reconstruction period, and underestimated the extent to which this had been made possible by the existence of under-employed labour and under-utilized capacity. These reserves were largely exhausted around 1953.

(ii) Investment requirements of the basic industries were under-estimated, if these industries were to develop at rates compatible with the engineering output required, given restricted import plans.

(iii) In drawing up the material balances on which allocations of materials and capacity were based, the estimated time scale for new investment projects was over-optimistic. There was a constant tendency for small investment projects, the initiative for which can hardly come from a level higher than that of the individual enterprise, to be neglected and for an undue proportion of investment funds to be devoted to new projects; the natural preferences of project makers in the ministries (mainly engineers) was, moreover, for balanced integrated

[49] See UN ESE 1955 (pp. 228-233). Unfortunately, apart from a short reference in Olivera (1960), this excellent piece of work remained unnoticed in the subsequent discussions on socialist investment cycles. The present author was the first to "rediscover" it at a 1986 Paris seminar - see Mihályi (1987). Although the authorship of a published UN document cannot be identified, I understand that this piece was in fact drafted by Messrs. R. Nötel and E. F. Jackson. (I am grateful to Mr. Nötel and Mr. Kaser for this information.)

plants, - that is, for large investment projects which could of their nature bear fruit only after a long delay.

(iv) Planners did not take account of the indirect impact of consumption growth on the efficacy of investments. The allocation of materials or foreign exchange to consumer-goods industries - materials which might otherwise have been used as inputs for the production of capital goods - may actually result in a bigger increase in national income because of its indirect effects on effort and productivity. In a pure capitalist system the limiting factor on the expansion of output is at times the morale of the entrepreneurs: if it can be raised, the investment multiplier comes into operation. In an economic system in transition to socialism the raising of the morale of workers and peasants may sometimes bring into operation a "consumption multiplier", less powerful but not negligible. It would probably now be agreed in all east European countries that, if consumption had been allowed to increase faster than actually happened in the years 1951-1953, more, rather than less, investment could have been accomplished, and progress would have been more regular. (Summarized from UN ECE 1956, pp. 231-232.)

A similar view was echoed in an early study by the Hungarian economist Bródy (1969b). In contrast to the position developed in subsequent decades, in this paper he did not look for any substantive explanation of the very large zigzags in investments. Referring to the Hungarian experience between 1949-1956, he emphasised the unwanted consequences of planners' hugger-mugger and lack of professional seriousness:

Imagine, for instance, the problems of staffing at all levels of skill under conditions where the labour force in state construction grew from some 60,000 in 1949 to almost 200,000 three years later, only to fall back to 114,000 in the following three years, while the regional and central distribution of construction activity was the subject of constant change. As can be seen from the statistics (though this is more difficult to prove), the same phenomenon affects other activities involved in investment: investment planning, the importation of equipment, engineering production, assembly and installation of plant and equipment (...). Ideas about the distribution of investment were likely to change every two or three years, and often were completely reversed thereafter. (*op. cit.* pp. 319-320)

On theoretical grounds the possibility of learning by doing was emphasized by the Yugoslav economist Alexander Bajt (1969, 1971, 1987). He presented this point in a manner different from that adopted by Bergson. Bajt thought that the more centralized the system, the more likely it was that the Centre would be capable of keeping investments under control. By contrast, once economic decentralisation is allowed to unfold - under the pressure of political forces in most cases - it must inevitably lead towards more instability, in the same way as in a market based economy. Beyond this point, of course, the pulsating pattern of investments has nothing to do with socialism any more.

I have no point of disagreement with the first part of his statement. It is a matter of fact that in the 1980s annual GINV fluctuations remained within narrower margins, in all countries for which comparable time series are available, than had been the case in the early decades of socialist planning. Nevertheless, developments in the Polish economy in the second half of the 1970s seem to present strong counter-evidence against the "learning-by- doing" hypothesis. In the fifteen years 1970-1985, this country experienced more forcible fluctuations than at any time in the past.

In the final analysis, however, I am inclined to accept Bajt's position. Poland is a case where the exception proves the rule. As illustrated with figures in Section 3.5 below, it was the very exceptional coincidence of a number of external factors which enabled the Polish planners to sustain high GINV growth rates between 1970 and 1975, and it was also an unusual combination of events that produced the very severe crisis after 1978.

2.4.3 Fluctuations Due to Campaigns. Still, Bajt is right only in the "final" analysis. One important question remains, which, if unanswered, can undermine his position: Why was the learning process so slow? Why did it take twenty years to learn how to keep GINV fluctuations within bounds?

The best answer to this illuminating question was given by Soós (1986). Elaborating and generalising propositions made by Wiles (1962, pp. 208-211), Levine (1969), Berliner (1971) and Marrese (1981), he convincingly argued for the incorporation of "campaigns" or "drives" into the economic theory of socialism.

A campaign is the deliberate creation of imbalance. As Wiles put it: "Heavy chemicals, virgin lands, maize, Chinese domestic steel; whatever it may be, the Communists cannot bear to do it by halves. (...) They could, within their system, quite easily advance on a broad front, (...) but they find it psychologically easier to advance on a narrow one." (*op.cit.* p. 208)

This idea gives us a key for understanding the mechanism which slows down the process of learning in the area of investment regulation. What happens is the following. After a few years of experience, the experts of a certain subject area (say investments in our case) would be able to avoid larger ups and downs but in the midst of sweeping campaigns, often supported by political intimidation and pressure, they are unable and unwilling to resist the wishes of the higher political circles. It is not only a matter of strength or civic and professional courage (although to a large extent it is). In a world of price distortions, due to visible and hidden subsidies and taxation, even the best expert cannot demonstrate with unquestionable certainty that the consequences of any given set of measures are detrimental to the economy as a whole.

Thus, the campaign is nothing but a consensus formation process, albeit involving a great deal of coercion to suppress dissenting views. Indeed, there is little else that politicians can do: "Basically, the absence of an agreed upon method of measuring trade-offs, inconsistencies among the incentives and «success indicators» of different levels of the bureaucratic hierarchy, and the lack of coincidence between nationwide goals and branch goals have produced a situation in which decision makers employ consensus formation as an alternative to marginal analysis." (Marrese 1981, p. 224)

Planners, when they listen to their own professional conscience, would perhaps be eager to avoid hugger-mugger, crude or sophisticated versions of stop-go type mechanisms but under the given socio-political circumstances this is not possible. Due to the hierarchical and bureaucratic nature of the system, the entire mechanism would be incapacitated without direct methods of political control; hence planners have to accept the wasteful consequences of such campaigns.

However, this is still not the full explanation. "The overlapping lines of command, the confusion of jurisdictions and the duplications of responsibilities" were also responsible for the campaigns. In addition to these loose formal organizational lines of command one has to add another element: "the imprecisions of the orders emanating from the top". These two institutional peculiarities of Soviet-type economies[50] were, by necessity, the hotbeds of competition among the lower level organs (branch ministries, trusts, regional authorities, etc.). This phenomenon is nothing else but the mechanism of positive feed-back, described in Section 1.2. When central orders were given to accelerate (or decelerate) the investment process the competing bureaucracies had a strong interest in going beyond all rational constraints. "This unusual amount of loyalty" that forced otherwise capable and well-trained technocrats to act against their better professional convictions was, under the given circumstances, an "entirely rational response to the structure of incentives facing these people". The "destruction of alternative opportunities for advancement" - and, in the final analysis, this is what the one-party system means - "was a powerful weapon to encourage people to further their careers by investing in loyalty to the regime".

2.4.4 The Cliff's Edge Thesis. Although, perhaps a pure coincidence, it is worth noting from our perspective that when Stalin solemnly introduced the new slogan, "building socialism in one country", he also touched in one and the same breath on the problem of cyclical developments. This occurred in 1925 at the XIV Congress of the CPSU. In his keynote address, he first explained that the Soviet Union must build its economy "in such a way as to prevent our country from becoming an appendage of the world capitalist system". Then he presented his "second proposition":

> We must on each occasion take into account the specific features of our management of the national economy distinguishing it from such management in capitalist countries. There, in the capitalist countries, private capital reigns; there the mistakes committed by individual capitalist trusts, syndicates, or one or other group of capitalists, are corrected by the elemental forces of the market. If too much is produced - a crisis ensues; but later, after the crisis, the economy resumes its normal course. If they indulge too much imports and an unfavourable balance of trade results - the rate of exchange will be shaken, inflation will ensue, imports will drop and exports will rise. All this in the form of crises. No mistake of any magnitude, no overproduction of any magnitude, or serious discrepancy between production and total demand takes place in capitalist countries without the blunders, mistakes and discrepancies being corrected by some crisis or other. (...) But we cannot live like that. There we see economic, commercial and financial crises, which affect individual groups of capitalists. Here, in our country, things are different. Every serious hitch in trade, in production, every serious miscalculation in our economy, results not in some individual crisis or other but hits the whole of our national economy. In our country, every crisis, whether commercial, financial or industrial, may develop into a general crisis that will hit the whole state. (Stalin 1954, pp. 305-306)

One can only admire Stalin's instinct. With so little experience behind him, he grasped the very serious implications of the fact that Soviet planners could not rely on the stabilising impact of market-induced positive feed-backs. Moreover, as Stalin correctly saw, "strains" can generate a crisis, even if planners themselves do their job faultlessly:

[50] In fact, Soviet-type bureaucracies showed a great deal of similarity to the functioning of the Nazi German state, which is brilliantly analyzed in Breton and Wintrobe (1986). The quotations in this paragraph are directly reproduced from their paper.

> Our entire work during the past two years has shown that we are not guaranteed either against fortuities or against errors. In the sphere of agriculture, very much depends in our country not only on the way we manage but also on the forces of nature (crop failures, etc.). (...) In the sphere of foreign trade very much depends not only on us but also on the behaviour of the West-European capitalists; and the more our exports and imports grow, the more dependent we become upon the capitalist West, the more vulnerable we become to the blows of our enemies." (*ibid.*)

If we adapt Stalin's line of thought to the problem of investment fluctuations, it is clear that for him this matter was not of central importance. The fluctuations themselves are not necessarily causally related to the system-specific rules of the investment process. Any kind of "crisis" - independently of its origin - can lead to a crisis in investment activities.

Now, after this excursus into the history of Soviet political thinking, let us return to Eastern Europe and to the first decade of debates on socialist investment cycles. In his book on the foreign economic behaviour of communist countries, Peter Wiles (1968) convincingly demonstrated the impact of the above-mentioned pre-capitalist traditions and the irrationalities thereof on the behaviour of policy makers. Wiles based his argument on the very same points as Stalin did. There was one difference, of course. Wiles presented his argument with a great deal of bitter irony, and a tiny amount of cynicism, which was very much in contrast with Stalin's heroic pathos.

According to Wiles,

> It is a Marxist prejudice to believe that important and dignified disasters must have important and dignified causes and cures; but there is no logic in this. The most philosophical remark the author can permit himself is that Stalinism is a politico-socio-economic phenomenon; so a precondition for the pre-1958 economy, successful or not, was a system of government by lies, terror and secrecy. Such a government might easily make policy errors and not correct them in time; it would be so prone to self-deception, so immune to criticism, that it would only halt at the cliff's edge." (p. 122)

In the remaining part of the book, I shall return to this important point made by Wiles. For the sake of brevity, I will refer to it as the "cliff's edge thesis".

About ten years later, Wiles (1982) once again returned to the subject of investment fluctuations. After a careful inspection of time series from EE7 and Mongolia, he took one "cycle" after the other and proved why these ups and downs in investment activities cannot be labelled as "cycles". On the basis of his historical analysis of the period 1950-1980, he distinguished four different types of investment waves. In Chart 2.4 I attempted to visualize Wiles' typology, while remaining faithful to the content of his verbal argumentation. In the most typical case (A), the starting point of the investment wave is a politically motivated investment peak. This is then followed by troughs that are, as he put it, "basically economic", and later by a recovery of stability through moderation. Sometimes - as shown in case B - the wave is initiated by a politically motivated investment trough. This is then followed by a "basically economic" revival, which, however, does not lead to a peak but to balanced, steady growth. Under exceptional circumstances it may happen (C) that the wave starts with a peak caused by economic reasons, followed by an A-type setback and - later - by steady growth. According to Wiles, the fourth type of these waves (D) was known only in pre-war Soviet economic history.

CHART 2.4 Four types of investment waves according to P. Wiles

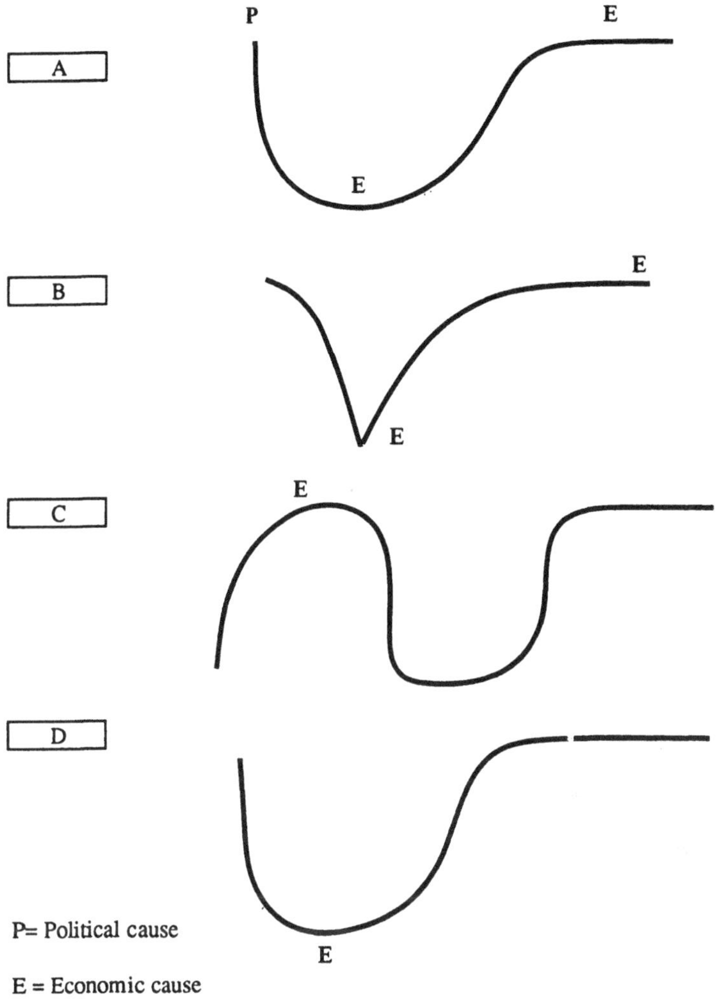

Source: On the basis of Wiles (1982)

Its logic is the following: the wave starts with an economic setback, and that leads to a stable recovery.

In Wiles' interpretation, everything that happens after the investment peak is essentially endogenous (economic). The peaks and troughs themselves, however, are purely political. Wiles accepts the findings of those who discovered certain regularities in the recurrence of taut investment plans, long lead times, dispersion and the ensuing balance-of-payments difficulties. His main point, however, is that when these strains appear under normal conditions, they are not, as a rule, followed by a spectacular fall in investments. What happens is rather simple: the Politburo reacts as a good manager, "plucks up its courage, defies the satraps and curtails investment starts".

Criticising ICM, as presented in Bauer (1978), Wiles put his finger on a hidden contradiction. Bauer had noted that some GINV peaks were "consumption-symmetrical" [51] - meaning that consumption is depressed but the trade balance remains firm - while some others were "foreign trade symmetrical" - meaning that consumption grows normally and the trade balance deteriorates. In the logic of ICM, there is no rationale for this important distinction.

What kind of endogenous reasons could explain why, under certain conditions, some governments opt for a "consumption symmetrical" adjustment, and not for a "foreign trade symmetrical" one? For Wiles, it is evident that the choice between these two alternatives must be political. In other words, the "exogenous explanation" - which was claimed to be superfluous by ICM in explaining the main regulatory mechanism of investment fluctuations - creeps back in the form of explaining a sub-regularity.

2.4.5 Investment Cycles or Business Cycles ? According to the "cliff's edge thesis", investments play no particular role in socialist economic development. Short-term fluctuations of output, exports and imports, the speed and direction of price changes are all the prerogative of the omnipotent Centre. Supply and demand and micro-economic profitability of production are not decisive in this respect.

Relying upon a very detailed analysis of Hungarian and Yugoslav investment fluctuations, Soós (1986) also came to such conclusions. As the reader follows his argumentation, he feels that the author's opinion is continuously shifting away from his starting position. There is less and less talk of investment cycles, and more and more about (administrative) business cycles. In fact, the sub-title of the book - *Regulation and Business Cycles in Hungary and Yugoslavia* - corroborates this feeling.

In his latest work on investment fluctuations Soós (1989) goes even further. His conclusion is just the opposite of what used to be the standard point of departure of the "cream" of east European economists of the 1970s. In those years, any explanation based on accidental political circumstances, the incompetence and indecision of planners seemed shallow to many of them. "The explanation of recurring investment waves cannot be so simple. Many experts in many countries cannot repeatedly make the same mistake" - ran their counter-argument at that time. "The periodical cycles of the capitalist system also have their genuine cause. The instability of supply and demand was never accepted as a sufficient answer by any respectable western economists, either. Therefore, there must be a deeper reason for such a regular occurrence of

[51] Interestingly, this type of sub-regularity of investment peaks was already noted by the 1955 report of the ECE, which analyzed developments in Hungary. "Given that output was increasing only slowly from 1951 to 1954 and that defence expenditure was moving in a similar fashion to investment outlays, there was necessarily a consumption cycle too, in the opposite direction." (UN BUL 1955, p. 88).

investment fluctuations in the socialist system as well." Indeed, this type of thinking guided the pen of János Kornai even later.

> Many tend toward the view that the socialist economy should be interpreted as a specific form of "administrative organisation". On this view, what happens in the system depends on economic management. Although certain physical and technological conditions are given, decisions are otherwise unconstrained. The philosophy of the present models (i.e. those presented in Kornai's book - P.M.) differs from this. The operation of the economic systems of the Eastern-European socialist countries reveals some characteristic regularities. At each level of decision-making *the behaviour of the decision-maker is in a certain sense "regular"*: definite impulses and signals lead to definite consequences." (Kornai 1982, pp. 125-126, italics in original)

Responding to such a line of thought, Soós rejected the idea of a regular investment cycle. It cannot exist because, in a typical socialist economy, the necessary conditions for a cycle contradict each other. Hence, their contemporaneous presence is a very rare, exceptional state of affairs. Those positive feed-backs which are a precondition of the emergence of a true cycle cannot usually come simultaneously into full view. There are possibilities at the two extremes which have to be taken into consideration.

(i) If the economy is essentially autarkic and producers are hermetically separated from the external world, then the revival in investments is bound to become fragmented and irregular due to the limited adjustment capabilities of domestic suppliers. Now, it often happens that the investment boom coincides with deblocking of import channels in order to sustain the investment boom but then the famous "foreign trade constraint"[52] comes immediately into play forcing its discipline on the planners.
Moreover, an economy characterized by inertia and lack of innovative capability is usually not able to restore its foreign trade position during investment slowdowns, to offset its deterioration during investment booms. Thus, the initial and subsequent "foreign trade symmetrical" investment cycles leave fewer and fewer possibilities for the emergence of later ones, due to the cumulated burden of indebtedness.

(ii) Another possibility worth thinking through is relevant when the domestic economy is already sufficiently interlinked with the external world. In such a situation, the economy is always vulnerable to external shocks, which in turn can have hundreds of different origins. Hence, in this case a genuine cycle cannot assert itself, because it is not very likely that these external shocks are synchronized with the endogenous, domestic pulsation of the economy.

[52] The concept of the "foreign trade constraint" was a key element in Kalecki's growth model of the socialist economy. The mechanism is the following. Rising NMP induces a higher demand for imports. This in turn generates the need for exports. Given the weak international competitiveness of a typical socialist country, this export drive, coupled with a reliance on import substitution, becomes less and less efficient in terms of domestic factor productivity. Hence, after a while there is no point in accelerating NMP growth. (For more details see Sawyer 1985, pp. 251-252, and Suba-Varga (1986, 1988))

With this conclusion, Soós pulled out the carpet from under the feet of his fellow Hungarian economists. The more or less regular investment fluctuations in Hungary, which received a particularly wide coverage both in that country and abroad, were now declared untypical.

2.4.6 GINV: Target or Control Variable ? As seen in the preceding section, administrative business cycles are not investment cycles, *proprement dit*. GINV is just one of the several control variables. This, of course, is not to deny the macro-economic importance of investments. Although investments are not considered as the "heart" or "engine" of the economy in the exogenous models, as portrayed in the endogenous models, they remain very important as a buffer. Investments function as a reserve in the hands of the planners. This interpretation was already implicit in Wiles' "cliff's edge" theory. Facing the danger of imminent economic collapse, planners always have this important trump card in their hands - this is an expenditure item, where cuts are easy.

In this logical framework, the Centre is not the prisoner of its own past decisions. As circumstances change, it enjoys considerable elbow room in determining the volume of next year's investment. It remains true that, *ceteris paribus*, the creation of new production facilities is a priority objective for the Centre and the SOEs alike. Once a crisis emerges - i.e. business is not as usual as the *ceteris paribus* condition would imply - the Centre will be motivated to and capable of imposing its will upon the economy.

If necessary, investments can be cut drastically from one year to the next or at least more drastically than other types of demand, such as consumption or exports. This does not immediately hurt anyone's vital interest. In normal circumstances workers[53] and consumers have no reason to complain or to resist. The continuity of current production is not seriously disturbed either. If new possibilities are opening up, or trade policy considerations force it, within one or two years spectacular results can be achieved in the acceleration of investment growth. Deblocking machinery imports, for example, usually enough to do the job.

Among the students of socialist investment fluctuations, the Yugoslav economist Branko Horvat seems to be the first author to have thought of the buffer role of investments. On the basis of a very detailed empirical investigation of his home country in 1955-1972, he found no evidence of causation leading from investment fluctuations to production instabilities. By contrast, he found that acceleration or retardation in production had systematically led to breaks in investment activity (Horvat 1975). Later research by Bajt (1989) confirmed this proposition.

A recent econometric study of the dependence of the Hungarian economy on the western business climate has shed some light on the details of this buffer mechanism. Using a weighted overall import index of Hungary's chief western partners, Szakolczai *et al.* (1987) found evidence suggesting that the Hungarian economic leadership used domestic investments as a buffer through which fluctuations in external demand were kept under control. According to Szakolczai, fluctuations in the Hungarian domestic economy were essentially caused by the regular fluctuation of the western countries' import demand. The periods of decisive acceleration of imports by Hungary's western trading partners tend to lead first to over-heating and then to a deep decline in the country's economic life. Throughout this period, the Centre concentrated its

[53] In the logic of the endogenous cycle models, a drastic fall in investments, or even a moderation in the growth rates of GINV, must provoke a change in the same direction in employment. In Section 4.1 below it is demonstrated that, in reality, no such simple relationship ever existed. Movements in the volume of investment are not strongly correlated with changes in the number of industrial or construction workers. The link between earnings and GINV is not particularly strong either.

efforts on stabilizing consumption, and allowed (or forced) investments to carry the total burden of adjustment.

Using a somewhat different technique, a model proposed by B. Balassa, Avramov (1990b) assessed the scope of external shocks for the Bulgarian economy and came to very similar conclusions. The author described the mechanism which reflected the interaction between investment policy changes and the impact of external factors on the evolution of domestic demand and found a very strong echo effect.

2.4.7 The Paradigm of Bureaucratic Regularity. In the family of exogenous models of investment fluctuations, empirical work has, to a great extent, been based on Donald Green's (1977) seminal paper.[54] His starting point was that in the case of Soviet-type economies, econometric modelling has to be built on different assumptions than in a market economy. One must rely upon the "law of large organisations" rather than the "law of large numbers" for the stability of macro-economic parameters.

There are two logical building blocks in this idea. One is the "contingency response" and the other is "central intervention". The first concept is essentially one of bureaucratic regularity (BR). It is understood very much in the same way as in Kornai (1982) or in any other endogenous model: definite impulses and signals lead to definite consequences. The second element, however, is new, and this is the point that invalidates the idea of a regular investment cycle. "Centralized intervention connotes a decision imposed by command through hierarchical channels and may override the process of contingency response." (Green 1977, p. 262)

An important ingredient of this concept is the "flick" and "drift" analogy, which Green borrowed from biology.[55] "Drift" results from bureaucratic administration of the status quo trends. "Flick", on the other hand, refers to sudden jump-like change in the direction of economic activity resulting from central intervention. The low-level bureaucracy has authority over certain drift facilities but they cannot operate flick. Flick has to come from the top, and it is here that irrationality may manifest itself. A flick, or a campaign, using Soós's analogy, can be initiated by all sorts of economic or political events. Hence it is fruitless to look for any time regularity in the process.

To demonstrate the usefulness of the BR approach, I have already cited some empirical results of Green (1978) on Soviet investment behaviour. Along these lines, Michael Marrese devoted a doctoral thesis to investigating the applicability of the theory of bureaucratic regularity. Shorter empirical studies, from the pens of researchers in Western Europe, such as Grosfeld (1987) and Roland (1987a), were also influenced by Green's work.

The three authors mentioned used econometrics to study Hungarian, Polish and Soviet investment fluctuations. Before going into the details, it is important to underscore that cyclicality is by definition excluded from the BR concept. These authors do not speak of any kind of time regularity. The models describe an "if-then" type of link, in which there is no

[54] Green's theoretical work served as a basis in the development of SOVMOD III, the Soviet Econometric Model built by a joint research project of the Stanford Research Institute and Wharton Econometric Forecasting Associates.

[55] Drift and flick mechanisms regulate the eye tracking of living species. There is a set of muscles whose task is to track something whose movement can be only partially forecast. At the same time, a set of muscle neurons is responsible for reacting with a flick when the target suddenly changes direction. For a discussion of this analogy see Hildebrandt (1985, pp. 17, 154).

mechanism to assure the recurrence of the "if" type of event. It will be recalled that recurrence was the first element of our cycle definition. If recurrence is not assured, we must reject the appellation of cycle. So, it was not by chance that the exogenous school was always careful to avoid using the word "cycle".

The empirical research of this school focuses on a single issue: modelling planners' behaviour. The efforts are aimed at estimating the impact of foreign trade, investment tensions, consumption and the climatic changes on GINV fluctuations. Using our symbols:

(2.6) $GINV = f_5 (Q_1, Q_2, \ldots Q_n)$,
where GINV denotes the volume of annual investments,
Q_1, Q_2, and Q_n denote foreign trade, investment tensions, the volume of consumption and climatic changes.

(i) Let us start the summary of findings of the three authors with the impact of foreign trade. One very important conclusion of the three independent studies is that - contrary to general assumptions and beliefs - there is no strong causal relationship between convertible currency trade and GINV fluctuations. Using Hungarian data, Marrese experimented with one- and two-year lags but the estimated regression parameters proved insignificant. Roland's estimates for the Soviet Union with a one-year lag produced statistically significant results but the size of the parameter was negligible. Grosfeld found that the influence of the western trade balance asserts itself only with a two-year gap on Polish capital formation. Even this linkage worked in an indirect way only. Notably, the western trade balance in year t had an impact only on investment plans formulated in year t+2.

It is not the actual fluctuation of GINV but rather the zigzags of the investment plans which stand in the centre of her investigation. Intentionally or not, Grosfeld's approach is related to Wiles "cliff's edge" hypothesis. Her starting assumption is that planners are not irrational but act in an atmosphere of panic - i.e. tensions have to pass a certain threshold value before the Centre is willing to make a move. In principle, macro-economic stability - equilibrium on the consumer market, the balance of foreign trade - are important, but in practice, small disturbance signals do not prompt reactions.

This is a model with switching regimes. The investment plan is determined by an equation in which the trade balance appears only under certain conditions as an explanatory variable. As long as the trade balance is below a certain threshold, trade does not appear in the equation as an explanatory variable.[56] In other words, it is a boot-strap model of planners' behaviour - an attempt to find regularities in planners' reactions and to identify those disequilibrium signals exogenous to the investment sector to which they are sensitive.

(ii) One of the most interesting contributions of Roland's study was the way he tried to quantify the impact of investment tensions on GINV. The indicator he opted for was ΣUGINV/GINV - the relative magnitude of the stock of unfinished investments.[57] The starting assumption was justified by his estimation work. An increase in the relative size of the stock of unfinished investments had a statistically significant simultaneous negative impact on investments.

[56] Note, however, that the coefficient of this variable proved to be small compared with those of lagged investment plans and realized investment.

[57] This is the same indicator shown in the first column of table 2.5 above.

According to this study, the size of its impact on GINV was many times greater than that of western trade.[58]

The state of equilibrium on the investment market played an important part in Marrese's research work, too. He started from the assumption, which later proved very fruitful, that investments in construction work have to be treated separately from investments in machinery. He found that - at least in Hungary - decisions on machinery investments are by and large unrelated to changes in other macro-variables. The effect of BR was statistically significant only for construction investment.

(iii) All three authors looked at the relationship between consumption and investments. This question is probably the oldest among those born out of the entire scientific discussion on socialist investment cycles. Olivera (1960) was the first to focus on this issue. His argument, which remained entirely abstract with no attempt made to quantify it, was based on the assumed contradiction between investment and consumption growth on the one hand, and the fundamentally different perception of this contradiction by the planners and the population, on the other. For planners, more investment is a pledge for future consumption growth, while the population considers that a bird in the hand is worth two in the bush.

Thinking seriously on this apparent contradiction as a possible cause of GINV fluctuations, Nove (1960) immediately challenged its validity. It is a pity that the point he raised escaped the attention of later students of the topic. Olivera himself, and later model builders following his line of thought, assumed that a continuous rise in the volume of investment provokes increasing dissatisfaction among households if their consumption does not grow in parallel. However, as Nove rightly said, there was no compelling reason to believe that explosive cyclical effects are generated by the fact that in a given period investments have risen by, say, 13 %, while the consumption of households grew by only 10 %. In reality, the problems intuitively associated with the excessive rise of investments appear only when living standards do not rise at all, or fall. But this is a different story.

Measuring the strength of an assumed causal linkage between the volume of consumption and investments at aggregate level, Marrese found nothing in Hungary which survived the hurdle of statistical significance. For construction investments, however, a certain amount of parallelism did prove significant.

Grosfeld focused upon real wage developments in the Polish economy between 1956 and 1980. Applying a lag of one year, she found traces of a parallel movement between the annual growth rates of GINV and that of real wages both in the simplified and in the more sophisticated version of her model. (In the latter, planners' behaviour was characterized by a non-continuous behavioural function.)

Alas, a meaningful analysis of the links between investments and the state of the consumer market is greatly hampered by the fact that, in a shortage economy, real wages do not reflect adequately changes in the volume of consumption. Hence, the planners' dilemma - consumption vs. investment - cannot be properly monitored with the real wage indicator. Grosfeld found herself also face to face with this problem. When she attempted to extend her sample period from 1980 to 1981, the inclusion of this single year reduced all the previous results to statistical insignificance. Her (probably correct) explanation was that at a time when imbalances on

[58] My reservations concerning the measurability of the true size of unfinished investments have already been mentioned above. Those concerns of course hold here, too.

consumer markets suddenly reached excessive levels, the real wage indicator loses its significance not only for households but for planners, too.

3. MEASUREMENT OF INVESTMENT FLUCTUATIONS

> Serious data analysis has to consider at least two data generation components: the economic behaviour model describing the stimulus-response behaviour of the economic actors and the measurement model, describing how and when this behaviour was recorded and summarized. While it is usual to focus our attention on the former, a complete analysis must consider them both.
>
> Griliches (1986, p. 1469)

In this chapter we delve deeper into the empirical enquiry. Before doing so, however, we have to take a closer look at our basic data and the conventional analytical tools applied in the cycle analysis. The rules of scientific disputes are somewhat similar to the rules of warfare. Before entering into battle, you make a survey of the battlefield and check your weapons.

3.1 DISTORTION OF GINV DATA

The production of coherent and unbiased time series on fixed capital formation has been always and everywhere a challenging task for statistical offices. As will be shown later, the difficulties in our case stem not so much from occasional imperfections of data, which are, to some extent, inevitable in all economic systems.

Time series can contain different types of error. A small part of them consists of genuine errors, sometimes as trivial as typographical ones.[1] Another type of error originates in the imprecision of the statistical estimating and computing methods applied. In terms of annual growth rates, for instance, differences of 1-2 percentage points can easily arise merely from a shift in the price base or in the weighting system.

The precise economic content of the data is another problem. GINV series may have a somewhat different coverage over time and also across countries. For example, it is questionable whether rural investments (private construction output of collective farmers) or private housebuilding in general have always been counted or treated in the same manner.

However, the truly important errors are systemic. Section 3.1 is entirely devoted to an investigation of this issue. It is very odd, as Ellman (1989, p. 260) noted in a somewhat different context, that until now comprehensive and sophisticated studies which aimed to throw light on systemic differences in investment behaviour did not examine the underlying data for systemic errors. In the context of market economies, the main source of confusion is that the data tend to be collected or reported by firms who have no stake in the correctness and precision of the observation they report. By contrast, in Soviet-type economies SOEs are involved in an intricate

[1] Between 1976 and 1982, the Hungarian statistical yearbook incorrectly stated the index number of net accumulation for the year 1956. Referring to 1950 as a base year (=100), the subsequent editions showed the figure 137, which visually fitted very well into its environment, but the correct - and indeed very low - figure was only 37.

rope-pulling game with the central authorities and this creates a unique type of interest in manipulating and doctoring the data reported.

Implicitly, the literature seems to reflect two types of response to this criticism of socialist statistics: (i) the data are not all that bad. (ii) the data are bad but economists have learned how to live with them.

In a reasonably stable institutional environment both arguments have their merits. The tradition in econometrics of allowing for "constants" in regression equations allows implicitly for permanent "errors" in the level of the various series (Griliches, 1986). Down-to-earth Sovietology works with the hypothesis of "equal cheating" (Nove, 1977, p. 352). This law states that exaggerated reporting of output, investment, or of any other indicator cannot affect the rate of growth unless the extent of exaggeration changes. In many cases this assumption is good enough to circumvent much of the data problem.

But if the size of the measurement error is known to fluctuate over time, it is impossible to distinguish between changes occurring in the underlying process and changes in the quality of the measurement process. The system of socialist economies is in permanent transformation. In most cases it moves in the "right" direction, from irrationality toward rationality. This implies, nevertheless, that the size of error is changing (diminishing). So the uncertainty built into our data disturbs the view formed about the subject of the measurement exercise. What we want to measure, for the purposes of cycle analysis, is the stability of the investment time series. In other words, my contention concerning the inaccuracy of GINV data should be taken here on its own terms: if and when data are unreliable, they are unreliable relative to what we purport to measure.

3.1.1 Revisions of Past Series. In contrast to western practice, statistical offices in the socialist countries usually handle their published data as if they were truth graved in stone. This policy is designed to make users of their statistics believe that these figures are perfectly accurate. Revisions of time series published earlier were carried out only by few countries, and in most cases even these modifications were rather cosmetic. Though it may sound surprising, there was a good reason behind this policy.

First, we should recall that the primary aim of statistics was to serve economic planning. For planners, however, retroactive modification of data from the recent past is undesirable. It brings an additional source of instability into the process of forecasting. Revisions of data published 5, 10 or 20 years ago would not create such difficulties. If, however, this revision implies a downward change in growth rates and production figures, then leaders running their countries for decades (see Section 2.4) would grumble, since they would have to acknowledge that their "historical successes" were partly built upon false or incorrectly calculated data.

Bulgarian statistics can serve as a good example to demonstrate the case. In 1989, this country was still steered by the very same T. Zhivkov who achieved his first political success between 1958-1960 by fulfilling a FYP in three years. This "unprecedented" success was underpinned by hardly realistic annual investment growth rates (22.3 %, 51.2%, 16.6%). In other cases, the false image of continuity was linked to the fate of politicians standing at one or two steps lower in the hierarchy. In the GDR, Prime Minister W. Stoph served in this capacity under two General Secretaries: first between 1964-1973 and then once again between 1976-1989. Developments in the GDR economy were also strongly influenced by the continued rule of G. Mittag, who was for more than thirty years the party's chief economic policy maker.

There are good reasons to hope that such outright falsification of economic data, which repeatedly occurred during the reign of the above-mentioned politicians, were not characteristic of every country at all times. Nevertheless, caution is fully justified in those cases where econometric analysis is based on time series containing the "old" dubious figures.

Another type of problem emerges when alternative GINV series are available, which ideally should depict the same fluctuation behaviour as the official ones but in reality do not. In the case of the USSR, the CIA has been working for decades to provide detailed estimates of the value of Soviet GNP, which of course includes an estimate for investments too. A distinguished Czechoslovak scholar, V. Nachtigal (1989), has made a heroic effort to build Western type GDP series on the basis of official NMP data for his own country. In the course of this exercise he computed an alternative GFCF time series for the period 1960-1988, which was directly comparable with GINV.

Table 3.1 reveals significant differences in the growth patterns of two sets of series for the two above-mentioned countries: there are differences in the average level and degree of fluctuation. In 1950-1980 the average growth rate of Soviet investments was 7.0 % per annum according to official data but 7.8 % according to the CIA estimates. The calculated compound growth rates, however, show a difference in the opposite direction: 8.2 % versus 7.7 %. The degree of fluctuation, as measured by the standard deviation, was only 4.3 % according to the official data but 6.5 % in the light of the CIA estimates.

TABLE 3.1 Czechoslovakia and USSR: Alternative GINV series

(A comparison of time series in annual percentage change form)

	Czechoslovakia		Soviet Union	
	Official data	Nachtigal's estimates	Official data	CIA estimates
Availability	1948-1989	1960-1988	1929-1989	1950-1980
Number of observations in the common sample period	28	28	30	30
Minimum	-11.2	-7.9	0.7	-7.8
Maximum	11.1	12.7	18.2	23.3
Arithmetic mean	3.9	3.9	6.9	7.8
Compound growth rate between two benchmark years	3.8	3.8	8.2	7.7
Standard deviation	5.2	4.9	4.3	6.5
Variance	26.6	24.4	18.5	42.8

Addendum:
Correlation (r) between the two series: 0.91 0.51

Source: Own calculations based on Table A.2, Nachtigal (1989, p. 221) and Joint Economic Committee (1982, pp. 65-67)

In the case of Czechoslovakia, the similarities of the two time series are greater but there are warning signs here as well. It is interesting to note that Nachtigal did not try to address the problem of hidden inflation. The compound growth rate of price changes calculated from his data were practically identical with the figure that can be obtained from the official GINV series. In terms of annual growth rates, however, the two sets of data reflect rather different scenarios. For the 1960s, the peaks appear to be higher and the troughs deeper than according to the official series. Later, as oscillations become more moderate in both series, such differences disappear. Within this dampened range of oscillation, however, there is little evidence for comovements. As we move forward in time, it is more and more apparent that the two time series cannot be used as proxies for each other. The correlation (r) for the period 1961-1978 is reasonably high (0.91) but during the years 1979-1988 it drops to an unacceptably low level (0.41).

3.1.2 The Treatment of Military Procurement. In Chapter 2 we already touched upon the question of armament expenditures. There it was mentioned that these outlays are systematically recorded as a part of public consumption. Unfortunately, after closer inspection, the conclusion cannot be so straightforward. Western military analysts suggest that Hungary - and probably Poland - recorded military construction work as part of investments, and to this extent these two countries depart from western statistical standards.[2] Hence, the "true" GINV figures for these two countries must be lower than those officially claimed.

It is impossible to be sure about the practices of other socialist countries. The official handbook on MPS, published by the United Nations but written by the CMEA secretariat in Moscow, gives no clear answers to such questions. The relevant paragraphs are open to two different interpretations. According to the first - which is in line with what is known about Hungarian, Czechoslovak and Polish practices - all military expenditures have to be registered as a part of collective consumption (NYUCC).[3] According to the second, which is more compelling in that it makes explicit reference to defence as such, these outlays have to be reported as a part of changes in (state) stockpiles.[4]

For evident reasons, this issue is particularly important in interpreting Soviet data. Some western analysts have suggested for a very long time that a considerable part of military expenditures must be hidden in the investment statistics. If this is so, it is sharply at variance with the practice of most east European countries. In some sense, of course, the Soviet Union had good reasons to depart from the agreed MPS methodology. It bore almost all the burden of high technology development in the Warsaw Pact, and this part of its military expenditures has

[2]See Crane (1988) and the literature cited there.

[3] "The material consumption of institutions and organisations satisfying the common collective needs of the community includes the consumption of material goods necessary for their operation, the depreciation of their fixed assets and consumption of road use and maintenance, provided to customers free of charge." (UN 1989b, p. 47). The reader is reminded that table 1.3 in Chapter 1 shows the skeleton of the national income statistics in terms of both SNA and MPS.

[4] "State material reserves consist of stocks of raw materials and consumer goods available to the Government to ensure uninterrupted production in the event of unforeseen difficulties and to ensure the country's defence capability." (*ibid.* p. 15.) Another authoritative UN document on national accounts explicitly states that "expenditures on fixed assets for military purposes are treated in MPS as a part of net fixed capital formation" (UN 1989a, p. xxii). This formulation, however, is probably incorrect.

more similarity with accumulation than consumption. If it is assumed that military expenditures are included in Soviet national accounts, although in a carefully disguised way, several arguments can be advanced for defending such a proposition.

This initial point is not trivial. In fact, it is rather doubtful in the eyes of some Western experts.[5] While it is almost certain - as Birman (1981, p. 18) says - that capital investment in the creation and development of the military industry are included in the investment statistics, there is less agreement on whether weapons procurement and construction work for the Ministry of Defence are also reflected here or not. In a methodological sense, the first solution is perfectly correct - and this is how it should be treated. Expenditures on weapons and miliary construction, however, must be included somewhere else. Where do they go, if anywhere? This is the question on which Western military analysts cannot agree.

To say that Soviet national accounts do not reflect this huge part of the total defence burden at all is a very sever blow to all types of macro-economic analysis.[6] If this is the case, then there is no point in speculating on links between the investment process on the one hand and changes in other macro-variables on the other. Asserting that the defence figures are totally (or largely) left out of statistics opens the way for any *deus ex machina* type of explanation. Changes in consumption, in foreign trade, or in the investment regime can all be explained by an assumed change in defence expenditures.

Interestingly, there were some years in the past when the Soviet statistical yearbooks did give an account of defence expenditures as a component of NYUAI on the utilisation side of NMP.[7] Later, however, this practice was abandoned, as the faultiness of these figures was only too apparent.[8]

Another fact worth noting is that even the lowest estimate for the size of armament expenditures is simply too high to fit into the envelope of R 60-70bn, the officially reported figure for collective consumption, where - according to the first interpretation of the MPS methodology - it should be. In any case, the share of these collective consumption figures within

[5] Such a position is reflected in Rosefielde (1990), which is the best account of the present state of the debate on these issues.

[6] According to D. Steinberg, a leading Western defence analysts, "it would be much easier for planners to conceal the total size of weapons production by excluding from GSP and national income altogether, rather than by trying to camouflage it among investment in producer goods." (quoted by Rosefielde (1990, p. 78.)

[7] See e.g., the 1922-72 jubilee edition of NH (p. 362) and the 1975 edition of the same publication (p. 566).

[8] Birman (1981, p. 18) pointed out that the published figures coincided exactly with the corresponding indicators of the budget. But this should not have been so on any account, since the NMP figures in the above-mentioned sources were given at 1965 prices, while the budget indicators were expressed in actual prices of the corresponding years. In other words, the published defence expenditure figures were forcibly "plugged into" the national accounts. The statistical office experts did not even attempt to convert them into comparable (constant) prices.

the consumption fund is inexplicably low in relation to international comparisons.[9] Hence, the least that can be said is that Soviet defence expenditures cannot be hidden among the items of intermediate consumption of the producers of services of the public administration.

To indicate the magnitudes involved in these disputes, a figure recently announced by the Soviet Prime Minister is of some interest. In June 1989, Prime Minister N. Ryzhkov acknowledged (*Pravda*, 8 June 1990) that the planned - and, in comparison with earlier years, already reduced - outlays for armaments purchases totalled R 33bn, quite a sizeable figure in comparison with annual GINV expenditures of about R 220bn (both at current prices). More recently, a Soviet newspaper quoted Birman, who claimed that the true figure was about twice as high. Birman, for his part, cited statements by two CPSU Central Committee secretaries which showed that the manufacture of military hardware alone amounted to R 70-80 bn in one recent year (*Moscow News*, No. 20. 1990.)

Now, on the totally arbitrary assumption that half of these expenditures were hidden in GINV statistics, we can easily come to a very surprising conclusion. A dynamically rising armament programme is capable of neutralizing the impact of any kind of "true" fluctuation in capital formation. This may be sufficient reason to explain why earlier students of investment cycles (Nove 1969, Bauer 1981) were unable to detect regular zigzags in Soviet GINV time series.

It would go much beyond the purposes of the present book to delve deeper into the secrets of Soviet defence statistics. The various schools of Western analysts are not in agreement on even the very basic facts either. The hypotheses advanced cannot be refuted but neither is the evidence sufficiently strong to prove them. Rosefielde is right to conclude that, under present circumstances, it is wisest to keep an open mind.

Another consequence of the conundrum of Soviet defence statistics is that any revision of Soviet GINV data for this type of systemic error would change the growth path of the time series. For the purpose of illustration, Chart 3.1 depicts the result of such an effort, based on Cohn (1973).

[9] The corresponding 1988 figures for the share of collective consumption in NMP used are as follows: 26 % (Czechoslovakia), 16 % (GDR), 12 % (Hungary), 11 % (Poland), 4 % (USSR). (UN ESE 1990, p. 113)

Chart 3.1

USSR: Alternative GINV series with and without adjustment for military hardware, 1951-1969

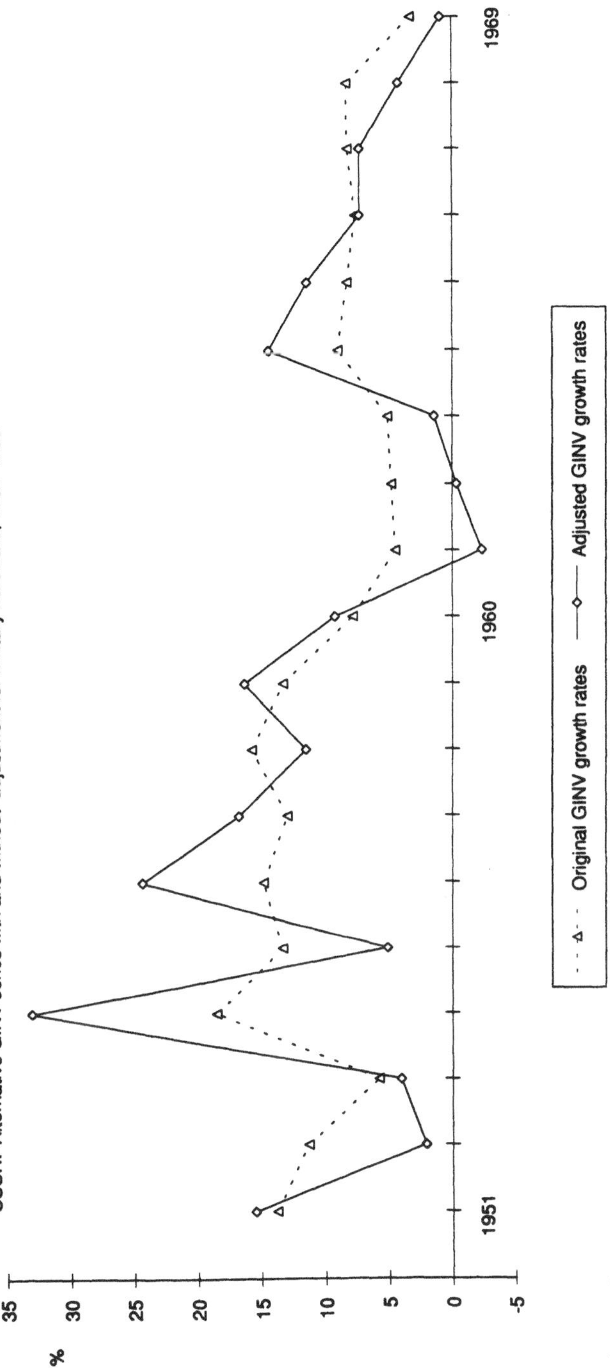

Source: Cohn (1973)

3.1.3 The Impact of Distorted Price Indices. As is well known, the estimation of price changes in order to obtain volume data is particularly difficult for the investment sector. Newly constructed projects are very different in technology and quality from similar plants built five or ten years earlier. The smaller the country, the more serious are the problems stemming from this simple fact alone. There are two possible types of distortion. The first is invariant to time, while the second varies in time with GINV itself. Let us look at these issues in order.

Time invariant biases of investment price indices. We may recall that the logic of physical planning requires price deflators rather than price indices proper. Planners' main objective is to eliminate the aggregate effect of individually approved price changes which are known by the authorities anyway. (This information is contained in the so-called price lists.) From this perspective, what matters most is the cost change of a given activity assessed from the supply side, rather than the price change of satisfying a given physical need as perceived from the demand side. The price deflator is used to measure the change in the volume of activities (output, investment or trade), otherwise the performance of the given enterprise cannot be assessed.

This approach explains the practice by statistical offices of deliberately excluding the price effect arising from product renewal. It is, therefore, more appropriate to speak of value data expressed at the price levels of a given year, instead of referring to them as being expressed in constant prices of that year.[10] It is of course impossible without a separate investigation to judge the total impact of such a method of measuring price change in a cross-country comparison. Though caution in interpreting these investment figures is probably not misplaced[11], there are no grounds for believing that such deficiencies could themselves create some kind of spurious fluctuations, let alone cycles. In other words, the underestimation of price changes is likely to be invariant to time in the short run. However, it is reasonable to assume that whenever officially acknowledged price rises are already quite significant (Hungary and Poland in the 1980s), the probability of an upward bias in the volume estimates increases.

Only four countries have recently published investment time series both at current and at constant prices: Czechoslovakia, Hungary, Poland and Yugoslavia. The Soviet Union and - since 1968 - the GDR have released GINV series only at constant prices.[12] Bulgaria made a backward step in 1984, when it returned to the practice of the 1950s, and published investment figures only at current prices.[13]

[10] As a matter of fact the Soviet statistical practice correctly refers to these prices as "Prices introduced on 1 January 19..".

[11] An overview of published implicit investment price deflators by sector and by industrial branch for 1970-1981 can be found in UN ESE 1982 (p. 178).

[12] With the 1990 revision, however, the GDR authorities released their new GINV figures for the period 1980-1989 in both forms. The problem with this series is that they were calculated according to the SNA methodology.

[13] Between 1984-1989, Romania also suppressed information about price developments in the sphere of investments. This shortcoming has, however, been corrected with the publication of ASR/90, the first yearbook in the post-Ceausescu area.

As noted, official investment price indices - if they exist at all - are likely to underestimate the real magnitude of price changes. Well-known Sovietologists - Stanley Cohn, Alec Nove, Peter Wiles and Philip Hanson - have gone so far as to suggest that in practice, Soviet investment statistics do not distinguish between current and constant prices, and Western recalculations (such as those done by the CIA) were so far not radical enough to get rid of this distortion. Others - A. Bergson, for example - do not see such a hopeless picture and appear to accept as a working hypothesis that a good part of price effects are removed from the investment time series by the Soviet statistical authorities and that there is nothing wrong with the CIA data.[14] The most recent CIA estimates (Pitzer and Baukol 1991) continue to argue for this conciliatory view. According to them, average inflation in GOSKOMSTAT's "constant price" series on machinery and equipment series was 2.3 % for the entire 1960-1987 period, which was a negligible magnitude. On the other hand, in construction the hidden inflation was measured at almost 1 % annually.

More recently, Soviet authors were also allowed to express their views on the matter. Unfortunately, so far none of them has been able or has had the possibility to publish alternative figures in a systematic and documented manner. Fragmentary reports suggest that among the well-known Soviet experts in this subject only Khanin (1988) and Faltsman (1991) are working on the revision of Soviet investment statistics. Generally speaking, they have much less confidence in Soviet official price deflators than the CIA experts have. Faltsman, for example, asserts that in 1960-1988, the hidden inflation in the investment sector was 3 % annually. If he is right, Soviet economic history and much of the empirical analysis done over the past 30 years have to be reconsidered. In fact, this work has already started. In the light of Western criticism and the improved contacts between Soviet and American official circles the CIA is currently revising its GINV series (CIA 1989, 60*n*).

In Czechoslovakia, recently published scholarly studies on macro-econ, receehaviour take it for granted that the officially reported investment statistics are seriously inflated. Authors such as Klacek *et al.* (1989) and Hájek *et al.* (1990) believe that between 1960 and 1988 the annual rate of hidden inflation in GINV was about 3.5 %.

In retrospect, it is not possible to establish the true size of such distortions with adequate precision. The only way to give some support to such surmises is to present alternative price indices for the given period and try to draw tentative conclusions from them. Table 3.1 serves this purpose.

Two observations can be made. First, these implicit GINV deflators, which are rather approximate because they were calculated from collated data, are always very similar to the size of the officially reported change in consumer prices. To some extent this is reassuring: the deflators are surely not absurdly wrong. On the other hand, these deflators are in all cases, except Yugoslavia significantly smaller than the annual percentage increase of nominal wages. This fact in itself is not enough to invalidate our first finding but may, nevertheless, give cause for concern.

[14] For an extended overview of this subject, see Bergson (1988), Sutela (1988) and Kontorovich (1989).

TABLE 3.2 Price indices and implicit GINV deflators, 1950-1989

(Percentage change)

	Period	GINV Implicit price index	Consumer price index	Nominal wages
Bulgaria	1952-1983	-0.1	0.2 a/	4.3
CSSR	1953-1989	0.9	0.5 b/	2.9
GDR	1950-1989	1.3	0.1 c/	3.8
Hungary	1950-1989	4.1	4.6	7.1
Poland	1950-1987	8.2	8.6 d/	11.3
Romania	1950-1989	0.4	...	5.8
USSR	1955-1984	0.9	0.3 a/	5.1
Yugoslavia	1960-1985	21.3	21.2 e/	23.4 e/

Notes: a/ Retail prices in the state sector.
b/ Cost of living index for workers and employees.
c/ Implicit NMP deflator.
d/ Cost of living index for workers and employees in the socialist sector.
e/ IMF data.

Source: Own calculations, based on national statistical yearbooks.

Price distortions as a possible "cause" of cycles. From the point of view of cycle analysis, inappropriately deflated value data may cause serious headaches. Unreliable price indices, if they happen to be asynchronous with the "true" but unknown volume changes, can neutralize the impact of volume fluctuations. This creates a false image of stability. By contrast, if price changes are contemporaneous with the volume changes - and statisticians fail to capture this effect in the price deflators - this will increase the apparent volatility of the zigzags.

On purely speculative grounds, there is some basis for believing that the second possibility is more likely than the first. In a period of rising investments, costs expressed in monetary terms can rise at a rate disproportionate to the increase in volumes for two reasons.

First, in an economy of shortages, an investment boom cannot be sustained without tolerating an increase in transport costs: construction materials have to be dispatched to the most important constructions sites from wherever they happen to be available at short notice. An upward drift of wages is also an inevitable part of the boom. Overtime, night shifts and work on holidays are all required if the Centre is truly determined to prolong the rise in investments.

These are the points where the peculiarities of investment price statistics come to the foreground. To be more precise, it is the peculiarity of construction statistics which counts in this respect.

When the price index for output or consumption is calculated, no one considers cost elements such as those above as components of the volume change. The baker's morning bread, made during the night, would not be recorded as a higher volume of output than the equivalent amount of afternoon bread just because the baker's workers on the night shift had to be paid better than those who worked in the daytime. In fact, this is exactly what happens in the construction statistics of the east European countries.

The second difficulty stems from the impact of "hidden" price changes disguised as a deliberate deterioration of product quality. Users of investment statistics, however, often tend to forget this, although such distortions have great importance in the investment process. Consumers - i.e. private households - resist buying half-baked bread or poorly tailored suits. In Soviet type economies, however, SOEs are not strongly enough motivated to refuse delivery of a half-finished new plant or building, or to return a newly-acquired machine if it fails to meet the technical specifications. Therefore it is quite common for investment work below the expected (average) quality to be priced as usual. Statisticians cannot subsequently get rid of this bias. At micro-level, of course, shortcomings of this type are usually made up by the customer firm later on. This implies further costs but they disappear among current outlays for the following year.

Both of these distortions are relevant to the present study, because they are more likely happen at around the peak of investments rather than in the trough. Furthermore, the impact of these factors probably distorts the "true" rate of project completions, too. If the completion of a large investment project coincides with a general investment boom, it is highly probable that the Centre will try to cut back "unnecessary" expenditures and economize on those imports and building costs which are not absolutely indispensable from the point of view of starting up operations. At a more relaxed time, expenditures to reduce costs, or for environmental or simply aesthetic improvements, are well tolerated.

In other words, investment blueprints and accomplished projects may differ greatly from one another, regarding both their technical parameters and costs. This additional factor, which goes beyond those already mentioned in the previous chapter, makes the quantification of investment commitment impossible for all practical purposes.

3.2 TRAPS OF TIME SERIES ANALYSIS

Many difficulties in the analysis of investment time series are of a very general nature. The ideas considered in this section are trivial for econometricians. Nevertheless, it is important to demonstrate their relevance to the example of our GINV time series, because economists are inclined to forget about them. They delude themselves with false hopes, assuming that simple approaches such as growth rate analysis or trend calculations require no special attention.

3.2.1 Precision of Growth Rate Figures. The inspection of growth rates is the simplest method of GINV analysis. It can give a very realistic, down-to-earth picture of underlying developments. It is simple, since little calculation is required. It is realistic as it is known that planners and statisticians of the Centre also work with such growth rate figures. It is almost natural that this approach should have been applied in such standard works as Bauer (1981) or Wiles (1982).

For several reasons, however, a time series consisting of annual percentage changes can also be misleading. First, extreme outliers - and as we can see from Table 3.3 the appearance of such figures cannot be excluded - have a distorting impact on the figures of the immediately following year. It is highly unlikely, that a - say - 30 % annual rise in GINV will be followed by a rise of similar magnitude in the next year. (In econometrics this is the so-called "negative autocorrelation" in a time series.)

TABLE 3.3 GINV growth rates: Maximum and minimum values, 1951-1989

	Maximum		Minimum	
	%	year	%	year
Bulgaria	51.2	1959	-2.2	1979
CSSR	21.1	1951	-11.2	1963
GDR	27.7	1952	-5.1	1982
Hungary	36.0	1959	-23.3	1954
Poland	25.4	1973	-22.3	1981
Romania	36.9	1951	-9.6	1954
USSR	18.2	1954	0.7	1979
Yugoslavia	23.7	1953	-17.0	1952

Source: Table SA. 1

According to an apposite formulation: "The rate of growth of an indicator during the reporting period relative to a base period characterizes the value of this indicator in both periods, hence in reality it does not properly characterize either of them." (Soós 1986, p. 237)

Second, it has to be recalled that growth rate indicators calculated in the form of annual percentage changes are not symmetrical. Starting from a given level, x per cent growth followed by an x per cent drop will not bring us back to the original level. For example, the data in table 3.3 show that in 1973 GINV fell by more than 22 % in Poland. In order to restore the 1973 level in 1974, instead of 22, a rise of 33 % would have been required. The higher is x, the more important will be this difference in percentage points.[15]

A third problem with growth rates was highlighted in the classical work of Morgenstern (1965). The difficulty stems from the fact that such figures reflect not only the volume of activity in both periods but also measurement errors which might have occurred on both occasions. Since these errors, as conventionally assumed, are random, one cannot exclude the possibility that pairs of errors do not cancel but rather strengthen each other's effect.

In table 3.4, a numerical example is presented using actual Soviet GINV figures to illustrate the potential size of distortions arising from a ±1, ±3 or ± 5 per cent measurement error on both occasions. The table shows GINV figures for the Soviet Union in 1983 and 1984, considering all possible variations.

According to official data, the annual percentage growth rate figures between 1979 and 1982 were as follows: 1979: 0.7 %, 1980: 2.2 %, 1981: 3.7 %, 1982: 3.5 %. It seems, therefore, that this was a period of upswing. In 1983, the rate was even higher (5.6%) but this was followed by a serious deceleration in the rate of GINV growth to 1.9 % in 1984.

TABLE 3.4 USSR: Alternative GINV series, assuming the presence of measurement errors, 1983-1984

	1984 174.3 ± error	166	169	173	174	176	180	183
1983	%error	-5	-3	-1	0	1	3	5
171.0 ±error								
162	-5	1.9	4.1	6.2	7.3	8.4	10.5	12.7
166	-3	-0.2	1.9	4.0	5.1	6.1	8.2	10.3
169	-1	-2.2	-0.1	1.9	3.0	4.0	6.0	8.1
171	0	-3.2	-1.1	0.9	1.9	2.9	5.0	7.0
173	1	-4.1	-2.1	-0.1	0.9	1.9	3.9	6.0
176	3	-6.0	-4.0	-2.0	-1.0	0.0	1.9	3.9
180	5	-7.8	-5.8	-3.9	-2.9	-2.0	0.0	1.9

Calculated growth rate on the basis of official data: 1984/1983 = 174.3/171.0 = 1.9 %

Source: Data: Table SA.1; Method: Morgemstern (1965), p. 288.

[15] E.g., 100x1.2x0.8 = 96, but 100x1.1x0.9 = 99.

Now, assuming that all these figures were precise and correct, the conclusion is straightforward: the boom ran out of steam in 1984 and a setback occurred. By contrast, after allowing for the possibility of a ± 5 % measurement error in both 1983 and 1984, the location of the peak becomes totally uncertain. For 1984 any figure between a 12.7 % rise and 7.8 % drop has the same probability. The assumption of a mere ±1 per cent measurement error - which is clearly a very optimistic scenario - is still great enough to produce a wide margin of uncertainty ranging between 0.1 and 4.0 %. It is not difficult to appreciate that the impact of measurement error does not depend on absolute levels. Only the difference between these levels and the assumed size of the error counts.

3.2.2 Theoretical and Practical Problems of Trend Analysis. There are good arguments for applying a trend approach - rather than looking merely at the annual growth rates, which is the simplest way to describe events. Year-to-year changes reflect only short term effects at best. However, extreme peaks and troughs are bound to have a longer - three to five year - impact on production capacities, on the balance of payments and, last but not least, on the behaviour of the planning organs. All this can be better captured by trend analysis. Furthermore, having defined a trend, different indicators can be computed to characterize the average size of peaks and troughs, thus facilitating cross-country comparisons.

Experimenting with trends. The sample mean values and the standard deviations of GINV growth rates are shown in table 3.5 for the whole sample period (1951-1989) and for three sub-periods. (I shall return later to the issue of periodization.) At first sight, it seems that investments in the eight countries can be characterized by a second or higher degree analytical function, because the mean values of growth rates are falling from period to period. The instability of the eight

3.5 GINV growth rates: Growth periods, 1951-1989

	Period I			Period II			Period III			1951-1989 (average)	
		AM	SD		AM	SD		AM	SD	AM	SD
Bulgaria	1951-60	15.7	14.0	1961-79	10.4	7.3	1980-89	4.1	5.1	9.2	9.9
CSSR	1951-61	11.2	6.7	1962-80	5.2	5.2	1981-89	0.7	3.5	5.9	6.5
GDR	1951-60	16.8	8.7	1961-81	5.5	3.8	1982-89	1.8	4.8	7.7	7.9
Hungary	1951-60	8.6	18.0	1961-79	7.4	6.6	1980-89	-1.4	5.4	5.3	11.2
Poland	1951-62	9.9	4.8	1963-78	9.5	7.4	1979-89	-1.4	10.3	6.5	9.2
Romania	1951-62	20.2	7.6	1963-80	10.2	3.6	1981-89	-0.5	3.5	9.7	10.0
USSR	1951-60	12.8	3.2	1961-78	6.5	2.1	1979-89	4.1	2.1	7.4	4.1
Yugoslavia	1951-64	8.7	9.7	1965-79	5.7	5.9	1980-89	-5.1	4.2	4.0	9.4

AM = Arithmetic mean SD= Standard deviation

Source: Table SA.1

series also appears to abate as we go forward in time. Standard deviation is smaller in the second period than in the first in all eight countries under review with the exception of Poland. However, in the third period - i.e. during the 1980s - the size of the standard deviation was greater than the mean in 7 cases out of 8.

The above casts some doubts on our chances of success in finding a good trend fit for our time series. In fact, after a series of experiments, Kyn *et al.* (1979) had already warned that no single trend can be fitted to the investment data of socialist countries. More precisely, a good fit can easily be achieved in the sense of having high R^2 values but the poor results of the Durbin-Watson statistics, reflecting autocorrelation in the time series, shed doubt on the reliability of the whole exercise.

The next two tables summarize the results of an experiment. In table 3.6 the estimated trend coefficients and other regression characteristics are tabulated assuming, first, a linear (y_1) and subsequently, a second degree exponential trend function (y_2). All in all, the two types of trends are equally good: t-values and the adjusted R^2 values are reasonably high. By contrast, as noted already, the Durbin-Watson statistics indicate the presence of positive autocorrelation.

Now, if we proceed with the removal of the trend and subtract the trend values from the actual values, we will have two different detrended time series - d(1) and d(2) - for every country. The question is, how similar are these pairs. If the two detrended time series are closely correlated, then - but only then - is it appropriate to assume that the technique of trend selection does not matter. In this case we can proceed. We can compare the comovements of this detrended time series with other macro-economic variables such as NMP, industrial output, foreign trade etc. In the opposite case, however, if we find little or no correlation between these pairs, further analysis is meaningless. If there is no way to find an analytical trend that fully satisfies the customary technical criteria of such a procedure, there is no room for compromise. Once we are ready to make compromises and tolerate the presence of autocorrelation[16], we have to make arbitrary choices between equally "faulty" trends and our further results will be very much dependent upon this arbitrary choice.[17]

After this general introduction, the message of table 3.7 will probably not come as a surprise to the reader. The table shows that the detrended time series are not correlated with one another: d(1) cannot substitute for d(2) or vice versa. Technically speaking, the difficulty stems from the autocorrelation of those neglected variables which were not taken into account in the procedure of trend fitting.[18]

[16] A good example for such a compromise is Marrese (1977, 1981).

[17] For those familiar with the classical literature of western business cycles this is not a surprise. In the early 1930s, researchers of the *National Bureau of Economic Research* assembled 23 trend lines fitted by various investigators to pig iron production in the United States and found that some of the trend lines over a standard time interval (1877-1914) yield cycles averaging 3 or 4 years in duration while others yield cycles more then ten times as long (Frickey, 1934). Commenting on these results, one can only agree with Burns and Mitchell (1946, p. 37) that "if an investigator fits a trend line in a mechanical manner, without specifying in advance his conception of the secular trend or of cyclical fluctuations, he may get «cycles» of almost any duration".

[18] See Pindyck and Rubinfeld (1981, p. 153).

TABLE 3.6 GINV: Alternative trend functions, 1950-1989

(Normalised series, 1975 = 100)

Regression equation: y1 = a + bT +e

N = 40	a	t(a)	b	t(b)	R**2/DOF	D-W
Bulgaria	-23.02	-6.39	4.71	30.76	0.96	0.24
Czechoslovakia	6.44	2.48	3.15	28.47	0.95	0.16
GDR	0.74	0.31	3.49	34.59	0.97	0.21
Hungary	5.91	1.49	2.92	17.39	0.89	0.18
Poland	0.99	0.20	2.42	11.26	0.76	0.16
Romania	-23.59	-4.99	4.67	23.24	0.93	0.12
USSR	-7.92	-3.49	4.13	42.85	0.98	0.12

Regression equation: y2 = a + bT**2 + e

N = 40	a	t(a)	b	t(b)	R**2/DOF	D-W
Bulgaria	11.11	6.84	0.11	51.29	0.99	0.65
Czechoslovakia	31.12	10.43	0.07	17.80	0.89	0.09
GDR	28.40	8.73	0.08	18.02	0.89	0.08
Hungary	29.60	7.47	0.07	12.18	0.79	0.11
Poland	20.95	4.70	0.05	8.90	0.67	0.12
Romania	11.06	3.11	0.11	22.93	0.93	0.14
USSR	22.60	14.76	0.10	47.19	0.98	0.13

Source: Table SA.1

TABLE 3.7 GINV: Correlation between alternative detrended series, 1950-1989

Coefficient of correlation between time series of deviation:

N = 40	R(d(1)GINV, d(2)GINV)
Bulgaria	-0.09
Czechoslovakia	-0.18
GDR	-0.36
Hungary	0.25
Poland	0.28
Romania	0.23
USSR	-0.39

d(1) = GINV/y1 ; y1 = a + bt + e   d(2) = GINV/y2 ; y2 = a + bt**2 + e

Source: Table SA.1

We meet similar obstacles if the analysis is carried out in terms of conventional growth rates and not on original GINV data, as shown above. If an attempt is made to fit linear trends to simple growth rates, as was done with somewhat shorter series by Staller (1964), Bajt (1969), Bauer (1981, pp. 291-295) and Summers (1990), the results will be unacceptable due to the presence of positive autocorrelation.[19]

The analysis of such detrended investment time series played a central role in Bauer (1981) and Summers (1990). Its function was to demonstrate the presence of comovements between detrended GINV data and other macro-variables. Bauer's conclusion was that investment fluctuations in Eastern Europe have a direct impact on several other macro-variables, while this link is weak or non-existent in the Soviet Union. Summers examined only the Soviet Union but came to opposite conclusions. In the light of the above, however, both sets of findings must be taken with a very great deal of caution. Much work is required, based on econometrically solid procedures, before a final conclusion can be drawn.

In order to circumvent the difficulties in finding a good analytical trend, an UN/ECE study defined the trend as a centred five-year moving average of the original annual data.[20] Bajt (1971) and Roland (1987a) also experimented with such solutions. The moving average approach has two obvious weaknesses. First, it gives an arbitrary definition of the length of the cycle. The correct procedure, at least theoretically, should be just the opposite. The length of the cycle has to be established through another method and this information can then be applied in the detrending procedure. In practice, this objection, however, may not be very pertinent: the two individual studies quoted above showed that the exact choice of the assumed length of the cycle does not very much alter the results of further analysis. Experiments with 5, 4 and 3 years showed very similar final results.

The second quandary is that the moving average approach offers no exact way to test the trend fit. Once again we have to face the risk that, if the trend is misspecified, the cycle so defined immediately becomes an artefact too.[21]

Theoretical arguments against detrending. Beyond the painful statistical experiences cited above, confidence in the trend approach has also been greatly undermined by the findings of modern business cycle analysts, equipped with more robust econometric tools than the classics of the 1930s.

In the past ten years a huge literature has been produced by econometricians working with western statistical data which question the legitimacy of the decomposition procedure. As Virén (1985) lucidly explains: "The problem with the whole decomposition is the fact that secular movements are not necessarily deterministic by nature. Or it can even be that the stochastic process of the secular (growth) component causes the main part of variability of the relevant time series." (p. 1)

[19] According to my calculations, performed on data in Table A2, the size of the Durbin-Watson statistics varied between 0.63 and 1.52, while R^2 fluctuates between 0.07 and 0.49.

[20] See UN ESE 1984-85 (pp. 138-143).

[21] In the already quoted NBER study the consequences of arbitrary decisions had already been demonstrated. Using once again the US data for pig iron production in the period between 1854-1933, it was found that the average length of the "cycle" increased more or less regularly as the period of moving averages was lengthened.

In speaking of a trend, the length of the series to which our statements refer must be always borne in mind. However long a series may be, we can never be certain, and often not even reasonably sure, that a calculated trend in a time series is not a part of a slow oscillation. For this reason, it is certainly more accurate to speak of slow or quick movements rather than trend and oscillation. But even so, as Kendall and Stuart (1966, p. 350) noted, the distinction between the two would remain a matter of subjective judgement to some extent.

The fact that deterministic trends "explain" much of the movement in macro-economic time series, "in the sense of producing high values of R^2, is in itself not convincing evidence of the existence of deterministic trends or the appropriateness of regression detrending for measuring the cyclical components." (Nelson 1985, p. 56)

It was shown by Nelson and Kang (1981), and later by others, that a *random walk* with a drift in itself can imply rather high R^2-s. Residuals from such a detrending procedure yield a measure of cyclical variation which is purely artificial. What is more, it was found that the period length of the cycle is entirely dependent on the number of observations.

This theoretical framework offers new ways to look at investment fluctuations. Random walks have the important property that there is no tendency for the process to return to any particular level or trend line once displaced by an external shock. This interpretation makes a lot of sense when looking at the historical aspect of the investment process of the socialist countries. It is not unreasonable to think of the sudden, often politically motivated, investment surges as a permanent shock, after which the system could never return to the previous growth path.

Looking for theoretical support, the proponents of the stochastic approach recall a wise warning from Hicks' *Capital and Growth.* The subject of this book is economic growth - i.e. the factor which cycle analysis wants to eliminate. Hicks's point of departure was the contrary - he wanted to discard short-term fluctuations. Nevertheless, on the very first pages of his book, he warned his readers that the distinction between these two factors is a methodological and not a real one:

> The distinction between trend and fluctuation is a statistical distinction. (...) Since economic theory is to be applied to statistics, which are arranged in this manner, a corresponding argument of theory will (no doubt) often be convenient. But this gives us no reason to suppose that there is anything corresponding to it on the economic side which is at all fundamental. We have no right to conclude, from the mere existence of the statistical device, that the economic forces making for trend and for fluctuations are any different, so they have to be analyzed in different ways. (Hicks, 1966, p. 4)[22]

All this is *a fortiori* true in Soviet-type economies. By forcing all the variation onto the cyclical component, the role of the cycle (if it exists at all) is magnified. Bajt (1971) was probably the first among the students of socialist investment fluctuations to conclude that the trend growth of investment and the short-term zigzags around it were inseparable from each other. Looking

[22] In this context it would be unfair not to mention that Marxists or sympathizers with the labour theory of value (e.g., P. Sraffa, J. Robinson) have always had serious reservations about another decomposition theory - namely, the production function. The issue at stake is analogous to the problem of eliminating the trend effect from a time series. These authors have doubts about whether a statistical procedure which explains economic growth by the increase of inputs on the one hand, and by the increase of productivity on the other, can shed light on something "fundamental" in the Hicksian sense of the word.

chiefly at the practical aspects of the problem, he saw no possibility of raising the secular growth of GINV at the price of short-term investment cuts.

The logic of the endogenous models suggested that a temporary cut at the top of an investment wave can help to improve the efficiency of capital formation. The elimination of tensions on the investment market should make a more solid base for the next period. In other words, the marginal efficiency of investments rises and this will secure higher average efficiency in the long run.

What is wrong with this assumption? The proponents of the investment cycle model transplant tacitly or subconsciously the logic of the market into the socialist environment. In the market economies, depression brings about a rising number of bankruptcies, ongoing investment projects are shelved, etc. Hence, for a market economy, the depression is a purgatory which eliminates weak and non-performing economic units. This is the price to be paid for the fruits of prosperity.

Bajt could not accept the validity of this logic in a socialist economy. He thought that the average and marginal efficiencies of investment were constant for a large part of the investment curve. It is the institutional setup, with all its deficiencies, which determines the relatively low average and marginal efficiency. Decreasing or raising the rate of investment (relative to output) cannot really alter the situation in this respect.

Approaching the problem from another angle, a Hungarian and a Polish economist - Major I. (1983) and Podkaminer (1989) - came independently to similar conclusions. Both authors noted that GINV fluctuations had lately become smaller and smaller. The peaks were lower and the troughs shallower than they had been earlier. This has often been interpreted as a positive development: planners were moving up on their learning curves.

The two authors, however, offer a different explanation. For them, learning-by-doing is only a partial elucidation. In a market economy, successive ups and downs in economic activity are more or less independent events. By contrast, in output and investment fluctuations of the socialist countries the symptoms of the very same problems and contradictions have remained unsolved for decades. There is no purgatory here: problems were not solved in an economic sense and were swept under the carpet. The moderation of oscillations reflects the continuously narrowing room for manoeuvre rather than the increasing intellectual capability of planners to manoeuvre.

3.2.3 Fluctuations at Random ? The use of mathematical and statistical methods to identify cycles requires very precise definition. As noted already in Chapter 1, the three R-s (recurrence, reinforcement and regularity) are not sufficient for this kind of venture. The concept of periodicity must also be built in. In other words, it has to be assumed that peaks and troughs follow each other with a certain time regularity.

In principle, statistical theory offers a number of ways to perform such a test. The paucity of the data, however, imposes a very serious constraint. GINV data at constant prices are available only on an annual basis. Thus the number of observations is not more, and often less, than 40. For this simple reason, robust testing methods such as spectral analysis, periodograms, etc. cannot be effectively used. Malinvaud (1969), for example, gives a strong warning against using periodogram testing for a time series when $n < 50$. Another widely used textbook - Box and Jenkins (1970) -, gives an indirect warning by using an example for such periodogram testing where $n = 224$.

In spite of such warnings, these methods can be experimented with in the sense that econometric software packages cannot physically prevent users from doing it[23] but the result is predictable. Using the standard east European time series in Appendix table A.2, periodogram analysis gave inconclusive answers. In three cases (CSSR, Hungary and Yugoslavia), the fluctuations have clearly remained within the pre-determined confidence limits, suggesting that the series contain nothing else but randomness (white noise). In other cases, the procedure yield no conclusive answer, even if the reservations concerning the small sample size are put aside.

Identifying the Number of Turning Points. When the secular growth component has been removed from the data in one way or another, we are left with a series which will represent fluctuations of a more of less regular kind. The question then arises whether this residual series is systematic in the sense that its values can be explained with a reasonable degree of certainty as a function of time, or, on the other hand, whether the values are random in the sense that they could occur in the observed order, by random sampling from a homogenous population.

Kendall and Stuart (1966) developed a very simple test, based on counting the number of peaks or troughs in the series. In what follows, I apply this method to analyze GINV data expressed in annual percentage changes. For the purposes of this exercise, a peak is a value which is greater than the rounded integer value of the two neighbouring data - i.e. differences in the first digit are neglected. If there are two equal values (e.g., the 1964 and 1965 data for the GDR) I regarded them as defining one peak.

Before applying the test, the first question is a general one. What is the distribution of peaks (or troughs) in a pure random series? Since the answer is the same for peaks and troughs - with a change of sign of the variate - our case can be formulated in a more general form. Peaks and troughs can be treated as turning points in the series. So, the reformulated question should be: what is the distribution of turning points in a random series? Without going into the details of proving the theorem for the general case, it is easy to see that in a series of 3 members, the values can occur in 6 ways. Only 4 of these would be a turning point. Hence the probability of a turning point in a set of three values is 2/3. For the general case with n values it is 2/3*(n-2).[24]

Consequently, if a time series contains significantly more or less turning points than the formula suggests, we have reason to suspect the presence of some systematic components.

The results of our computations are presented in table 3.8. They suggest that in three countries out of eight, namely in the Soviet Union, CSSR and Yugoslavia, fluctuations in the annual growth rate of GINV series are likely to be random, because the observed and the expected number of turning points are not significantly different. The same cannot be said, however, with regard to Romanian, Polish and GDR data. Nevertheless, it should be mentioned that experience showed that the above method is rather sensitive to changes in sample size. (This

[23] There have been repeated attempts by Bulgarian economists - Dimitrov (1980,1987), Antonov (1987), Vesselinov (1991) - to use spectral analysis to detect cyclical behaviour in various time series (industrial output, NMP and, in Dimitrov (1987), also GINV) for their national economy. These authors must have worked with 20-35 original observations. Vesselinov (1991) and I. Kostov used pseudo-quarterly indices, generated with the help of cubic spline functions. This method, however, has not offered convincing proof of the existence of pronounced fluctuations. (For precise references on Kostov's work see Avramov 1990, p. 35.)

[24] For a full demonstration see Kendall and Stuart 1966, pp. 351-352.

is an obvious consequence of the shortness of the time series.) As the reader can easily verify himself, the removal of the last or the first observation of the time series will yield somewhat different results from those reported above. Thus, all these findings should be interpreted with a great deal of caution.

All in all, perhaps the outcome of applying the Kendall-Stuart procedure is still plausible despite the simplicity of the method applied. Other authors, following totally different lines of argument, also came to similar conclusions. Bauer, for example, found that in the GDR and the Soviet Union the evidence for the presence of cyclicality was weaker than in the "classical" cases, such as Czechoslovakia, Poland and Hungary.[25]

TABLE 3.8 GINV growth rates: Number of turning points, 1950-1989

	Number of observations	Number of turning points expected	Number of turning points observed	Concordance ratio
	N	2/3*(N-2)		
	<1>	<2>	<3>	<3>/<2>
Bulgaria	40	25	19	0.75
Czechoslovakia	40	25	21	0.83
GDR	40	25	19	0.75
Hungary	39	25	19	0.77
Poland	40	25	18	0.71
Romania	39	25	16	0.65
USSR	40	25	23	0.91
Yugoslavia	40	25	20	0.79

Source: Table SA.1

[25] Writing on the GDR, Bauer (1981) concluded that "for the 1960s and the 1970s, only the existence of fluctuation can be established with full certainty. It would be difficult to take a definite stand whether in this period two long or four short cycle occurred, let alone to identify the phases of these cycles." (p. 229) His position was similar with respect to the Soviet Union. "During the 1950s, the observed changes in the volume growth of investments were sufficiently robust to suggest the existence of some cyclical movement below the surface. In the 1960s and the 1970s, however, the growth rates of investments became even more stable than before." (p. 375)

Exogenous shocks. It is a truism that unforeseen developments (e.g., the death of Stalin, the rise of Khrushchev or Gorbachev, the erection and the crumbling of the Berlin Wall, the tenfold increase in international oil prices between 1973 and 1982, an earthquake or a drought etc.) can have a sudden, persistent and incalculable impact on the economies of socialist countries. Nonetheless, the methodological consequences of this are not yet deeply rooted in the minds of students of the socialist economists in general or those of investment cycle specialists in particular.

To avoid misunderstanding, it is important to emphasize that any previous or forthcoming reference to "random fluctuations" or "random shocks" does not imply that every turning point is accidental or haphazard in the sense of the outcome of a lottery or the throwing of dice. Randomness is understood only in the context of the presence or non-presence of any systematic time pattern of the investment process itself as it is reflected in GINV series. In a sense, there is nothing revolutionary in this position - the present formulation is fully in line with the tenets of the important work of Slutzky (1937), which interprets ups and downs in economic activity as the accumulation of random events.

Let us recall the second element of our cycle definition: reinforcement means that any turning point stands in a causal relationship with the subsequent one. Randomness is understood in this context only. The turning points are random if this condition is not met.[26]

In the previous section, a very simple method was used to test for the presence of randomness in GINV series. A more rigorous procedure will now be applied to show that the assumption of random shocks in a number of cases is sufficient to describe annual changes in the volume of investments.

The following hypothetical question will be tested: is it true that annual variations in the investment process exhibit a regular time pattern, as the deterministic cycle theory suggest? The answer here is based on an analysis of the autocorrelation characteristics of the GINV series. First, an attempt is made to exploit the negative experiences with the trend approach summarized earlier. It will be recalled that the autocorrelation of residuals (as shown by the Durbin-Watson test) casts doubts on the trend fit. Now, having abandoned the trend approach, we return to scrutinize annual growth rates of GINV. We then look at the autocorrelation structure of lagged GINV variables. Our starting point is that lagged variables in a regular cycle are necessarily autocorrelated and the level of this regularity can be measured by conventional econometric tests.

The sample autocorrelation values derived from GINV data after a transformation in log difference terms are reported in table 3.9. (The use of logarithmic differences is advantageous for two reasons. First, it produces variable elasticities directly over time; secondly, it is symmetrical over time. This means that an X unit decrease after an X unit increase will bring us back exactly to the same level, whereas, as seen in the previous section, this is not true if changes are measured by conventional growth rates in percentage terms.) Though the analysis of these figures cannot yield a definitive answer to our question, they allow a tentative

[26] One of the statistical horror stories quoted by Griliches (1986) may help to illustrate this point. The total number of patents granted by the U.S. Patent Office in a particular year was found to depend rather strongly on the total number of patent examiners available for the job. For various reasons, their number has gone through several cycles, inducing concomitant cycles in the actual number of patents granted. The observed fluctuation in patents granted are random if the analysis is focused, for instance, on measuring the impact of GDP growth on this process. Looking at the same process from another angle, there is nothing random in the time series. If the impact of changes in the number of patent examiners is tested, we have a perfect model.

judgement. Typically, only the first-order autocorrelation coefficients deviate from zero at standard levels of significance. In the case of three countries (Bulgaria, Czechoslovakia and Hungary) the random walk hypothesis cannot be rejected, because the Box-Pierce statistics for five lags fails to pass the critical level of significance.

TABLE 3.9 GINV: Autocorrelation coefficients, 1950-1989

N = 34	R(1)	R(2)	R(3)	R(4)	R(5)	X^2_5
Bulgaria	0.32	-0.19	-0.12	0.04	0.08	5.37
Czechoslovakia	-0.29	-0.18	-0.29	-0.17	-0.29	10.88
GDR	0.48	0.19	0.44	0.38	0.27	22.94
Hungary	0.23	-0.12	0.22	0.10	-0.32	7.71
Poland	0.72	0.33	0.08	-0.33	-0.24	27.21
Romania	0.61	0.26	0.31	0.15	0.10	19.34
EE6 (unweighted)	0.60	0.24	0.32	0.09	-0.02	17.82
USSR	0.64	0.59	0.47	0.43	0.42	45.25
EE7 (unweighted)	0.62	0.29	0.34	0.14	0.07	20.78

Notes: R(i)-s denote the autocorrelation coefficients of di.
di = lnGINV - lnGINV<-1>
X^2_5 are the Box-Pierce statistics.
The critical value of the chi-square statistics at the 95 % level is 11.07.

Source: Table SA.1

A more powerful test, following a procedure suggested by Dickey and Fuller (1979), scrutinizes the autocorrelation function of the di series (di being dln GINV). This method is based on the assumption that the time series contain nothing else but a random walk. The test requires estimating the following equation:

$$(3.1) \qquad di = C + a_1I(-1) + a_2T + a_3di(-1) + a_4di(-2) + e\ ,$$

where I = ln GINV T denotes the time trend and e is the error term. Since di = I - I(-1) by definition, the above equation can be rewritten in the following form:

$$(3.2) \qquad I = I(-1) + C + a_1I(-1)\ a_2T + a_3di(-1) + a_4di(-2) + e.$$

Now, let us note that (3.2) is nothing but the composition of a random walk with a time drift and real shocks, provided that $a_1I(-1) = 0$, which in turn is the case if a_1 is not significantly different from zero. The regression results in table 3.9 show that the estimated a_1 parameters are in fact very close to zero. Typically there is a negative drift in time ($a_2 < 0$), which corresponds to the known fact of falling growth rates.

It is perhaps not superfluous to emphasize that the findings in tables 3.9 and 3.10 should also be treated with caution because of the small sample size.[27] Furthermore, the evidence found here does not in itself call into question the validity of endogenous cycle theories. Not rejecting the random walk hypothesis does not prove that the series are random walks. On the basis of the above test, we cannot legitimately claim more than that various real shocks hitting the east European economies at random seem to generate fluctuations so big that the impact of internal cyclical forces, in terms of time regularity, is discernable only to a very limited extent, if at all.

TABLE 3.10 GINV: Parameter estimates for the Dickey-Fuller test procedure, 1950-1989

Regression equation: di = C + a<1>I(-1) + a<2>T +a<3>di(-1) +a<4>di(-2) + e

N = 37	C	a<1>	a<2>	a<3>	a<4>
Bulgaria	0.17	0.00	0.00	0.33	-0.43 *
Czechoslovakia	0.02	-0.04	0.00	0.04 *	-0.19
GDR	0.35 *	-0.07	0.00	0.02	-0.24
Hungary	0.23	-0.06	0.00	0.38 *	-0.27
Poland	0.13	-0.03	0.00	0.96 *	-0.39 *
Romania	0.08	0.03	-0.01	0.19	-0.14
EE6 (unweighted)	0.05	0.02	0.00	0.48 *	-0.34 *
USSR	0.30 *	-0.08 *	0.00	0.25	0.00
EE7 (unweighted)	0.06	0.01	0.00	0.49 *	-0.34 *

I = lnGINV di = lnGINV-lnGINV(-1)
* Significant at the 5 % level.

Source: Table SA.1

[27] The above results were first presented in Mihályi (1986b) at the 1986 Paris cycle colloquium, mentioned in the Introduction. On a slightly different data set (n=25) Ickes (1990) repeated the above test procedure and obtained identical results.

The impact of harvest fluctuations. Among several possible random factors that may have an exogenous impact on the investment process, the agricultural crop harvest is the most obvious. It will be recalled that in the period under investigation, the size of the annual harvest was of considerable macro-economic importance in all countries of the region. It had a noticeable impact on NMP growth in the given year.[28] It also influenced the domestic food[29] and fodder supply - as well as the countries' export potential - in the given and in the subsequent year. Windfall gains in exports or reduction in import needs could always open channels for additional machinery imports. In bad years this mechanism worked in the opposite direction.

The size of the crop harvest is not known with satisfactory precision before the ninth month of the year.[30] Not surprisingly, investments in the year in question are hardly influenced. Investment plans for the following year are usually elaborated at just about this time. To set its likely influence in proportion, it is worth mentioning that the crop harvest's gross value in the periods under discussion was equivalent to 70-100 per cent of GINV in those countries (GDR, Hungary, Poland and Romania) for which comparable data were available. In these economies the total gross value of annual agricultural output was about 50-80 per cent above GINV levels.

The importance of the harvest is crucial in understanding the reinforcement mechanisms which operate during the downward phase of GINV fluctuations (Eckstein 1960, 1968). The effects of a harvest downturn tend to operate throughout the economy, generating a cumulative contraction. Obviously, the magnitude of this impact is inversely related to the level of development. From our perspective, however, it is pertinent, as most of the socialist countries had a relatively large agricultural sector in the period under discussion. The fact that this mechanism seems to have worked only in the downward phase of the cycle explains why simple regression tests (with or without lags) cannot detect significant correlation between annual GINV changes on the one hand and fluctuations in agricultural indicators (AGRT, AGRC, AGRL) on the other.

In the past, little attention has been paid to this subject - either in the socialist countries or outside them. For reasons discussed later, planners were inclined to underestimate the impact of weather fluctuations. Outside experts, most of whom were critical in their orientation, also neglected this subject, since for them each poor harvest was a demonstration of the failure of collectivised agriculture. A notable exception was Montias' account of Romanian investment policy formation. In his interpretation the harvest prospects were the third among three basic factors explaining the levels set by planners for state investments.[31]

Recently, however, considerable research has been done on the effect of the weather on harvest results both in the USSR and China. This body of literature is surveyed in Ellman (1989,

[28] In 1965, according to contemporary CMEA statistics, the net contribution of agriculture to NMP varied between 12.0 per cent (Czechoslovakia) and 32.5 per cent (Bulgaria).

[29] In the second part of the 1960s food accounted for about 50 per cent of total retail trade in these countries.

[30] The issue is somewhat more complicated in the Asian socialist countries, where the main crop (rice) is harvested twice a year. Hence, a proper analysis for these countries would require quarterly or monthly data.

[31] The first two were: the political climate of the moment and the state of the balance of payments (Montias 1967, p. 233).

pp. 124-127). It is a terrible indictment of collective farming that the worst famines of the 20th century (China 1958-61, the Soviet Union 1932-34) occurred under socialism. This is undoubtedly the main lesson of the new findings.

It seems, however, that the severity of these harvest failures was due, to a large extent, to exceptionally unfavourable weather conditions. Beyond this, there was one more common, truly system-specific feature of these tragedies: when it occurred, the gravity of the problem was completely concealed and no external help was accepted to overcome the food shortage. Decades elapsed before their true dimensions became known.

The Chinese famine of 1958-1961 was the more severe case. According to harvest data first released in 1983 (!), grain production dropped by 15 % in 1959 and then to about 25 % below its previous levels for two further consecutive years (Ashton et al., 1984). The other necessary condition for revealing the truth was the publication of the first post-famine census. The 1980 census report has generated a number of studies which permitted a historical reconstruction of the events. On this basis, today's estimates for the number of excess deaths resulting from the famine and its consequences vary between 17 and 30 million.

This unprecedented tragedy resulted in a sharp fall in state investments: 62.5 % in 1961 and an additional 44.1 % in 1962. Of course, these figures, which were first released in 1983, reflect a totally different picture of the investment front compared with what had been known or postulated by contemporary analysts (Eckstein, 1968).

Similarly, the 1933 Soviet famine was a classical example of a random shock, after which the system never returned to its previous growth path. Indeed, in a certain sense, it is still valid to say that in 1990, more than half a century after the event, the combined impact of the freakish weather and the catastrophic collectivisation campaign of 1933 has never been fully absorbed by the Soviet economy.

The results of the official 1937 census, the uncontestable evidence of the magnitude of this tragedy, had been suppressed and surfaced only recently (*Vestnik Statistiki*, 1990. No. 7.). It turned out only then that the number of deaths in 1933 surpassed the level of the previous year by about 6.5 million. This was the direct and indirect consequence of the large scale famine which devastated the country. According to official Soviet data, first published 30 years (!) later, the volume of investments in 1933 fell by 17 % - the largest annual drop in peace time throughout 70 years of Soviet economic history.

Freakish weather (drought, flood, plant disease) is, of course, much less than a full explanation for the volatility of harvest fluctuations. Appropriate crop structure and carefully implemented development programmes can help to stabilize the harvest independently from the level of technological development (which is given in the short run). The fact that this did not occur, or not to a very great extent, can also be explained on system-specific grounds. Planners act inconsistently, which is reflected in short-term changes in the structure of the sown area. As Brada (1986) showed for five east European countries, the structure was more volatile in the period after 1945 than before - at least in the case of seven major crops. He found strong statistical evidence linking this fact on the one hand, and the volatility of fluctuations on the total harvest on the other.

From our perspective it is the consequences of, rather than the reasons for, harvest fluctuations which are decisive. As noted above, the size of the annual agricultural output was large enough in all socialist countries to exert an impact on the national economy as a whole. What we still need to demonstrate is that the total harvest - and its crop and livestock components - are more volatile than investment itself. The data are set out in table 3.11.

TABLE 3.11 Fluctuations in GINV and agriculture, 1951-1987

(Calculated from time series in annual percentage change form)

N = 37	Investments	Agricultural output		
		Total	Crop	Livestock
Bulgaria				
Standard deviation	9.73	10.46	15.76	4.82
Coefficient of variation	0.99	2.89	4.32	1.20
Czechoslovakia				
Standard deviation	6.68	4.08	8.53	5.29
Coefficient of variation	1.11	2.28	5.27	2.37
German Dem. Republic				
Standard deviation	8.06	6.15	11.30	6.20
Coefficient of variation	1.03	2.32	5.17	1.85
Hungary				
Standard deviation	11.03	8.32	15.05	6.95
Coefficient of variation	1.89	3.40	5.25	2.58
Poland				
Standard deviation	9.32	4.59	6.70	4.96
Coefficient of variation	1.37	2.31	3.33	2.36
Romania				
Standard deviation	9.77	9.70	14.30	5.56
Coefficient of variation	0.94	2.03	2.67	1.30
Soviet Union				
Standard deviation	4.17	5.73	9.30	4.60
Coefficient of variation	0.55	1.87	3.39	1.27

Source: Own calculations based on ECE/DEAP Common Data Base

As noted, a bad harvest is bound to have a negative impact on economic developments in the given year and an even stronger one in the subsequent year. If this does not happen, special circumstances can be adduced in explanation. In Yugoslavia, for example, the harvests were particularly poor in 1952 and in 1956. Agricultural output fell by 29 and 17 %, respectively (Cobeljic and Stojanovic 1969, p. 142). Though the volume of investments fell immediately in both years, the country managed to avoid famine and disastrous macro-economic consequences in general due to the prompt and generous support measures of Western governments.[32]

Bad weather appears to have taken planners by surprise even in years following several years of good harvest, when probability alone might have been expected to suggest caution. In Yugoslavia, as noted, agricultural production had its own exogenously caused cycles, which until 1960 - according to Horvat (1975) - recurred every second year. How can this shortsightedness be explained?

The so-called "ratchet principle" - i.e. planning from achieved results - has much to do with this. Since planners cannot see precisely in advance which geographical areas and which crops will be affected by unfavourable climatical developments, the losses expected nationwide cannot be quantified at the level of regions and product balances. In addition, the Centre had good reason to believe that if agricultural plans made allowances for possible adverse weather conditions, the harvest would diminish automatically even if expected weather calamities did not materialize. This is because plans are, in a way, self-fulfilling prophecies. Hence, there is a certain logic behind taut plans. If a plan is less ambitious than in the previous year, it is likely that each level of the planning hierarchy - down to the level of the cooperative farmers - will lessen its efforts to implement the plan, hoping that bad weather will hit someone else while they can easily fulfil the lowered targets.

Since annual plans did not usually set aside sufficient reserves to cover unexpected developments, ad hoc measures were required when losses became known to the planning authorities, to ease tensions. In most cases, the foreign trade sector alone cannot eliminate the consequences of a really bad harvest. Reducing exports and increasing imports are usually not enough. Other chapters of the plan have to be modified as well.

Among the authors of the "bureaucratic response" school mentioned in Section 2.3 above, only Green (1977) and Marrese (1981) directly addressed the subject of weather fluctuations. Green found that in the Soviet Union, in a period when about 20 % of all investments were allocated directly to agriculture, the annual volume of agricultural investments (and hence total investments) was influenced by the outcome of the harvest in two ways.

The state of the harvest in the previous year (measured by the percentage deviation of actual from normal output) has a negative effect upon the planned growth of agricultural investment and the realization of those plans. According to Green this observation should be interpreted as a compensatory response by planners. The state of the current harvest had a direct positive impact on the actual investment growth in the sector, primarily in construction work carried out by state and collective farmers.

To the present author these econometric results suggest that - in contrast to general belief - money and monetary results do play a certain role in Soviet planning. At the sectoral level, and further down at the level of cooperatives, a bumper harvest means windfall profits. This extra

[32] Between 1951-1969, cash donations and other grants worth about $ 100 million were provided annually to Yugoslavia by the US government alone. (U.S. Department of Commerce 1975, p. 874). To set this figure in the right perspective, it should be compared with the total value of imports in the period: $ 300 mn in 1950 and still only $ 800 mn in 1960.

income is spent immediately on additional investments (and probably on consumption as well). In the following year, total investments directed to the agricultural sector are lowered, since the Centre does not feel the pressure of urgency to come to the help of the cooperatives. Planners assume that, after a good year, the agricultural sector will have enough monetary and other reserves to fulfil output plans without additional central support.

This interpretation of Green's findings is corroborated by a study by Hungarian agricultural economists (Borosznói *et al.* 1978). They also established a positive link between harvest results and sectoral investment activity. Interestingly, their results suggested that the feed-back mechanism is not symmetrical: a bad harvest exerts a stronger negative impact on next year's investment, in comparison to the positive feedback triggered by a bumper harvest. The key element of the Hungarian story at the micro level is similar to the macro explanation, described above. Cooperatives and state farms are also "born optimists", in the sense that their plans always reckon with a constant rise in harvests. When this forecast proves to be wrong, they are forced to cut investments disproportionally in order to protect other type of expenditures which were originally expected to be financed from an overall rise in incomes.

Marrese's analysis, stemming from his econometric model of Hungarian investment behaviour, follows a somewhat different logical path. Bad weather in his sense means a harsh winter. One result of cold spells is possible harvest loss but the construction sector can also suffer through the loss of working days. Indeed, it was found that bad weather adversely affected the spending of construction investment funds (GINV-C), while the opposite occurred with respect to machinery investment (GINV-M). For understandable reasons, therefore, the link between bad weather and GINV, which consists of construction plus machinery investment, proved to be statistically insignificant.

These findings are thought-provoking and perhaps even surprising. Certainly, they deserve further examination. In the absence of such studies, it is not possible to establish the general validity of the Chinese, Soviet and Hungarian results. Chapter 4 takes up this issue again. The analysis will use conventional, non-econometric methods to investigate - *inter alia* - the role of agricultural harvests in the rise and fall of investments. It will be shown that harvest failure, recurring every second or third year, usually play an important role in triggering a cut in GINV growth. This logical feedback mechanism seems to work in the opposite direction, too. If, as a result of sheer good fortune, a socialist country has good harvests 4-5 years in a row, this creates the impression of a protracted investment boom. But it is only an impression. When the bad harvest finally arrives, the consequences are usually even more devastating.

3.3 East-West comparison of GINV fluctuations

An analysis of investment fluctuations under socialism would be incomplete without inter-system comparisons. Indeed, such an exercise could have been placed with good reason at the very beginning of this book. It could be argued that any discussion of investment cycles in the socialist economies is meaningless without a yardstick obtained from an examination of the same phenomenon observed in the market economies.

Variation of GINV Series. There are several methods for measuring the stability of a time series. The academic literature on investment cycles prefers those where variation is measured according to the size of deviation from a calculated trend. In Section 3.2.2, however, it was shown that fitting a trend to our GINV data cannot be done with any reasonable degree of confidence. This, of course, excludes the possibility of measuring stability in this way.

The coefficient of variation (σ) calculated from growth rates is one of the least objectionable methods for the purposes of an East-West comparison. Unfortunately, this method has an important weakness. It is easy to see that as the rate of growth slows down, σ approaches infinity. Fortunately, in our sample for East-West comparison, this problem does not occur, as the mean of the time series never falls close to zero.

The limits of the comparison are drawn by data constraints on the Western side. Since the UN standard for national accounting (SNA) was introduced in the mid-1950s, there are very few Western countries where comparative investment series were made available for the period 1950-1960. This explains the time horizon 1960-1989 chosen for the data presented in table 3.12.

On the basis of historical facts and the methodological explanation presented in previous sections, it will probably not surprise the reader that the Soviet Union exhibits the smallest variation in GINV. The coefficient of variation is about 1/5 or 1/6 of those exhibited by some Western countries. By contrast, σ proved to be much higher in Yugoslavia, Poland, Hungary and Czechoslovakia than in the Soviet economy. More importantly, the size of the observed variation in these four economies does not appear significantly different from Western norms.

These results were achieved by a very simple calculation. Regretfully, table 3.12 in itself does not provide much support for determining the direction of further research. The data do not reveal any standard pattern for explaining the country-specific differences. It is easier to discard some factors from the possible list of causes than to find a good candidate for explanatory variables in a regression fitting exercise. It appears, for example, that the level of development is probably not a good explanatory variable judging by the pair-wise comparisons for USA-Canada, Spain-Greece, Denmark-Finland. The size of the economy is not a good candidate either (cf. France - FRG, Denmark-Switzerland). Similarly, the idea that higher average growth rates are always accompanied by greater instability can also be jettisoned. In all the three European sub-regions, roughly identical average growth rates were concomitant with widely different σ-s.[33]

[33] It is true, however, that there is for the sample a healthy correlation between average growth rates and the measured variation of growth rates (r = 0.68). I am indebted to Mr. Gy. Molnár (Hungarian Academy of Sciences) for drawing my attention to this relationship.

TABLE 3.12 East-west comparison: GINV and GFCF time series, 1960-1989

(Calculated from time series in annual percentage change form)

Country/ Region a/	Average growth rate rate	Coefficient of variation b/
France	4.1	105.8
FRG	2.4	198.2
Italy	3.0	175.9
U.K.	3.4	154.7
Total-4	3.1	110.9
Austria	3.7	126.9
Belgium	3.2	178.6
Denmark	2.6	315.6
Finland	3.6	155.5
Ireland	5.1	158.9
Netherlands	3.0	186.2
Norway	3.6	243.5
Sweden	3.0	129.5
Switzerland	3.6	160.1
Total-9	3.3	105.5
Western Europe	3.2	105.7
	5.2	
Canada	5.2	94.1
Japan	8.2	90.0
US c/	3.5	179.3
Greece	3.7	233.6
Portugal	4.5	179.2
Spain	6.0	121.5
Turkey	5.7	140.1
Southern Europe	5.5	106.5
Bulgaria	6.7	96.2
CSSR	3.7	130.9
GDR	4.4	97.9
Hungary	4.0	171.1
Poland	4.8	186.8
Romania	7.1	84.8
EE6	5.1	47.1
Yugoslavia	2.5	277.7
USSR	5.4	47.1

Notes: a/ Weighted averages
b/ (Standard deviation/mean)*100
c/ Private sector investments only

Source: Table SA.1,SA.5.

Investment Ratio: High or Low? Calibrating the optimum size of the investment effort as a percentage of NMP has always been one of the most important policy decisions of socialist planners. This is a normative question and thus goes beyond the scope of this book. Nevertheless, this issue is worth considering, because behind the normative question there is always a descriptive one: is the investment ratio (IR) higher or lower in the socialist countries than in Western market economies? The academic discussion on cycles was also confronted with this problem in modelling planners' behaviour.

Most authors assume, or simply state without further examination, that the investment ratio (investment relative to GDP or NMP) is higher in socialist than in market oriented economies. At a theoretical level, this is explained by the insatiable investment hunger of the system, while as empirical evidence the slow growth in consumption can be mentioned.

It is well-known that intra-system comparisons in this respect have very serious limitations. According to conventional explanations, the difficulties stem from price distortions, which in turn are the results of planners' interference in price formation. In reality, however, there is an additional and equally important problem: system-specific differences in sectoral productivity levels. In particular, relative productivity levels in the production of consumer and investment goods can be very different in countries with different economic systems and this, as well as government intervention, can produce differences in relative price levels.[34]

Consider the following example. Countries A and B have two types of output: cows, which are consumed, and one cow-shed which constitutes the annual investment effort. Annual output in both countries is 10 cows and 1 cow-shed. In A, the amount of labour required to build 1 cow-shed is equal to the labour requirement of raising 2 cows. In B, however, labour productivity in construction is lower and the prevailing labour need for 1 cow-shed is 3 cows.

The statistician wishing to measure IR in both countries will have to realize that there are two answers to his question. In volume terms, the ratio is 10 cows to 1 cow-shed in both countries - i.e. there is no difference. In value terms, however, country B has a higher IR than country A. Because of the lower level of labour productivity in construction work, in country B a bigger share of annual output has to directed to investment than in country A. In country B, the IR will amount to 23.1 per cent (3/(10+3)), while A can get along with the lower ratio of 16.7 per cent (2/(10+2)).

Broadening the perspective, what can be said about relative productivity levels in the socialist countries? In intra-system comparisons the conventional wisdom would assert that productivity in the socialist countries is relatively lower in the investment sphere than in the production of consumer goods. If this is true, this factor alone can justify the assumption of higher IRs.

What can be said in support of this assumption? Investment goods are typically customer-designed, individual products. It is more difficult to implement effective control by bureaucratic means over this type of production as compared to the manufacture of standard consumer items. The lack of market discipline leads to disproportionate and unjustified cost rises in the investment sphere. By contrast, in the market economies, there is no such difference; cost discipline depends on the strength of market forces and not on the skill of plan bureaucrats. Since the data provided by national statistics permit cross-country comparison only in value terms, the impact of differences in price relatives on the one hand, and productivity differences on the other, become inseparably intermingled.

[34] In the following paragraphs I draw heavily on the unpublished manuscript of Drechsler (1983). The numerical example which follows is also his.

In the first instance, the whole issue might appear to the reader as an irrelevant technical detail of interest only to a few specialist statisticians. However, this impression is mistaken. In fact one of the most important and most scholarly discussions in Soviet academic life was directly related to the above.[35] And, of course, the issues raised in this debate were of great relevance to any other socialist country.

According to the first school, Soviet official statistics gave a wrong impression about the relative size of the investment effort. Due the lack of discipline in this area, investments registered at comparable (constant) prices had a much smaller volume content than the deflated value figures suggested. Hence, as argued by such prominent authors as Valtukh, Krasovskii, Khanin and Faltsman, the "true" IR was much lower than the official data (about 25 %) indicated.

The other school, represented by Selyunin and Shmelev, insisted on the contrary. Their argument was based solely on the price distortion factor. For them, the problem was the different valuation applied to investment goods on the one hand and to consumer goods on the other. In the first case, as these authors rightly pointed out, data were calculated at factor cost, while in the second, the state's net revenues - realized through turnover taxes levied on consumer goods - also become part of the measured magnitudes. For this reason, the authors concluded that a consequent evaluation in both sectors would result in a much higher rate of accumulation - not 25 % but perhaps as high as 40 %.

It is very interesting to note, although it might be sheer coincidence, that CIA figures give support to the second view. In the latest CIA assessment (1989, p. 60) of the proportions of Soviet GNP for 1988, the ratio of gross investment to GNP falls close to 33 %. This can be (roughly) approximated as a 40 % IR calculated as a percentage of NMP.

For the moment, there is no way to decide this debate. True volume-type comparisons can be made only in the framework of a complete re-pricing exercise, where the peculiarities of various the countries' price systems are eliminated. These comparisons have been made but the Soviet Union has never been a party to an exercise of this kind, or if it was, the results were never published. Several international organizations participated in the so-called International Comparisons Project (ICP) conducted under the auspices of the United Nations, which covered a large number of Western and a few Eastern countries for the purpose of such volume-type comparisons. In the past, similar investigations have also been carried out by the CMEA secretariat but the results of this work were never published in detail.[36]

A condensed summary, based on the several phases of the ICP project, is given in table 3.12. Within the ICP, value data are expressed in terms of a common, fictitious currency (the international dollar), thereby removing distortions of national price systems. All participating eastern countries were included in the sample but, on the western side, only economies with roughly similar development levels were retained.

The ICP method has drawbacks as well as advantages. First of all, it is a very labour intensive, time consuming and hence costly exercise. It cannot be repeated more than once in five years. The list of participating countries constantly changed. The figures presented in table 3.13 are thus somewhat accidental in the sense that a selection of other years or other western countries might have yielded slightly different results.

[35] For a detailed account of this debate, see Nove (1989).

[36] I am grateful to Mr. Gy. Szilágyi (UN/ECE) for this information.

TABLE 3.13 East-West comparison: Investment ratios in countries with similar development levels, 1970, 1975, 1980, 1985

	1970		1975		1980		1985	
	National statistics	ICP results	National statistics	ICP results	National statistics	ICP results	National statistics	ICP results
	GINV or GFCF as a percentage of GDP (At constant prices)							
Hungary	29.6	27.1	28.1	32.8	28.0	27.8	23.8	20.1
Poland	...	...	...	37.1	19.3	29.7	21.1	23.8
Romania	...	...	...	34.4	...	...	...	...
Yugoslavia	...	...	...	28.8	...	34.0	...	16.1
Italy	29.5	25.4	...	...	...	...	...	...
Ireland	...	...	23.5	21.7	...	...	23.4	22.5
Mexico	...	...	21.7	24.6	...	...	...	...
Greece	...	...	...	...	19.6	26.0	16.3	17.4
Portugal	...	...	...	...	26.2	18.2	19.9	15.8
Uruguay	...	...	11.2	8.3	17.8	20.9	...	...
Argentina	...	...	...	...	22.1	28.8	...	...
Chile	...	...	...	...	17.6	25.1	...	...
Turkey	...	...	...	...	...	...	19.9	18.0

Source: Own calculations, based on Kravis et alia (1975) tables 14.4 and 14.5;Kravis et alia (1982) tables 6.4 and 6.5; UN-Commissions of... (1987) tables 6-8.; UN (1986) pp. 18-19, 239-240, 1023-1024, 1650-1651. OECD (1987) and unpublished ICP documents.

In broad terms, table 3.13 corroborates the conventional wisdom. For 1970 and 1975 the ICP showed that IRs were higher in the socialist countries than in those Western market economies at about the same development level. The evidence is less robust for such a statement for the years 1980 and 1985. In the last year of comparison Ireland had a higher IR than Hungary, the figure for Turkey surpasses that of Yugoslavia, etc.

3.4 Synchronization of Investment Fluctuations

There are a number of good *a priori* reasons to assume that individual country cycles - if they exist at all - are independent of each other, at least with regard to their length and amplitudes.

(i) Despite political homogeneity, there were significant differences among socialist countries as far as their levels and pace of development were concerned. Consequently, they must have somewhat different investment absorption capacities. It is logical to assume that, if the gestation period of investment projects is an important explanatory variable in the cycle model, the timing and length of the cycle should differ from country to country.

(ii) As shown in Chapter 2, some authors claim that the artificial five-year planning process is in itself sufficient to explain the cyclical pattern of investments. Since inter-country harmonization of FYPs and the strict adherence to the policies outlined in them was more an exception than a rule, this would imply a de-harmonization of the cycles.

(iii) The importance of the primary sectors (agriculture, mining), where output and export revenues are strongly influenced by exogenous factors, is again different from country to country. Though it is true that changes in weather may influence agricultural output similarly in neighbouring countries, the synchronization effect stemming from this is probably small. The same may hold for the influence of world market fluctuations and, *a fortiori*, for the combined effects of the two.

However, the idea of regional synchronization has been present from the outset in the academic literature on socialist investment cycles. Allusions to such effects are to be found in Goldmann (1964), Portes (1969) and Bajt (1971). Wiles (1982) makes this point very strongly, although for him the synchronizing force is clearly political: the direction of the wind in Moscow. Bauer (1981, pp. 29-30, 85) and Boot (1984), however, expressed doubts concerning the overall importance of this factor.

The first systematic work known by the author to have focused on the synchronization problem is a 1966 UN/ECE study.[37] The conclusion was favourable to what the study called the "Goldmann hypothesis". This forced the ECE experts to abandon their earlier contention (see Section 2.4) that investment fluctuations resulted from planning errors.

> Bearing the shortcomings of investment planning in mind, it would generally seem that a considerable part of the fluctuations observed in the past has been primarily policy determined. This same factor accounts to a very large extent for the concordance of major fluctuations in individual countries. Allowing for the effect of specific factors, the similarity of planning strategies, the coordination of medium-term economic plans and economic foreign policies, and the more or less parallel phasing of investment programmes seem indeed to provide the main explanation for the simultaneity in practically all the eastern European countries of the high pressure phases of 1950-1951

[37] This was published in UN BUL (1966, pp. 31-64). I am grateful to Mr. R. Nötel, the author of this paper, for directing my attention to it.

and 1958-1959, as well as the consequent relaxation periods of 1953-1954 and around 1963. (UN ESE 1966, p. 34)

More recently, the subject has aroused interest in academic circles once again. An ECE study (UN ESE 1985, pp. 138-143) as well as the writings of Mihályi (1987, 1988b) and Ickes (1986a, 1990) shed some light on the weight of factors supporting the concordance of investment fluctuations among the socialist countries.

First and foremost, bilateral trade with the Soviet Union is of crucial importance for EE6. Past experience showed that large shifts in Soviet behaviour tended to affect them in a rather similar manner. It happened very rarely that Soviet policy decisions were calibrated on a case-by-case basis, favouring or penalizing any particular country. (The treatment of Yugoslavia was different after the Tito-Stalin break in 1948. This affair had long-term consequences, in the sense that the ties between Yugoslavia and the USSR never became really close again.) The behaviour of Soviet exports to the east, calculated in annual percentage change form, perfectly reflected these developments. Pair-wise correlations (R^2) for the period between the performance of Soviet export to the region as a whole (EE8) on the one hand and to the countries concerned on the other, give the following results: Bulgaria (0.50), CSSR (0.88), GDR (0.76), Hungary (0.56), Poland (0.59), Romania (0.21), Yugoslavia (-0.03), Albania (0.05).[38]

To a lesser degree, the same could be said regarding the impact of East-West trade relations. Since the first oil shock of 1973, this link has been growing in importance. International price developments and the fluctuation of West European import demand are exogenously determined factors for the EE6, and it is not surprising that the macro-economic data, to some degree, reflect a synchronization effect.

The third factor worth noting is that at an earlier stage of development, the Soviet Union played a crucial direct role in the investment process of several less developed socialist countries. During the first FYP (1953-57) of China, for instance, total imports from the Soviet Union accounted for 49 % of total domestic construction investment (Dernberger, 1968, p. 740). In Mongolia, investments in the 1961-65 quinquennium were financed up to 47.1 % from credit, 90 % of which came from the Soviet Union. The proportions for 1966-70 and 1971-75 were 50.3 and 49.8 respectively (Sanders 1987, p. 87). The first FYP in Viet Nam, after unification with the South (1976-1980), reckoned with similarly high foreign participation. It was assumed that out of Dong 35 bn of investments 15 bn (43 %) would come in the form of foreign aid (Will G. 1987, p. 76).

Table 3.14 confirms some parallelism in the change of GINV time series up to the present. In fact, both planned and actual figures for the period 1986-1990 show once again that when investment optimism appears, it tends to prevail throughout the region. After the first five-year planning quinquennium (1951-1955), the next four periods saw rises of 40-80 per cent (or even higher) in GINV, relative to the cumulated volume of investment achieved in the previous period. This process seemed to be an unbreakable rule until the mid-1970s. Then every country - with the exception of Bulgaria and Romania - succumbed to slower growth rates. In the EE6 region as a whole, the growth rate diminished to 40 % and in the Soviet Union it fell below 30 %.

The loss of momentum in 1981-1985 was of historical importance. A long period of recession had started. In EE6, the total volume of investment was smaller than during the

[38] The calculations were performed on the basis of Soviet foreign trade data expressed in current transferable rouble terms and covered the period 1951-1989.

previous five years and there was a clear deceleration in the Soviet economy, too. The plans for 1986-1990 reflected a bold but vain attempt to reverse this process. According to the preliminary 1989 and 1990 data, performance remained behind plan targets in every east European country but the GDR.

3.14 GINV growth rates in five-year periods, 1951-1990

(Cumulative percentage change)

	1956-60	1961-65	1966-70	1971-75	1976-80	1981-85	1986-90 Plans	1986-90 Actual
Bulgaria	72.5	84.0	83.3	43.1	39.4	24.9	32--40	18.0
Czechoslovakia	59.1	31.5	32.2	44.1	32.7	-2.1	10--12	9.2
GDR	98.8	40.3	50.0	38.3	27.2	-0.3	8--10	13.4
Hungary	12.7	59.1	53.3	46.8	30.9	-9.7	3--5	-
Poland	47.8	46.7	47.3	89.0	33.6	-32.1	24.0	22.9
Romania	61.8	98.4	67.0	65.9	67.4	6.6	19.5	-4.0
EE6 (weighted)	59.5	46.8	63.3	...(a)	39.5	-6.6	20.5	9.4
USSR	90.4	44.4	42.4	41.2	27.7	17.5	23.6	26.3
EE7 (weighted)	83.8	45.3	42.7	...(a)	31.3	9.7	22.8	21.7

Notes: Weights for regional aggregation: 1950-1965 (1965), 1970-date (1975)
a/ Not available due to changes in weights.

Source: Table SA.1

Table 3.5, presented earlier, can also be of use in explaining the process of region-wide synchronization. The main message of that table was that in each of the three periods there was at least one crisis-ridden country. In most cases, this led to an absolute fall in production levels:

I. period
- Yugoslavia: 1952, 1956
- Hungary: 1952, 1954, 1956
- Romania: 1956

II. period
- Czechoslovakia: 1963

III. period
- Poland: 1979-1982
- Yugoslavia: 1983, 1987-1989
- Hungary: 1979, 1985, 1988-1989
- Bulgaria: 1989
- Romania: 1989

As Wiles (1982) noted, these were "important and dignified disasters" but they were provoked by a number of reasons, among which system-specific economic, political and totally exogenous random factors all played a role.

The problem of recurring harvest failures in Yugoslavia, which were a permanent feature of the 1950s, has already been discussed above. The 1956 harvest in Romania was nearly catastrophic. Crop output fell by more than 25 % and livestock production remained 6 % below the previous year's level. The situation was further aggravated by a Soviet decision to cut export deliveries by more than 20 % in a single year. (Note that this happened when the Soviet Union was Romania's main trading partner.)

The common element in these crises is the "cliff's edge" effect. As soon as the first serious signs of imbalance surfaced, the Centre did not hesitate to react by curtailing domestic investment expenditures. In Czechoslovakia and Hungary, these measures always sufficed, in the sense that debt servicing and payment capacities were maintained and a disintegration of production processes was avoided; the engines of economic growth could have been reactivated after a temporary halt. At the end of the 1970s, Poland failed in this respect. If left alone, Yugoslavia would probably have suffered the same fate but the country was saved on two occasions in the 1950s by the generosity of foreign creditors.

The other common element in these crises was the learning effect. Although it would be difficult to document conclusively, some evidence suggests that a crisis in one country served as a signal to the leadership of "fraternal" neighbouring countries. Clearly, the 1956 economic crisis and uprising in Hungary prompted the leaders of other countries to improve the living standards of their own population. The fiasco of the Gierek leadership in 1981 was an equally important sign to the leaders of other countries.

This said, the salient parallel movements in the data displayed in tables 3.5 and 3.14 still cannot be explained to a sufficient extent. Closer inspection of the figures suggests that the above-mentioned short-term adjustment measures do not fully explain long term comovements.

TABLE 3.15 Correlation coefficients of IR time series, 1950-1989

		1950-1962	1963-1979	1980-1989	1950-1989
Bulgaria		0.94*	0.72*	-0.22	0.92*
CSSR		0.95*	0.92*	0.96*	0.96*
GDR	relative to	0.86*	0.93*	0,95*	0.96*
Hungary	the unweighted	0.47	0.94*	0,96*	0.90*
Poland	average of	0.91*	0.89*	0.26	0.89*
Romania	EE6	0.92*	0.91*	0,85*	0.96*
USSR		0.73*	0.65*	-0.47	0.77*
Yugoslavia		0.70*	0.11	0.94*	0.32

Notes: IR = GINV/NMP
* denotes significance at the 1 % level.

Source: Table SA.4

A simple calculation of IRs (table SA.4) already reveals a noteworthy characteristic. Until 1975 they tended to rise in all the countries concerned. Since that year, however, IRs stagnated or declined. It is interesting to consider the results of a calculation in which the investment ratios in a given country were compared to that calculated from the non-weighted average ratios of the remaining countries (table 3.15).[39]

As we know, IRs in the first period rose quite dramatically in EE8 and this explains the very high levels of correlation (r). Hungary was, quite plausibly, an outlier since its IR had fallen between 1953 and 1958. Economic policy-making in Yugoslavia went its own way, as reflected in its relatively low correlation coefficients. In this particular case, however, there was only a differentiation in timing. The Yugoslav planners had launched their unscrupulous investment drive somewhat earlier than in the other countries. Thus, the IR reached 30 % around 1950. After that there was simply no more room for further rises.

In the second period, covering the 1960s and 1970s, the synchronization of IRs gathered new momentum. By this time Yugoslavia was following a totally different growth path. This is reflected, among other things, in the almost continuous reduction of IRs between 1962 and 1974. In the third and final period, only Bulgarian, Soviet and Polish investment policies departed from the common path. In the first two countries, the tendency towards a further increase in IRs survived into the 1980s. The explanation of the Polish case is different again. Here the rising ratio merely reflected the temporary recovery of the Polish economy between 1982 and 1988.

[39] For the sake of simplicity, an attempt was made to retain the periodization of table 3.5. This was not entirely possible, however, as regional aggregates cannot be meaningfully calculated with shifting terminal years. For this reason, the break years chosen - 1962 and 1979 - are somewhat arbitrary.

4. COMMON PATTERNS AND PARTICULARITIES - A HISTORICAL ANALYSIS

4.1 THE METHOD

The next step is to attempt a cross-country analysis of investment waves using the exogenous model approach. Three objectives are laid down. The first is to present data in a systematic manner, drawn from computerized data bases, for a small sample of the "cycles" experienced by six East European countries (EE6). This approach provides us with an approximate measuring instrument to assess quantitatively the changes in the relevant macro-economic variables in country "A" and to compare them with those in the other five countries. The second is to perform a rough consistency check on these widely used data. It is assumed that certain macro-variables should meet certain coherency criteria in a national accounting sense. For example, growing investments *plus* growing consumption requires a rise in the domestic utilization of national income (NMPUT). The third objective is to draw attention to common behavioural patterns during various phases of the fluctuation, and also to significant time and country-specific differences among them.

It is assumed that GINV is treated as an exogenous control variable in the hands of the planners. The aim here is to focus on the immediate short-term consequences of its fluctuations. The results generally confirm the findings of the endogenous models but only partially. Some cycle-relevant variables (e.g., construction, machinery imports) do exhibit a behavioural pattern, as this theory suggests, but in other cases (e.g., trade balance, allocation of NMP) surprisingly little evidence has been found for any systematic behaviour. More importantly, it will be shown that the fluctuations of some important segments of the economy are unrelated to the investment climate - in other words, there is no multiplier effect.

Apart from a few exceptions forced upon us by data constraints, the analysis was conducted in terms of annual growth rates (expressed in percentage form) at constant prices. At one point, however, I deliberately deviated from this approach - namely, when trade balances were examined. Here current price data only were used to illustrate better the difficulties that the countries' economic decision makers actually faced.

For each country one and only one period was chosen. In the selection, the following criteria were applied.

(i) The period must consist of two or three years of marked acceleration of GINV, preceded and followed by one or two years of conspicuously restrained or negative investment growth.

(ii) Years when the country in question was hit by a sizeable adverse external shock or by a severe domestic political crisis were excluded from the investigation. For this reason, and because of data availability constraints, the first 15 years of socialist development (1945-1960) were not analyzed. The years after 1973, when dramatic changes in relative world market prices disadvantageously affected five countries out of six, were represented in our sample by Poland, the only country of the region to benefit from changes in the terms of trade. For the other five economies, the periods were chosen from the normal, uneventful times between 1960-1973.[1]

(iii) Out of ten clearly discernible GINV waves those six which had the highest peaks were selected. Thus four cases were omitted: two in Hungary (1965-1967-1968, 1968-1970-1972), one in Bulgaria (1961-1963-1965) and one in Poland (1963-1967-1970). The years in brackets

[1] As already noted, the economic policies of the east European countries were, until the late 1950s, to a great extent, subordinated to capricious changes in the policy stance of the Soviet Union. Therefore,

indicate the timing in a trough-peak-trough scheme. For the sake of precision, it should be noted that the 1961-1963-1965 wave in Hungary had a slightly lower peak than the second one omitted. In many respects these two periods were equally regular, closely resembling a bell-shape curve. Thus the choice here was somewhat arbitrary. On the other hand, the year 1968 coincided with the start of the New Economic Mechanism and this fact in itself spoke in favour of the earlier period selected.

For the purposes of this exercise, 32 different macro variables were chosen in order to depict the consequences of GINV fluctuations throughout the entire economy. Some of these variables served only for control purposes (e.g., mirror statistics of partner countries in foreign trade), while others proved irrelevant in the course of the investigation. All these figures were deliberately retained in tables 4.1-4.5 and 4.7 for the sake of completeness but their message has often not been analyzed in the text.

Two important areas remain in the shadows. First, restrictive policy measures were generally explained and defended at the time of their introduction as a necessary response to changes in the debt situation, or in the balance-of-payments. Secondly, it is known from anecdotal evidence that military considerations were often the decisive motive behind an investment upswing. Unfortunately, none of these countries have published adequate debt or balance-of-payment figures for the years prior to 1970 and even less is known about defence policy decisions.

Given the short-term nature of the periods selected, econometric measurement methods were not applied in the analysis. Thus - at least at this stage of research - we had to be satisfied with qualitative statements concerning the strength of the association between changes in cycle-relevant variables.

4.2 CONSTRUCTION OUTPUT

Given the large share of construction work involved in the investment process - ranging between 42 per cent (GDR) and 64 per cent (Czechoslovakia) in the period under review - it seems appropriate to start our investigation in this area. In table 4.1 three variables are displayed: employment in, and net output of the construction sector, as well as gross output of the construction materials-producing branch of industry. It can be observed that the upswing in investments was in general strongly associated with a noticeable rise in construction work variables, Hungary and Poland being the exceptions. Employment showed a vigorous adjustment to growing demand for construction work almost everywhere. As for employment growth, the picture was similar in Poland but the developments in Hungary were unique: after a short lived surge in 1962, employment appears to have really started to expand only when the investment boom was already over.

After a closer inspection of the complete employment time series (EMPC), however, it cannot be excluded that the observer is misled by the apparent impact of a partially implemented change in statistical classification. The difficulties start with the fact that Hungary reports employment data reflecting the situation on 1 January, while other east European countries give annual averages, or estimated mid-year figures. Thus, for the sake of comparability the original Hungarian data had to be transformed. The averaging procedure squeezed the size of the change from 13.1 to 6.5 per cent. Nevertheless, this is still a surprisingly high figure.

In all six countries but Hungary, the behaviour of net output of the construction sector paralleled changes in GINV. (This seems to confirm our doubts concerning the reliability of the 1965 EMPC figure for Hungary.) Also, rising investments were supported by a dynamic expansion of output by the construction materials branch nearly everywhere: here, the notable exception was Poland - where the growth rates of the output variable (CONSTMAT) remained practically unchanged despite the trebling of reported GINV rates. The picture was similar but not so marked in the German Democratic Republic: at the peak of the investment boom, when GINV grew by almost 16 per cent, building materials output grew by a very modest 2 per cent - down from the 6 per cent annual rate registered in the previous year. Moreover no substantial turnround occurred until 1970, by which time, however, the GINV rate had halved.

TABLE 4.1 GINV and the development of the construction sector, 1961-1979

(Annual percentage change)

		GINV	EMPC	CONST(N)	CONSTMAT
Hungary					
	1961	-2.7	-0.2	2.2	5.8
	1962	10.3	3.4	2.3	2.4
	1963	13.7	3.3	3.6	2.1
	1964	3.6	0.1	4.2	5.1
	1965	1.5	6.2	0.7	4.2
CSSR					
	1963	-11.2	-2.7	-15.6	-8.7
	1964	11.1	0.7	12.3	7.1
	1965	7.5	2.4	13.0	9.0
	1966	9.5	3.9	19.0	7.9
	1967	3.0	3.0	7.3	8.2
Bulgaria					
	1965	7.4	3.3	2.8	11.0
	1966	19.6	6.5	16.1	17.0
	1967	23.6	5.3	16.7	13.0
	1968	9.0	4.6	14.4	10.0
	1969	1.0	-2.5	5.3	4.0
Romania					
	1965	9.0	2.3	5.2	14.0
	1966	9.9	7.0	8.0	9.0
	1967	16.6	11.1	14.6	14.0
	1968	11.7	4.2	13.5	17.0
	1969	6.6	2.1	7.3	12.0
GDR					
	1966	6.5	0.5	7.3	5.0
	1967	8.9	1.0	5.8	4.0
	1968	10.9	8.1	11.4	6.0
	1969	15.5	5.7	7.6	2.0
	1970	6.8	3.3	4.9	13.0
	1971	1.7	1.7	4.7	6.0
Poland					
	1970	4.0	0.4	3.3	6.0
	1971	7.4	4.4	5.0	6.7
	1972	23.0	6.5	21.4	8.6
	1973	25.4	10.2	16.3	8.0
	1974	22.3	7.5	13.7	8.6
	1975	10.7	1.0	11.0	8.7
	1976	1.0	-1.2	2.5	5.8
	1977	3.1	-0.3	1.0	4.1
	1978	2.1	0.3	-0.3	2.1
	1979	-7.9	-1.6	-6.2	-4.6

GINV	Gross investments
EMPC	Employment in the construction sector
CONST(N)	Net output of the construction sector
CONSTMAT	Gross output of the construction material producing branch of industry

Source: ECE/DEAP Common Data Base; UN Commodity trade data (COMTRADE); Statistisches Bundesamt, Warenverkehr mit der DDR und Berlin (Ost), Reihe 6, Wiesbaden

4.3 Industrial output

The performance of industry can also be assumed *a priori* to be closely linked with the investment cycle. Needless to say, no simple correspondence in growth rates was expected. Since the volume of gross industrial output (INDT) is numerically about four to five times larger than that of GINV, a noticeable but not necessarily spectacular growth in INDT can, in principle, easily be compatible with a very buoyant rise in GINV (accelerator effect). In fact, an unquestionably close relationship between the two was found only for Czechoslovakia and Poland (table 4.2). In Bulgaria, Hungary and Romania, industrial output showed a clear decelerating tendency throughout the periods under review, irrespective of what happened in the investment domain. In the German Democratic Republic, output growth rates were high - but they showed no sign of acceleration as the investment boom was asserting itself. In fact, the same high but stable rates (around 6-7 per cent) were reported for industrial production in all years of the 1964-1976 period, while the growth rates of investment continued to fluctuate in the later years (1972-1974: 4.3 %, 8.5 %, 5.5 %).

Table 4.2 offers some information also about the performance of the so-called Group "A" sub-sector of industry (output devoted to producing investment and intermediate goods) - an indicator closely watched in many east European countries and duly reported by the CMEA statistical sources. The findings about the behaviour of total industrial production, summarized in the previous paragraph, hold for this variable, too.

Regarding the industrial export performance, it is generally believed that it behaves asymmetrically to GINV. Without further qualifications, however, this proposition seems to lack empirical grounding. In Czechoslovakia, the GDR and in Hungary, it was found that a surge in GINV provoked a slowdown in the expansion of socialist machinery exports and, conversely, weakening domestic investment demand allowed (or required) a strengthening of this type of exports. But no solid evidence with respect to any systematic behaviour of non-socialist machinery exports was found.

TABLE 4.2 GINV and the development of industrial output, 1961-1979

(Annual percentage change)

		GINV	INDT	IND(A)	XSOC	XSOCMACH	XNSOC	XNSMACH
Hungary								
	1961	-2.7	8.3	12.3	21.8	18.5	9.6	3.0
	1962	10.3	7.0	11.0	5.8	3.4	10.4	48.2
	1963	13.7	6.7	5.9	4.2	0.1	27.6	25.3
	1964	3.6	7.1	9.3	13.0	24.3	5.0	34.3
	1965	1.5	4.0	5.1	11.4	9.1	24.0	17.1
CSSR								
	1963	-11.2	-0.6	-1.1	12.4	14.9	1.6	-7.3
	1964	11.1	4.1	5.1	3.1	2.5	20.1	4.9
	1965	7.5	7.9	9.2	2.9	5.8	9.4	14.9
	1966	9.5	7.4	8.2	0.1	1.0	19.4	30.9
	1967	3.0	7.1	7.5	7.8	6.0	1.0	-10.7
Bulgaria								
	1965	7.4	14.7	16.8	17.7	39.7	15.0	30.9
	1966	19.6	12.2	12.8	9.2	15.0	28.5	4.8
	1967	23.6	13.3	14.1	13.4	17.5	11.3	39.1
	1968	9.0	10.1	10.6	11.6	17.4	12.2	56.1
	1969	1.0	9.4	9.9	9.6	15.5	5.5	21.2
Romania								
	1965	9.0	13.1	13.7	9.8	3.7	13.0	18.4
	1966	9.9	11.4	12.4	-5.4	2.8	39.6	41.7
	1967	16.6	13.6	14.3	12.6	12.1	29.8	39.0
	1968	11.7	11.7	14.1	7.3	11.7	-1.5	15.2
	1969	6.6	10.6	10.3	17.3	12.2	11.7	24.7
GDR								
	1966	6.5	6.5	6.2	6.2	2.3	9.1	11.0
	1967	8.9	6.8	7.2	11.0	13.3	4.8	7.2
	1968	10.9	5.9	6.7	10.7	12.4	1.8	5.1
	1969	15.5	6.9	8.7	3.7	4.6	30.3	29.8
	1970	6.8	6.7	7.7	9.9	7.2	-0.1	11.3
	1971	1.7	5.7	6.4	12.4	11.4	2.4	13.4
Poland								
	1970	4.0	8.1	9.0	9.0	15.7	0.0	40.6
	1971	7.4	7.9	8.3	10.1	2.6	9.1	26.2
	1972	23.0	10.7	10.6	13.7	13.0	12.6	18.5
	1973	25.4	11.2	11.6	12.4	16.9	14.6	9.3
	1974	22.3	11.4	12.0	14.0	19.2	18.4	26.3
	1975	10.7	10.9	10.7	10.8	13.2	5.5	39.7
	1976	1.0	9.3	9.7	-1.1	-0.5	7.8	9.6
	1977	3.1	6.9	6.4	10.0	12.1	5.6	10.4
	1978	2.1	4.9	4.4	5.6	5.9	1.6	7.0
	1979	-7.9	2.7	2.6	8.8	16.6	2.2	0.3

GINV	Gross investments
INDT	Gross industrial output
IND(A)	Output of group "A" in industry (Hungary: Heavy industry excluding mining)
XSOC , XNSOC	Socialist (non-socialist) non-agricultural export
XSOCMACH	Machinery exports to socialist countries.
XNSOCMACH	Machinery exports to non-socialist countries

Source: See table 4.1

4.4 Imports

Except for the two less developed economies of the region (Bulgaria and Romania) the investment wave is positively associated with fluctuations in machinery imports.[2] This finding (table 4.3) seems to hold for purchases in socialist and non-socialist countries alike. Mirror data - taken from OECD sources - confirm this relationship at least as far as imports from the West are concerned.

It is interesting to note, however, that for three countries (Czechoslovakia, GDR and Hungary) machinery imports from non-socialist countries continued to show an acceleration one or two years after the peak of the GINV growth rate. This is all the more surprising since it is generally believed that long lead times between orders and actual deliveries are typical of intra-CMEA trade but not of imports originating in the OECD countries. This phenomenon could be explained by the fact that Western machinery tends to be installed at the end-phase of investment projects. Thus, in times of slowing overall investment growth, when efforts are concentrated on the completion of projects, western machinery imports continue to expand further for one or two years. In Bulgaria, the positive association of machinery imports with investments can be established only for imports originating in the socialist countries. In this case, but also in Romania, imports of Western machinery were allowed to jump only in a single year in the upward phase of the period (1966 for Bulgaria, 1967 for Romania). This was followed by an immediate downturn.

[2] The long term specificities of these imports were described in great detail in a recent UN study (See: "Eastern imports of machinery and equipment, 1960-1985", UN BULL 1986).

TABLE 4.3 GINV and the import of machinery, 1961-1979

(Annual percentage change)

		GINV	SOCMACH	NSOCMACH	OECDMACH
Hungary					
	1961	-2.7	25.7	16.7	...
	1962	10.3	20.5	2.3	...
	1963	13.7	12.8	24.1	26.4
	1964	3.6	-2.6	49.5	26.3
	1965	1.5	-2.2	7.7	-3.7
CSSR					
	1963	-11.2	-0.1	6.1	-11.5
	1964	11.1	26.3	20.3	13.5
	1965	7.5	14.2	33.4	26.4
	1966	9.5	3.6	55.7	49.0
	1967	3.0	-6.5	-15.1	-9.4
Bulgaria					
	1965	7.4	16.6	29.5	...
	1966	19.6	20.0	117.2	97.4
	1967	23.6	10.2	-10.1	-6.6
	1968	9.0	9.1	-28.6	-36.0
	1969	1.0	-1.4	-20.3	-7.7
Romania					
	1965	9.0	-17.1	20.4	24.5
	1966	9.9	14.7	18.8	25.2
	1967	16.6	4.2	41.4	100.3
	1968	11.7	12.6	-7.0	-5.5
	1969	6.6	5.2	9.6	-10.3
GDR					
	1966	6.5	19.7	32.9	58.5
	1967	8.9	26.1	6.7	7.7
	1968	10.9	29.4	-4.9	-18.4
	1969	15.5	31.0	40.8	34.0
	1970	6.8	5.2	58.1	29.5
	1971	1.7	4.5	1.5	-1.9
Poland					
	1970	4.0	25.6	-14.0	-20.0
	1971	7.4	-3.6	16.8	6.1
	1972	23.0	17.3	88.0	66.8
	1973	25.4	26.3	52.4	52.1
	1974	22.3	12.9	21.7	24.3
	1975	10.7	-4.3	18.7	12.5
	1976	1.0	8.5	-3.3	-5.1
	1977	3.1	7.1	-13.7	-20.0
	1978	2.1	6.8	-9.9	-15.2
	1979	-7.9	4.9	-20.6	-20.3

GINV Gross investments
SOCMACH Machinery import from socialist countries
NSOCMACH Machinery import from non-socialist countries
OECDMACH Machinery import from OECD countries
(SITC 7 at 1975 constant US $ prices)
Hungary, CSSR at current US $ prices.

Source: See table 4.1

4.5 Standard of Living

It is often argued that large increases in investment are usually coupled with a slow-down in consumption growth, while a moderation of investment growth allows more resources to be allocated for the purpose of improving the supply of material goods to the population (see e.g., Bajt (1971)). Table 4.4 displays some figures to test this hypothesis. As far as the most aggregate variable - personal consumption of material goods - is concerned, it appears that such a relationship simply does not exist. In fact the evidence points in the opposite direction. Increasing investment goes hand in hand with rising private consumption. Thus the textbook example of a trade-off (more investment *or* more consumption) cannot be demonstrated. On the contrary, as soon as the expansion of GINV is curtailed, consumption growth rates also start to weaken.

The behaviour of the Group "B" sub-sector of industry (consumer goods) offers no conclusive evidence in either direction. In fact, to some extent it seems to contradict the findings related to changes in consumption. In the developed economies - Czechoslovakia, the GDR and Hungary - changes in output growth of the consumer goods-producing industries were clearly asymmetrical with respect to the fluctuations in GINV, as the text book example would suggest. The opposite was true for Poland. In Bulgaria, the slow-down of output growth seems to be completely independent of GINV, while in Romania, the figures oscillate so widely that no clear relationship can be asserted.

As is well known, imports of consumer goods never amounted to significant volumes. Typically, the annual machinery import was 5-10 times higher than the volume of imported consumer goods in the periods under investigation. Thus it is no wonder that fluctuations in the growth rates of these types of imports are rather independent of changes in GINV.[3] A more uniform picture emerges if the fluctuation in housing construction is analyzed: here a rather strict asymmetrical pattern seems to prevail in all countries apart from Poland.

[3] Outside of this group of countries, in the Soviet Union, there was always a strong trade-off between imports of food and imports of Western machinery.

TABLE 4.4 GINV and the developments of living standards, 1961-1979

(Annual percentage change)

Hungary	GINV	NYUCP	IND(B)	MSOCCON	MNSOCCON	OECDCONS	HOUSING
1961	-2.7	1.1	8.5	1.3	10.6	...	16.3
1962	10.3	3.4	4.1	26.0	3.0	...	-19.9
1963	13.7	4.7	5.0	1.1	23.3	10.6	-2.5
1964	3.6	5.4	7.6	-2.7	-3.7	16.8	1.3
1965	1.5	1.5	3.6	16.1	-0.7	15.8	2.2
CSSR							
1963	-11.2	1.1	0.1	-11.9	6.3	0.0	-3.6
1964	11.1	3.0	2.6	5.5	30.6	37.3	-5.9
1965	7.5	5.1	5.7	47.6	73.0	35.7	0.7
1966	9.5	5.3	5.9	17.5	39.7	26.2	-2.9
1967	3.0	3.5	6.4	-10.3	11.9	9.5	5.0
Bulgaria							
1965	7.4	7.2	12.4	-6.0	50.4	...	-4.6
1966	19.6	6.3	11.5	31.3	51.4	36.2	-4.0
1967	23.6	9.6	12.4	4.9	0.2	-7.6	-1.6
1968	9.0	8.6	9.6	23.5	-2.9	-24.2	-0.1
1969	1.0	5.0	8.9	-2.9	-8.9	11.6	10.3
Romania							
1965	9.0	7.9	11.5	-25.0	24.8	30.0	...
1966	9.9	10.4	9.8	18.2	28.6	27.5	...
1967	16.6	11.0	13.1	20.8	100.2	74.7	...
1968	11.7	8.9	7.7	-2.2	4.1	17.4	...
1969	6.6	4.7	10.1	14.5	-16.0	2.1	...
GDR							
1966	6.5	5.4	7.2	35.1	7.4	6.9	-8.5
1967	8.9	3.4	6.2	11.8	13.8	25.8	10.8
1968	10.9	3.3	4.5	11.1	2.7	-21.7	4.7
1969	15.5	5.6	1.7	25.9	84.7	63.9	-8.6
1970	6.8	3.8	3.8	-2.3	8.4	22.9	16.3
1971	1.7	4.4	4.5	-1.4	9.6	10.1	-1.2
Poland							
1970	4.0	4.0	7.6	36.9	162.4	6.1	-1.4
1971	7.4	7.0	8.2	14.6	-41.0	23.0	-1.9
1972	23.0	8.7	11.0	16.2	79.5	36.7	7.8
1973	25.4	8.5	10.8	-8.1	23.7	23.4	10.5
1974	22.3	6.8	10.6	11.6	11.2	23.7	10.0
1975	10.7	11.4	11.4	18.5	-13.8	-4.8	-0.7
1976	1.0	8.7	8.8	-2.1	40.2	28.5	6.2
1977	3.1	6.6	7.3	23.3	3.2	-13.7	1.0
1978	2.1	1.0	5.3	8.1	-24.4	-5.0	6.6
1979	-7.9	3.2	2.2	-1.6	23.4	-14.1	-2.0

GINV	Gross investments
NYUCP	Personal consumption of material goods
IND(B)	Output of group "B" in industry (Hungary: Light industry)
MSOCCON	Import of consumer goods from socialist countries
MNSOCCON	Import of consumer goods from non-socialist countries
OECDCONS	Import of ind. consumer goods from OECD countries (SITC 8 at constant 1975 US $) Hungary, CSSR: current US $ prices
HOUSING	Number of new dwellings

Source: See table 4.1

4.6 Domestic utilization of NMP

Rapidly growing investments often provoke tension in the allocation of national income (NMP). Out of five countries which publish comparable NMP data at constant prices, the peaks in GINV coincide in all cases with significant excess spending (Table 4.5). In other words, the volume of NMP used is greater than the volume of NMP produced. In this regard, the GDR proved to be the most notorious "excess spender": in two consecutive years, NMP used surpassed NMP produced by more than 12 per cent.

Perhaps this is what lies behind the fact that in the past, the absolute level of NMP used was one of the most closely guarded secrets in the GDR. On the basis newly published data, however, this can be now estimated with reasonable confidence for the period in question.

At this point, it is necessary to note that our analysis was carried out on time series expressed in terms of the currently used constant price level of the country in question. Thus in this case 1985 prices were applied for GDR. It is very likely that the same ratios expressed at current prices of some earlier years would have shown somewhat different (lower) magnitudes. Here we face a practically insurmountable difficulty for any time series analysis. The construction of a useful data base requires the creation of time series consisting of absolute figures (rather than indices, or growth rates) but after manyfold repricing of the time series, the relative proportions may change quite drastically, due to huge shifts in relative prices.

In Czechoslovakia, the NMPUT/NMP ratio appears to have been close to 100 per cent throughout the entire 1963-1967 period[4], in spite of considerable variations in GINV. Interestingly, changes in net fixed investments clearly followed GINV. Its share in NMP used (NYUAF/NMPUT) peaked in 1964 and dropped in each year thereafter. However, changes in stocks (which include the changes in uncompleted investments) almost entirely offset its impact on the accumulation ratio. In the GDR, developments were similar to those in Czechoslovakia, though excess spending was more pronounced. It is also noticeable that fluctuations in stock building were so intensive that the zigzags in net accumulation (NYUA/NMPUT) have shown no parallelism with changes in GINV.

As already mentioned above, it is impossible to reconstruct the true balance-of-payments consequences of investment fluctuations from published sources. The maximum that outside research can provide is a separate analysis of aggregate trade balances according to trading partners: (1) trade with the socialist countries, (2) trade with the Soviet Union, and (3) trade with the OECD countries (table 4.5). This seems to be a justified simplification, since trade flows with socialist countries other than the Soviet Union, as well as those with developing countries, are too small to be relevant from our point of view.

In Bulgaria and Czechoslovakia, the reaction pattern of trade balances to changes in investments was uniform for all three types of trade. As the pace of investment quickened, trade balances deteriorated but they improved as soon as GINV rates started to fall. By contrast, in Poland and in Romania only the trade balances with western countries deteriorated simultaneously with GINV. In these cases, as well as in Bulgaria, the evidence is fairly robust: in peak years the value of total imports surpassed that of exports by 40-90 per cent. In the GDR, the trade position with the socialist countries proved to be slightly positively correlated with the cycle, while trade balances with the Western economies as a whole (including intra-German trade) behaved asymmetrically to GINV. No clear picture emerges in the Hungarian or Romanian

[4] For the reasons explained above, the shift of the price base from 1977 to 1984 resulted in a 3-4 percentage point rise in the NMPUT/NMP ratios. Thus, to obtain meaningful data in table 4.5 the underlying Czechoslovak figures were recalculated at 1977 levels.

TABLE 4.5 GINV and the allocation of NMP, 1961-1979

	GINV	NMPUT / NMP	NYUA / NMPUT	NYUAF / NMPUT	NYUAI / NMPUT	M/X (SOC)	M/X (USSR)	M/X (OECD)	M/X (OECD) - M
	% change				Percentage				
Hungary									
1961	-2.7	109.1	18.1	10.5	7.3	92.9	110.0	126.0	...
1962	10.3	109.6	18.4	10.7	7.5	101.4	105.7	113.2	110
1963	13.7	110.9	19.8	12.4	7.1	106.8	104.8	111.0	105
1964	3.6	112.6	20.2	12.0	7.8	103.7	102.3	125.8	111
1965	1.5	109.8	18.1	12.4	5.4	96.6	105.9	112.0	100
CSSR									
1963	-11.2	99.9	19.0	12.6	6.8	85.5	89.3	98.3	82
1964	11.1	101.2	17.7	16.0	0.5	92.8	93.0	110.3	87
1965	7.5	102.1	16.9	15.0	1.0	99.8	89.4	109.3	98
1966	9.5	101.6	20.6	13.5	7.5	99.7	97.2	114.0	114
1967	3.0	101.2	20.8	12.7	8.9	94.1	98.5	99.5	99
Bulgaria									
1965	7.4	101.6	28.3	15.0	13.3	93.6	95.6	140.8	132
1966	19.6	106.2	34.3	16.1	17.8	103.1	106.6	171.0	173
1967	23.6	105.7	33.9	20.4	13.6	102.6	98.6	143.9	162
1968	9.0	105.8	32.2	18.9	13.4	107.6	106.5	135.0	140
1969	1.0	102.8	33.2	22.7	10.8	98.0	100.0	98.0	130
Romania									
1965	9.0	...	...	...	...	87.3	91.3	131.5	112
1966	9.9	...	...	...	...	94.4	95.3	130.7	113
1967	16.6	...	...	...	...	95.5	93.0	165.0	148
1968	11.7	...	...	...	...	94.7	91.3	156.6	146
1969	6.6	...	...	...	...	91.5	106.0	147.9	135
GDR									
1966	6.5	112.6	26.5	20.1	6.5	96.7	113.6	120.2	118
1967	8.9	111.7	27.0	21.8	5.1	92.1	100.3	109.5	104
1968	10.9	109.2	24.8	23.5	1.3	88.1	93.8	97.1	87
1969	15.5	112.2	27.6	26.1	1.4	98.5	106.7	105.4	87
1970	6.8	115.2	29.9	25.4	4.6	99.3	111.6	129.3	108
1971	1.7	114.1	28.3	23.7	4.7	90.4	99.3	128.4	108
Poland									
1970	4.0	100.4	35.8	26.9	10.4	109.1	107.0	92.4	86
1971	7.4	102.0	37.5	27.0	12.6	111.4	105.3	95.4	87
1972	23.0	103.8	40.3	30.4	11.6	104.2	87.4	121.1	107
1973	25.4	107.1	45.1	34.0	13.0	104.1	92.9	158.8	133
1974	22.3	108.6	48.5	37.1	13.3	100.5	105.3	176.6	147
1975	10.7	109.1	47.4	38.0	10.6	93.2	101.7	190.7	152
1976	1.0	108.8	45.5	35.3	11.6	98.8	110.7	192.4	135
1977	3.1	105.9	41.7	35.5	6.8	102.7	111.3	165.1	118
1978	2.1	103.4	40.6	33.9	7.4	101.0	95.8	147.6	116
1979	-7.9	101.9	34.1	29.8	4.7	96.4	103.2	131.8	105

GINV	Gross investments	M/X (SOC)	Import/export ratio (soc.)
NMPUT/NMP	National income used vs. produced	M/X (USSR)	Import export ratio (USSR) (from Soviet statistics)
NYUA/NMPUT	Net accumulation ratio		
NYUAF/NMPUT	Fixed asset ratio	M/X (OECD)	Import/export ratio (OECD)
NYUAI/NMPUT	Stock ratio	MX (OECD) - M	Import/export ratio (OECD) (mirror statistics)

Source: See tabe 4.1

cases. In both countries trade with socialist partners resulted in growing deficits as domestic investment picked up. At the same time, however, both countries improved their trade positions *vis-à-vis* the Soviet Union.

In the remaining cases the countries' positions *vis-à-vis* the Soviet Union and the countries of the socialist community as a whole behaved similarly. The two above-mentioned cases were somewhat surprising, since in the middle of the sixties the Soviet Union was the most important supplier of machinery imported by socialist countries from other socialist countries (around 30 %).

Needless to say, the coincidence of the GINV movements with changes in the trade balance does not prove that the former was the cause of the latter. An examination of the size of the increments of machinery purchases relative to the absolute increase in total imports can help to come closer to a conclusion. As regards the changes in imports from the socialist countries, it appears that only in two cases (Czechoslovakia and Romania) were machinery imports largely responsible for the deterioration of the trade balance. In other cases, absolute increments in this variable accounted for only 30-40 per cent of the rise in total imports. The results were similar for machinery imports from non-socialist countries.

The findings of our examinations of the link between ups and downs in GINV and the role of imported machinery are summarized in table 4.6. The emerging pattern suggests that there

TABLE 4.6 Machinery imports and the foreign trade balance, 1961-1979

	Trade with socialist countries (a)		Trade with OECD countries (b)	
	Trade balance co-variate with GINV (c)	Increment of machinery import as % of total import increment	Trade balance co-variate with GINV (c)	Increment of machinery import as % of total import increment
Bulgaria	YES	44%	YES	57%
CSSR	YES	55%	YES	35%
GDR	YES	37%	NO	(.)
Hungary	YES	33%	NO	(.)
Poland	NO	(.)	YES	41%
Romania	YES	61%	YES	66%

Notes: a/ From national statistics
b/ From OECD partner statistics
c/ From trough to peak, as shown by M/X (SOC) and M/X (OECD) variables in table 4.5

Source: See table 4.1

was only a single case (Romania) where the zigzag of machinery imports can be directly blamed for the deterioration of trade balances with both group of suppliers. In two cases, the deterioration of the socialist trade balance can be largely, but in three cases only partly, explained by the fluctuation observed in machinery imports. In trade with the OECD countries, tensions in the trade balance were provoked by the sudden rise in machinery imports also in two instances. In Romania this factor accounted for 2/3, in Bulgaria for more than half of the rise in total foreign purchases. In all the remaining cases, either the changes in the balances were independent of GINV, or their movements were largely attributable to other factors. Though it was not tested in a systematic manner, it appears that in these cases fluctuations in the trade balance were largely attributable to changes in raw material and semi-finished products imports.

There is also some evidence pointing toward a link between consumer goods imports (at least from the western market economies) and GINV but given their small weight in trade, they cannot play a decisive role.

TABLE 4.7 GINV and the development of agriculture, 1961-1979

(Annual percentage change)

		GINV	CROP	LIVESTOCK	XSOC	MSOC	XOECD	MOECD
Hungary								
	1961	-2.7	-6.3	5.6	22.0	-0.5	...	...
	1962	10.3	6.1	(-)	8.4	20.8	...	...
	1963	13.7	8.3	0.9	4.0	3.4	27.3	38.5
	1964	3.6	0.8	9.9	18.8	4.8	-6.5	-36.0
	1965	1.5	-7.0	-3.3	-1.0	24.3	21.1	14.2
CSSR								
	1963	-11.2	16.2	-0.7	30.7	11.7	29.1	-5.1
	1964	11.1	-0.8	7.9	-26.5	-16.3	-15.5	13.9
	1965	7.5	-15.5	2.8	1.4	7.3	3.1	39.8
	1966	9.5	21.7	3.4	-14.6	19.1	-5.8	25.1
	1967	3.0	4.6	5.8	20.9	4.4	13.9	-33.1
Bulgaria								
	1965	7.4	-1.5	8.3	21.4	-37.3	41.5	49.3
	1966	19.6	19.0	5.8	7.0	42.4	27.9	26.9
	1967	23.6	1.8	6.9	19.6	9.8	-4.4	-38.1
	1968	9.0	-10.3	-1.1	9.1	36.8	-4.6	113.1
	1969	1.0	6.8	-1.6	12.9	-1.5	-7.4	-40.6
Romania								
	1965	9.0	6.7	4.7	8.6	-43.4	20.6	9.2
	1966	9.9	16.1	12.1	-3.5	22.0	-3.9	-2.5
	1967	16.6	-2.1	7.7	2.8	50.6	74.5	67.3
	1968	11.7	-3.4	-0.9	0.2	-3.4	-28.6	-28.6
	1969	6.6	5.3	-0.5	-1.4	7.8	15.8	3.7
GDR								
	1966	6.5	1.8	5.1	3.8	17.9	73.8	-15.2
	1967	8.9	12.6	1.4	42.6	19.7	20.0	-29.3
	1968	10.9	-1.9	4.2	-4.0	-13.2	-27.1	-29.2
	1969	15.5	-16.1	-0.7	11.7	19.9	26.7	34.2
	1970	6.8	10.8	(-)	138.2	21.1	-0.8	-11.7
	1971	1.7	-6.2	4.0	-0.2	-5.3	2.2	18.5
Poland								
	1970	4.0	4.3	-1.1	8.3	-14.4	11.4	45.5
	1971	7.4	1.1	6.6	-18.8	53.2	4.1	11.3
	1972	23.0	7.8	9.0	59.0	-26.7	26.0	21.2
	1973	25.4	6.5	8.2	-8.5	-12.4	40.7	28.7
	1974	22.3	-0.7	4.2	70.8	52.8	-9.6	2.4
	1975	10.7	-3.0	-1.0	-12.0	-10.8	-8.9	26.4
	1976	1.0	5.0	-8.7	-26.8	-37.9	20.4	37.0
	1977	3.1	-7.2	13.7	-6.1	44.7	4.3	-23.3
	1978	2.1	5.4	2.6	1.2	-6.4	14.3	65.0
	1979	-7.9	-3.7	1.3	9.0	-7.6	13.3	24.1

GINV	Gross investment
CROP	Crop output
LIVESTOCK	Livestock output
XSOC,MSOC	Export (import) of agric. goods from (to) socialist countries
XOECD,MOECD	Export (import) of agric. goods from (to) OECD countries (SITC 0-1 at current US $)

Source: See table 4.1

4.7 ROLE OF THE HARVEST AND FOREIGN CREDITS

As shown in table 4.7, marked fluctuations in crop harvests were registered in a number of countries in the periods examined. This fact, however, does not imply straightforward or identical consequences in all the countries concerned.

In Hungary, for example, the trade impact of the poor harvests in 1964 and 1965 was ambiguous. Agricultural exports to the socialist countries grew fast in 1964, while sales to the West (which were about the same size in volume terms) fell back. In the following year, when crop output actually fell by 7 per cent, only exports to the socialist countries suffered, while exports to the West grew by more than 20 percent. (Partly as a consequence of these efforts but also for other reasons, the country almost balanced its trade with the OECD countries by 1965, while according to OECD partner statistics it even attained a small surplus in 1966.) The domestic impact of the 1965 harvest was quite brutal: the growth rate of NMP produced was virtually zero, much lower than in any other year in the historically long 1957-78 period.

The years 1964-1965 were also difficult in Czechoslovakia. After a year of stagnation, the 1965 crop harvest fell by more than 15 per cent - an unprecedented magnitude in the entire post-war history of the country. Accordingly, NMP growth was adversely affected too (1964: 0.6%; 1965: 3.4%). Agricultural exports to the OECD countries were also hit but given their small weight in hard currency earnings (around 14 %), these consequences were not very severe. In trade with the socialist countries, however, the changes in the following year were already noteworthy. The growth of machinery imports almost halted, while food imports - representing about one third of all imports from socialist countries - grew by nearly 20 %.

In Bulgaria, bad harvests in 1967 and 1968 were presumably one of the chief reasons behind the fall in agricultural exports to the OECD countries. By 1968, the amount of total machinery imports (SITC 7) originating in this area effectively fell below the level of the country's food exports (SITC 0-1). NMP growth also reacted sensitively. After two years of high rates, close to 10 per cent on average, the 17 per cent fall in net agricultural output pulled down the 1968 NMP growth rate to 6 per cent. The peak year of the GDR's investment boom, 1969, coincided with a very bad harvest. Crop output fell by more than 16 per cent. (In fact this was the second worst year in the country's history, after the harvest shortfall of more than 27 per cent recorded in 1961.) Nevertheless, given the small contribution of the agricultural sector to NMP, aggregate output performance was not severely affected. Despite the small harvest, the level of food exports to the West increased considerably in that year[5] and it was then maintained over the next two years.

The motives behind this decision are not difficult to see: in good years - even for the relatively industrialized GDR economy - food exports accounted for more than 20 per cent of total export incomes originating from western trade. Hence, the government simply could not afford to cut them, if the level of hard currency earnings was to be maintained. Poland and Romania were fortunate not to be hit by any larger harvest shortfall during the periods analyzed here.

The case of Poland merits further discussion, since here the run up period was exceptionally long (1970-1975). To the present author, this can be explained by two factors. First and foremost, the country was lucky with the weather: the harvest was good for several consecutive years. No significant shortfall occurred until 1977. Finally, this did happen in 1980: crop output plunged by more than 15 per cent, causing additional hardships to the conflict-ridden Polish society, where the normal rhythm of production was already greatly disturbed by strikes, civil unrest and internal struggles among the country's leaders. Secondly, the 1970s opened the way for Eastern Europe to obtain sizeable foreign credits - a possibility simply non-existent for other

[5] The surge of food exports to the socialist countries was spectacular in percentage terms, but it was nonetheless a negligible development given the small absolute size of the trade flow.

countries in the earlier periods. After 1973 western credits poured into Poland. This created an entirely new situation.

4.8 CONCLUSIONS

The statistical account presented above indicates a number of country and time-specific differences among the investment booms and the subsequent halts, albeit only a small sample was analyzed. This fact in itself is an obvious warning against precipitate generalizations concerning the "typical" course of east European investment cycles. There are at least three popular fallacies in this regard.

First, it is often said that an upsurge in investments has to have a stimulating impact on domestic industrial activity. Secondly, both planners and outside observers are inclined to accept the existence of a trade-off between more investments and more consumption. Thirdly, it is often claimed that after a few years of increased investment activity, the halt is inevitable because the accompanying machinery imports cannot be counterbalanced with exports.

However, systematic analyses of six investment waves showed that these assertions lack satisfactory empirical grounding. Nonetheless, a few common features - valid in the majority of the cases investigated above - still remain.

Taking as a starting point a year when GINV expands very slowly or even contracts, and assuming that during the next 3-4 years no external shock or internal political crisis shakes the economy, the following scenario seems to be rather typical. As the investment process quickens, non-residential construction activity and machinery imports also start to grow at accelerated rates. So far, this is in line with the received wisdom. Surprisingly, however, it is found that personal consumption goes hand in hand with GINV changes. The dynamic impetus originating from rapid increases in investment does not lead to sustainable investment-led growth. Industrial output often remains invariant to changes in GINV. On the other hand, experience from the past shows that there is a great probability that within a five-year period one or two bad crop harvests may occur. Needless to say, this a purely exogenous development, which has very little to do with system-inherent factors. However, given the tendency to taut resource allocations, where a sudden drop in harvests cannot be pre-planned (even if, on a probability basis, it is very likely), urgent policy modifications are required when it actually occurs. In numerous cases this is the real reason - and not the stepped-up machinery imports - that provokes the halt in investments. Thus after 2-3 years of investment boom, its immediate curtailment appears to be the quickest and least painful remedy to restore the overall balance. Nonetheless, the easing of these tensions typically does not come about within one or two years.

In a search for further common explanations, the disturbance free "golden years" (roughly 1960 to 1975-1978, see table 4.8) of the pre-crisis period were scrutinized country by country. In that decade and a half, investments and IRs grew practically everywhere. Between the beginning and the end year of the various individual country sample periods, GINV grew by a factor ranging from 2.5 (Czechoslovakia, Soviet Union) to 7.0 (Romania). It seems logical to assume that other explanatory variables, if they existed, should have clearly manifested themselves in such a period. Nearly a dozen possible unlagged explanatory variables were tested. Perhaps surprisingly, little significant correlation was found in most cases between the annual increases of GINV (in log difference terms) and that of the other macro-economic variables. In these "golden years", GINV in Hungary and in Poland proved to be positively correlated with total domestic demand (NMPUT), with industrial output (INDT) and with certain import variables. However, in the other five economies practically no systematic relationship seems to have existed with the selected macro-economic variables.

TABLE 4.8 Correlation coefficients (r) of changes in GINV and in some macro-economic variables, 1961-1978

(In log. difference terms)

Cycle-relevant variable	Bulgaria 1961-1977	CSSR 1964-1975	GDR 1961-1976	Hungary 1962-1976	Poland 1961-1974	Romania 1961-1978	USSR 1963-1975
NMPUT	**	-	**	****	***	...	-
INDT	-	(-)	-	*	***	-	-
NYUCP	...	-	-	***	***	...	...
Total import	-	-	-	-	****	-	-
Import from the USSR	-	-	-	-	-	-	-
Import from the FRG	-	-	-	-	***	-	-
Total socialist import	-	-	-	***	-	-	-
Socialist import :machinery	-	**	*	****	-	-	-
Total non-soc. import	-	-	*	*	**	*	-
	-	-	-	-	***	-	-

Note: All variables measured at constant prices, except for "Import from the USSR", which is measured at current TR prices.

Symbols used:

*****	r>0.9
****	r>0.8
***	r>0.7
**	r>0.6
*	r>0.5
-	r<0.5
(-)	r<0.0

Source: See table 4.1

5. CLOSING REMARKS ON MEASUREMENT AND CONTROL

The main purpose of this study has been to provide a comprehensive theoretical and statistical analysis of the major features of investment behaviour in the socialist countries. In doing so, an attempt has been made to identify some general patterns which can, it is hoped, be used in the analysis of other aspects of socialist economies (e.g., foreign trade, monetary policy, etc.).

The principal contribution of the first two theoretical chapters was to provide a broad comparison of the findings of earlier quantitative research. It was shown that many of the results were contradictory - various authors, talking about the same countries, have come to widely differing quantitative results. The efforts to produce replicable results to buttress a general theory of socialist investment cycles yielded much less in the way of results than was generally expected.

The data analysis in Chapter 3 has led to several conclusions but their substance can be summarized in four main contentions.

(1) The reliability of our basic investment data (GINV) is questionable for certain periods and for some countries. The presence of cyclical bias is particularly worrisome.

(2) Conventional time series analysis methods are also problematic, if it is acknowledged that the underlying data contain measurement errors. The presence of autocorrelation was also a cause for concern, since it prevents proper detrending of the basic GINV series.

(3) East European and Soviet investment time series do not exhibit cyclical patterns in a strict econometric sense, even if all data reservations are discarded.

(4) In the context of inter-system comparisons, the fluctuation in GINV time series is not particularly strong or weak. In general, it could be appropriate to say that there is nothing system-specific in this fluctuation at all.

In Chapter 4, an attempt was made to combine quantitative methods with the ingredients of historical analysis. It was found that elements of the exogenous fluctuation theory provide a better explanation of the underlying processes than the various versions of the endogenous cycle models. On the one hand, we have seen that the Keynesian multiplier was not allowed to work, and therefore investment fluctuations could not reverberate throughout the economy. On the other hand, the turning points of the investment process were always very sensitive to external shocks, such as weather and political developments.

Before concluding the present study, I would like to illustrate these points from a slightly changed angle in order to indicate one possible direction of future research. We may start by introducing two concepts: the measurement trap and the definition trap.

5.1 The measurement trap

Measurement and control are intertwined concepts. The accuracy of the measuring equipment sets the limits of the accuracy of the control process. In other words, control itself cannot be more precise than the measuring equipment. However, the measurement process itself presupposes a certain degree of regularity in the process under investigation. The more complex the subject it is intended to measure, the truer is the above statement.

Let us recall the ideas presented in Chapters 2 and 3 on the inherent difficulties of compiling investment price indices or measuring investment starts and completions. To determine the total costs of all simultaneously running investment projects at constant prices, a detailed methodology is required first, to fix the date of the start and completion of the project. Second, there is a need for reliable performance on the part of the various administrative organs responsible for aggregating data on thousands of ongoing projects. In turn, the price index needed at the macro-level for eliminating the cost changes which arose from the variation of prices alone assumes that we have a predetermined set of criteria to distinguish between value and volume effects at the micro-level.

An important ingredient of this complex process can be characterized by an analogy borrowed from nuclear physics. The *uncertainty principle*, introduced by W. Heisenberg, is a conception of the measurement process at sub-atomic levels. It emphasizes the active role of the scientist who, in making measurements, necessarily interacts with the object observed and thus causes it to be revealed not as it is in itself but as a function of measurement.

Compared to that of nuclear physicists, planners' curiosity, as manifested in looking after the details of the investment process, is much less innocent. The centre collects information because it wants to interfere in the investment process. This leads to a situation in which micro-level data are inherently distorted by the nature of this relationship.[1] State owned enterprises (SOEs) try to doctor the information which they forward to the centre, according to their own best interests. From an analytical point of view, two questions emerge that are worth considering:

(1) Is it logical to assume that hundreds of occasional distortions mutually neutralize each other? Our answer is a cautious "no", because year-to-year changes in the government's policy stance usually imply several modifications in economic regulators and neither *ex ante* nor *ex post* can one easily tell what is the total impact of all these changes on the interests of SOEs. Moreover, as already argued earlier, it is not self-evident to assume uniform behaviour for all SOEs throughout the economy and even less to generalize such findings to all other firms (e.g., industrial and agricultural cooperatives).

(2) Are there any limits to such manipulations? The answer is yes. The proportions to which the supervising authorities have been accustomed in the past cannot be drastically changed overnight. This would strike one's eye. However, if manipulations are confined within the 10-15 percentage point range, the firm can remain within the domain of credibility and legality. Since year-to-year GINV fluctuations usually remain within the same band width, it is impossible to make a precise distinction between real policy-induced changes and policy-induced cheating.

[1] This aspect of the situation is often discussed within the framework of the *principal-agent theory*. Nevertheless, the concept of "uncertainty principle" appears to be more illuminating for the present analysis.

5.2 The definition trap

The essence of this second type of trap is that a statistical information system originally conceived to serve certain goals will become increasingly dysfunctional when these objectives become unimportant or less relevant.

The best example is the Soviet statistical treatment of defence expenditures. In the economic sense the accumulation of weapons is obviously not an investment, but in the past a good part of military hardware acquisitions were registered as such for political reasons. This manipulated figure then started to live its own independent life, since beyond a very narrow circle of experts, nobody knew precisely how big this distortion was. The planning apparatus, hundreds and thousands of decision makers, could do nothing else but accept the published GINV figures at face value, although - in very broad terms - they were all aware of its imprecision. This situation would not, in fact, have been different, if for a given year the true size of defence expenditures had appeared in the published budget data. Economic analysis, the assessment of the effectiveness of the investment process etc., cannot be carried out on the basis of one single correct number. It is not enough to publish the total GINV figure; meaningful analysis and decision-making require correct branch data, unbiased price indices, etc. Such corrections, however, are very difficult or simply impossible to implement retroactively.

Let us consider a more complicated case, what we will call the "maintenance-reconstruction" dilemma. In the mid-1960s the Hungarian statistical and planning authorities defined and elaborated a new methodology of investment statistics. It was, of course, designed for contemporary conditions and not for the late 1980s, when those regulations were still in force. In 1966 - and even after the introduction of the 1968 economic reform - the lion's share of investment was centrally-determined. SOEs were accorded means sufficient to maintain their already achieved level of operation - but no more. At the same time, it was hoped that day-to-day operations would be self-financing and autonomous, so the Centre would be relieved of the burden of everyday control of firms. The amalgamation of maintenance and reconstruction expenditures, on the one hand, and their clear separation from investment expenditures, on the other, was conceived according to this logic.

Later, the independence of SOEs became much wider and the autonomy of the centre has greatly diminished. Under such circumstances, sound economic decision-making would have required more than a set of statistically reported investment data. In the late 1980s, economic policy formation aimed at regulating the investment market in its entirety. Hence it would have needed data which characterize the true state of this market. It is true that the very last table in the investment chapter of the annual *Statistical Yearbook* did contain a small table on maintenance expenditures of the socialist sector. But, as we have seen in the case of the Soviet defence figures, one single number is insufficient to bridge the information gap arising from definitional ambiguities.

The definition trap has another interesting property. The chosen names for statistical terms have a certain force in influencing the mind-set of users of the data. A well-trained statistician, for example, might be fully aware of the inherent methodological problems of investment definition and might therefore suggest that everybody adjust reported GINV data for the impact of maintenance expenditures or the presence of hidden military outlays. However, this warning will never reach nine users out of ten. The tenth may know and understand this problem but he will still refrain from following the advice, as he will rightly suspect that the use of such "corrected" investment data - parallel to the conventional ones - will lead to confusion and misunderstanding.

5.3 MICRO-ECONOMIC CONDITIONS OF MEASUREMENT

Central control and the measurement of economic processes in the socialist economies relied upon two broad sources of micro-economic regularity: (i) technological and (ii) behavioural.[2]

(i) Among *technological regularities*, standards and quality norms played the most important role. If we say that in country A, *per capita* meat consumption has grown, for example, from 70 to 90 kilograms, this makes sense only if it can be assumed that in the meantime the quality of the product consumed (composition, fat content, etc.) did not change. In the context of a well-functioning market economy, such an assumption is normally justified. Competition among producers is an effective guarantee that every seller will produce goods of a certain standard quality. In this sense, it can be rightly said that in a market-based system the validity of micro-economic and macro-economic statements are independent of each other: 1 kg meat is always equal to 1 kg meat, irrespective of the overall economic conditions.

In the area of consumption, such compelling mechanisms also operated under the socialist systems, although certainly less strongly than in the market economies. Except in extreme situations, a half-baked loaf or a shirt without buttons will not find a buyer in a socialist economy either. In the service sector, even the most seasoned and apathetic socialist consumer will not remain silent if a waiter pours wine on his trousers or a barber cuts his face with a razor. However, this type of "flesh and blood" sensitivity was almost totally absent in the sphere of investments.

During an investment upswing, when excess demand for investment goods was higher than usual, constructors, manufacturers and importers were usually able to persuade their customers to accept and pay for poor and/or expensive work. This was possible, of course, only because the customer - another SOE - was not spending its own money. SOEs were usually more interested in meeting certain plan deadlines than securing good quality work and realistic prices. In the absence of real markets, the Centre was almost powerless against such anomalies.

This deficiency of the socialist investment system can be partially cured by means of more sophisticated rules and regulations. If the Centre is really determined to keep an eye on costs, it is possible to avoid cost overruns. In this case, builders may build something different (worse) than the plan postulated. The housing estate will be built but the schools will be "forgotten", the planned imported western machinery will be commissioned on time but there will be no money for accessories, etc.[3] In a way, the whole issue is analogous to the well-known saucepan paradox of traditional central planning: if the output plan target is determined in units, the typical SOE will produce nothing but very small saucepans; if, however, the plan is given in tonnes, only super-size saucepans emerge from the factories.

[2] This terminology is borrowed from Green (1977). In the context of western market economies, he distinguishes a third type of regularity, the so-called statutory regularity. This involves monetary relationships determined by a legal statute (e.g., tax-revenue proportions).

[3] All this is more than mere speculation. According to a National Bank survey carried out on a sample of 200 Hungarian industrial investment projects, the cost target proved to be the only target which was really achieved. On average, the cost overrun was less than 3 per cent in the period 1975-1982. However, in other areas (gestation period, profitability, hard-currency earning capacity, etc.) a 30-50 per cent shortfall was typically registered relative to targets (Antal and Várhegyi 1987, p. 185).

The general experience - and this was amply demonstrated in the previous chapters - was that over time even the most standard technical regularities did not assert themselves with a reasonable degree of rigour. As it was shown, the relationships between investment costs and gestation periods, between reported outputs and inputs were astonishingly weak. Thus, it would not be an exaggeration to conclude that in a system where the logic of planning, politically motivated campaigns, real and simulated markets were all present, measurement at the micro-levels was always problematic: the quantitative characteristics of individual investment projects were recorded differently during the period of peaks than in troughs.[4]

(ii) In a market economy, *behavioural regularity* is based on profit-orientation and the rules of competition. There is a single (though never precisely known) objective function derived from the principle of profit-maximization. In this model, changes in certain conditions trigger typical behavioural patterns. By contrast, as we have seen, simple assumptions concerning the behaviour of SOEs do not work properly.[5] Why? The mere fact that no mechanisms based on profit-seeking exist, does not, of course, exclude the presence of a different type of behavioural regularity. Indeed, the entire theory of socialist investment cycles is built on the assumption that such system-specific behavioural rules do exist in the investment process.

The traditional interpretation of socialism, as described in Section 1.3 above, explains the expansionist attitude of SOEs, the so-called "investment hunger", in terms of the motivations of managers.

> The most important motive is that the leader - whether he is the responsible manager of a workshop, a producer firm, a hospital or a school - *identifies with this job.* He is convinced that the activity of the unit under his charge is important. Therefore it has to grow. He is pressed by the internal problems of the unit and believes that they could be solved, at least partially, by investment. The machines are out of date - it is time to replace them. The foundry is unable to supply enough castings to the metal cutting workshop - it ought to be enlarged. The surgery needs new equipment. Projectors ought to be acquired in order to modernize education. (Kornai 1980, p. 192, italics in original)

This very fundamental assumption about the behaviour of enterprises (or senior enterprise management) was nowhere questioned in the previous chapters. The control theory models and the endogenous models, as well as most of the exogenous models discussed, are all based on this assumption but I deliberately avoided any quarrel on this matter. Throughout the book, my attention was focused, first, on challenging the views of the first two schools by means of

[4] If allowance is made for quality fluctuations in the theoretical perspective of socialism, new horizons therefore open up in many areas. Podkaminer (1989, p. 21), for instance, suggested the introduction of the concept of "quality adjusted consumption". It is perfectly possible that, if it is assumed that quality of consumer goods and services deteriorates during periods of investment expansion and improves during periods of contractions, then quality-adjusted consumption levels would also exhibit more fluctuation than conventionally perceived. In a similar manner, one could rightly talk about "quality adjusted" GINV time series as well.

[5] I am grateful to Mr. A. Madarász (*Institute of Economics*, Budapest) for helping me to formulate the question in this sharp and clear form.

quantitative methods - i.e. contrasting their hypothesis with the statistical reality. Secondly, it was equally important to show that these two schools were unable to present a convincing behavioural model of the central decision makers (planners), while the third school, using exogenous models, was more successful in this respect.

Surely, if managers' behaviour can be modelled by a single objective function (the investment hunger paradigm), then this can be generalized for the representative or typical SOE. The question is, can we accept this assumption?

In a very broad, general sense there is not much point arguing that in Soviet-type societies politics determines economics, since at this high level of abstraction the opposite view (i.e. that economics determines politics) can be also accepted. However, when we descend from this high level of abstraction to the analysis of the investment process, it cannot be said that the argument works in both ways. In the previous chapters, it was shown by various means, why the causation runs more strongly from one direction (i.e. from to politics to economics) than *vice versa*, but now I would like to add one more argument to support this contention.

Historically, managerial behaviour changed over time too. At the outset, the political system of the socialist countries was intensively competitive everywhere, so that managers' positions were insecure. A second important feature of the early years was that the loyalty of managers was based on sincere intellectual convictions. The majority of these people believed in the supremacy of central planning, so they willingly became enthusiastic and obedient servants of the central planning apparatus. As time passed, both tendencies weakened. The unconditional belief in central planning vanished and the relentless industrialization drive abated, opening the way for a variety of different individual strategies among enterprise managers and political leaders.

The salient point here is that due to the absence of market forces, the socialist system tolerated (and often encouraged) the co-existence of significantly different managerial strategies. The performance and efficiency of managers, and therefore their enterprises, exhibited variations which were much greater than those observed in the market economies. So, it would be ill-conceived to assume the existence of a single-variable objective function for socialist managers, which is - at least in its form - similar to the profit-maximization goal of managers in a market economy.

There was, therefore, no such thing as a representative or typical socialist manager. These men and women had vastly different educational, moral and political standards. Some of them, indeed, were motivated *à la* Kornai, identifying themselves with their firm. If they had a specialized engineer-type background, they might have rightly felt that their own fate was inseparably linked to the good fortune of their enterprise or industry.[6]

In Soviet-type economies the socio-economic texture was interwoven with the warp of personal obedience and loyalty at every level of the hierarchy. This was, of course, a semi-feudal heritage, which was reflected in the *nomenklatura* system: in the servility of the apparatchik-class on the one hand and insane despotism on the other. Such managers were not motivated to take risks or fight for additional resources. Instead they tended to keep a low profile and simply

[6] But even this fact would not necessarily generate insatiable investment hunger. Directors and senior managers of SOEs usually did not remain in their posts for more than 2-3 years. However, the construction of large investment projects took longer than this, and their benefits (in the forms of easing plan fulfilment) were thus enjoyed not by those who initiated the investment, but by their successors. For a detailed exposition of this point, see Stankiewicz (1991).

cultivated their own personal connections, hoping for a further opportunity to move them forward, or rather upward, in the *nomenklatura* hierarchy.

Although much more could be written on this subject, this does not seem to be the appropriate place for an in-depth discussion. In science, just as in everyday life, any definite statement on a particular issue can rightly be followed by another "why-type" question. Nevertheless, at some point every research study must come to an end.

The epoch of Soviet-type economies has ended and, as I tried to argue in the introductory chapter of this book, we still do not fully understand why the end came. If we are to reach a new, better understanding, we probably need a new micro-economic foundation of our general knowledge. I am fully aware that the ideas presented in this closing chapter are still conjectural but I hope that at a later stage they will stimulate further research.

APPENDIX I: TWO HUNGARIAN CASE STUDIES

As a Hungarian author, I am most familiar with the Hungarian scene. My knowledge, based on first hand and secondary sources, is necessarily more limited with respect to the other socialist countries. The objective of the previous chapters has nonetheless been to offer a comprehensive overview and not to limit the argumentation and the collection of evidence to Hungary alone. This effort, I am afraid, was not as successful as I had wished, but that is perhaps understandable. In many cases I simply failed to find illustrations or proofs drawn from countries other than Hungary, although I strongly believe that they exist.

By contrast, this short note is based entirely upon Hungarian experience. I am confident that the core of the ideas which will be presented is applicable in other socialist countries as well. However, given the case-study character of the two investigations presented below, no attempt has been made to supplement the findings with such examples.

1. THE IMPACT OF INVESTMENT FLUCTUATIONS ON THE LABOUR MARKET

As already noted several times, the endogenous cycle theory assumes the presence of a *multiplier* effect within the investment cycle. Using Bauer (1981) as a source of evidence, several Hungarian labour market specialists stated as a commonplace that there had been a direct link between investment behaviour and changes on the labour market in the traditional, unreformed socialist system.

According to Fazekas (1988, p. 92), for instance, "demand for labour rises at the top of the cycle and the growth of the industrial labour force accelerates." Real wages and the volume of overtime are also believed to speed up in such periods. During the downward phase, the labour market is believed to be slacker: there is a slowdown in the rise of real wages and the volume of overtime is thought to fall back in absolute terms.

Indeed, this line of thought appears to be straightforward at first sight. This explains, perhaps, why no attempt was ever made to test the validity of this logic in the light of empirical data. My suspicion is that the idea that the unfolding investment cycle must have a direct impact on the labour market appeared attractive because such relationships do exist in market economies.[1]

However, once we step outside the framework of investment cycle theory, the question can easily be turned around, as two non-Hungarian authors have rightly pointed out. Podkaminer (1985) and Sapir (1987) tried to think through mechanisms operating in the opposite direction. Although these models remained at a high level of abstraction, in the sense that no effort was made to test them empirically, they merit closer examination.

In a shortage economy, when investments peak the expanding state enterprises meet difficulties in retaining their labour force. This is the starting point of Leon Podkaminer's theory. Growing shortages exert increasing pressure on the workforce to quit and join the semi-legal or illegal

[1] The correlation between GFCF and employment time series (both expressed in the form of annual percentage changes) appears to be rather high in some but not all western countries. For the period 1961-1988, the following r values were obtained: Switzerland (0.90), Denmark (0.81), Finland (0.76), Canada (0.76), FRG (0.74), USA (0.72), Spain (0.71), Belgium (0.62), France (0.59), Netherlands (0.50), U.K. (0.50), Ireland (0.43), Austria (0.35), Turkey (0.32), Sweden (0.29), Italy (0.16), Norway (0.11), Portugal (0.04) and Greece (-0.23).

TABLE AP.1 Hungary: GINV and the development of labour market variables, 1957-1965 (I.)

Panel A	Gross investment	Changes in employment: Industry	Changes in employment: Construction	Changes in employment: Non-agricultural sectors total	Change in overtime in the state sector of industry	Changes in the socialist sector of industry: Wage fund	Changes in the socialist sector of industry: Average nominal wage
	%	in 1000s	in 1000s	in 1000s	%	%	%
			Second Three-Year Plan (1958-1960)				
1957	-11.1	99.0	6.0	88.0	...	17.2	17.2
1958	29.0	39.0	17.0	100.0	0.0	4.8	0.9
1959	35.9	115.0	27.0	227.0	15.5	8.5	3.0
1960	11.0	40.0	4.0	93.0	-19.2	8.4	1.6
1961	-3.7	32.0	2.0	50.0	4.4	4.1	0.8

Panel B	Gross investment in the soc. sector	Changes in employment: Industry	Changes in employment: Non-agricultural sectors total	Change in overtime in the state sector of industry	Changes in the socialist sector of industry: Wage fund	Changes in the socialist sector of industry: Average nominal wage
	%	%	%	%	%	%
			Second Five-Year Plan (1961-1965)			
1961	-6.9	2.3	1.7	4.4	4.1	0.8
1962	15.5	3.3	3.0	9.8	5.8	2.4
1963	13.2	4.2	3.7	...	7.4	3.5
1964	4.8	4.4	1.9	7.1	6.1	2.4
1965	0.4	0.8	1.5	-22.0	0.7	0.1

Source: Bauer /1981/ pp. 114, 121, 133, 134.

private sector. This move gives workers a better chance to raise their incomes and/or to improve their access to goods and services in short supply. In this model, the manpower shortage is the main factor which triggers the reaction of central planners. Investments are cut and imports of consumer goods are increased in order to stop the exodus from the state sector.

Jacques Sapir's first analysis (which was later developed into a booksize historico-sociological study of the Soviet Union) sought to model specific Soviet conditions in a very abstract manner. For him, the main effect of the investment boom is a massive transfer of the agricultural labour force into industry. This results in a sharp deterioration of the food supply, which in turn compels the planners to slow down the investment process.

As mentioned, these models were never tested systematically either on Hungarian or on any other countries' data, and for this reason they are not directly relevant to this chapter. I refer to them, however, for the purpose of illustration. Such studies are excellent examples of how sometimes trivial and very appealing trains of thought are rooted in a given model framework - but as soon as we leave this framework, the logic working in the opposite direction can become just as trivial and appealing as the original one.

Two Investment "Cycles" in the Pre-reformed Hungarian Economy. The figures displayed in Appendix table 1 below are reproduced from Bauer (1981). There they served the important end of defending his contention concerning the causal link between investments and the labour market. In a 50-page chapter, he scrutinized two subsequent investment waves (or cycles as he called them) and came to the following conclusion.

> As far Hungarian investment fluctuations are concerned, some authors have claimed that these fluctuations did not spill over into the behaviour of other macro-economic indicators.[2] The data presented in this chapter (as partially reproduced here in Appendix table 1 - *P. M.*) do not support such assertions. We saw that the fluctuations of investment outlays are more or less echoed in construction output, in employment in industry and construction, in overtime, in wages and consumption, in retail trade, in the use of raw material inputs and in the import and export of traded goods. (*op. cit.* 149.)

When one looks at Bauer's argumentation in its original place, his data seem rather convincing. This is partly to be explained, however, by the fact that his data are presented in four blocks separated from each other by several pages of text. Once all the relevant figures are "squeezed" into a single table, they immediately become less plausible.

In fact, a glance at a time series consisting of less than ten elements provokes a more general objection. Is it justified to draw any conclusion from such a short series? For now, let us put aside this question. In defence of Bauer's original position, there is an argument to be made for replacing a "strong" theorem by a "weaker" one. It makes good sense, for instance, to say that the relationship linking investments with the labour market functions only in those years when a regular sine-curve investment wave occurs. If there is no such development and investments exhibit a steady growth, then the dampened random zigzags do not necessarily have an impact on other variables. If this "weak" theorem is true, it can still be argued that the investment cycle theory has furnished us with an important discovery.

My reading of the data, however, does not lend much support to this weaker theorem, either. In those years when investments took off - i.e. in the years 1958-1960 and 1962-1964 - Bauer was right to see a link between this on the one hand and the rise in industrial employment and overtime on the other. However, a closer inspection of the underlying processes and breakdown of aggregate figures into their components indicate that these undoubtedly parallel movements do not imply a true, causal relationship.

Appendix table 2 may seem to be a repetition of the previous table. Indeed, partly it is, though there is one important difference. In the second table, the indicators are perfectly comparable in Panels A and B - i.e. between the two planning periods - which was not the case in the first table.[3] This simplifies matters and aids understanding.

[2] At this point, Bauer makes explicit reference to a study by a Hungarian author - Zala (1968) - and the standard Western position as formulated in Portes (1969). In the places quoted by Bauer, both authors had stated clearly that in their view the Hungarian employment fluctuation was "almost completely independent" of the investment waves.

[3] For example, Appendix table 1 (Panel A) refers to total investments (GINV), while Panel B worked with data covering the socialist sector only; Panel A presented some series in absolute terms, while the same data appeared below in percentage form, etc.

TABLE AP.2 Hungary: GINV and the development of labour market variables, 1957-1965 (II.)

(Annual percentage changes in the socialist sector)

	Construction investment	Changes in the construction sector			Machinery investment (home-produced)	Changes in industry		
		Employment	Manual workers' overtime	Per capita real wages		Employment	Manual workers' overtime	Per capita real wages
	(GINV-C)	(EMPC)			(GINV-MD)	(EMPI)		
Panel A			Second Three-Year Plan (1958-1960)					
1957	-5.9	-3.3	...	20.9	...	0.0	...	15.6
1958	19.4	1.6	....	-2.1	...	3.9	1.9	0.3
1959	27.6	12.7	...	5.5	27.9	5.2	15.3	4.4
1960	10.7	-1.23	...	0.3	14.5	6.6	-19.1	0.4
1961	2.2	-2.8	-9.5	-0.2	-9.0	3.3	4.4	-0.4
Panel B			Second Five-Year Plan (1961-1965)					
1961	2.2	-2.8	-9.5	-0.2	-9.0	3.3	4.4	-0.4
1962	5.8	5.2	6.9	2.4	38.5	3.3	9.7	1.8
1963	6.8	3.2	208.7	6.2	11.9	3.8	39.9	4.0
1964	4.0	3.2	-42.5	0.3	2.1	3.4	7.1	1.5
1965	1.2	-2.5	-13.9	-0.2	4.9	0.5	-22	-0.6

Sources and notes: See table AP. 3.

First, let us consider the not very likely possibility that investment fluctuation is explained only by movements in the volume of imported machinery. If this is the case, there is no need to assume any kind of pre-determined sequence of change. Increased imports can be financed from loans and/or improvements in terms of trade. Another possibility is that increased export earnings by the agricultural or service sectors cover the costs of the higher machinery import bill. In the contrary case, a contraction of machinery imports may lead to balance-of-payments improvements or to a lessening of shortages on domestic markets. A more realistic assumption would be that a rise in investment is always accompanied by a similar change in domestic machinery production and construction activity. Thus, if the "weak" theorem holds, one can expect that

(1) Construction investment (GINV-C) will exhibit a correlation with the labour market indicators of the construction industry, and

(2) Investments of home-produced machinery (GINV-MD) will fluctuate in parallel with the labour market indicators of industry.

In other words, an attempt is made to follow the advice of Marrese (1981) by examining the investment data at a somewhat less aggregated level (Appendix table 2). The analysis was carried out on the basis of original data, published in various specialised yearbooks and compendia of the Hungarian Central Statistical Office (KSH). Although on some occasions Bauer worked from secondary sources (studies, newspaper articles), this proved to have little detrimental impact on his results apart from one small but important detail concerning overtime. I will revert to this issue later. The fact that the analysis covers the socialist sector only brings a small bias into the results, as the fluctuations of most macro-variables appear slightly stronger than those of the economy as a whole. This is particularly disturbing since the analysis revolves around the labour market as a whole, and the amount of labour tied up outside the socialist sector was quite significant over most of period covered.

During the first investment "cycle" which, in Bauer's view, took place during the Second Three-Year Plan (Panel A), there was a certain degree of comovement between changes in construction work (GINV-C) and changes in employment within that sector (EMPC). Let us note, however, that in 1960 and 1961, when construction investment still grew by 11 and 2 % respectively, the behaviour of the employment and overtime variables was not identical. Moreover, considering the cumulative impact of changes in these two years, the sign of the changes was negative with respect to these labour market indicators. The behaviour of real wages is a more clear-cut case: they were independent of the GINV-C level. Unfortunately, lacunae in the data prevent us from seeing whether there was any link between the machinery component of investment (GINV-MD) on the one hand and changes in the number of industrial employees (EMPI) on the other. Nevertheless, on the basis of available data we can be reasonably sure that this relationship was weak at the best.

Considering the historical circumstances of the period under examination (1957-1961) these findings should not appear surprising. It is well-known that after the brutal suppression of the 1956 uprising, the Hungarian government tried to appease the urban working class with extraordinary wage rises and various types of liberalisation measures. What is less well known is that the lion's share of the "improvements" was not distributed in cash - i.e. in nominal wage rises.

The main method was the relaxation of work discipline, the abolition of piece-work wages, the introduction of profit-sharing schemes, etc. In fact, wages went up as well. In the first three quarters of 1957, average industrial wages rose by almost 20 %, while output was just 1 % above the previous year's level (Pető and Szakács 1985, p. 314). It goes without saying that there were no massive lay-offs - despite larger-than-normal shortages of raw materials and semi-finished goods. The wage drift in the state sector was partly motivated by the regime's sudden opening toward the private sector. Early in 1957, the political leadership launched a supportive campaign for the benefit of private artisans.[4] In sum, managers and central planners had to close their eyes to the increasing gap between productivity and wages if they wanted to retain their best workers.

A year later, however, when political power had already been consolidated, there was no further need for such permissiveness. The widening of the private sector was immediately halted.[5] Work discipline was strengthened and investments were stepped up. As a result, the country's investment performance in 1958 surpassed the previous year's level by almost 30 %, although real wages in the two key sectors of the economy stagnated or even fell.[6]

During the period of the Second Five-Year Plan the story more or less repeated itself (Panel B in table 2). The enlargement of the construction work force was proportional to the rise in construction demand but changes in real wages and overtime were independent of GINV-C. In industry, by contrast, the employment changes behaved autonomously, while real wage changes were apparently sensitive to changes in the demand for domestic machinery. As far as overtime is concerned, the variation in yearly growth rates was so wild that it was probably independent from the state of the investment market.

For this second period all the necessary data are available. This enables them to be tested for the presence of lagged relationships. It is conceivable, for example, that a part of the investment of home-produced machinery manufactured in year t will not be installed until year t+1. Such a delay is less likely to occur in the construction sector, since this type of output is not storable. A closer examination of the data in Appendix table 2, however, does not support the hypothesis of a lagged relationship.

The Explanation of Overtime. In an approach which favours the endogenous cycle theory it is reasonable to assume a link between GINV fluctuation and changes in overtime. In macro-economic terms, an investment cycle means by definition a relatively sudden rise in investment activity. At the micro-level, according to the advocates of the endogenous cycle theory, construction firms and domestic machine builders have no alternative but to increase the number of hours worked by their manual labourers.[7]

In the preceding analysis of the developments in the 1960s, it was demonstrated that reality does not follow such simple logic. As Appendix table 2 showed, annual changes in overtime

[4] In the words of the party newspaper (*Népszabadság*, 5 January 1957), "Private artisans of the construction industry, carpenters, bricklayers, house-painters, electricians, etc. will get their trade licences in the shortest possible time, within one or two days." (quoted from Berend T. (1988, p. 99).

[5] Before the year ended, on 17 December 1957, the Politburo gave its (secret) verdict. "New trade licences will be given out in those areas where the socialist sector is unable to satisfy the needs of the population. The disproportionally high windfall profits of artisans will have to be creamed off through appropriate steps, such as more stringent taxation measures." (quoted by Ungvárszki (1989, p. 157.) on the basis of documents, which were released two decades later).

[6] As Appendix table 2 showed, there are lacunae in our data for 1958. The volume of domestic machinery investment is unknown. Detailed figures available for industry can, however, be used to assess the situation. Per capita nominal wages in the machinery industry, for example, rose by only 0.5 per cent in 1958, but productivity went up by 12 per cent. (KSH, 1966, pp. 100-101, 296-297).

[7] Hungarian statistics provide no record of the amount of overtime worked by and paid to white-collar employees.

displayed wild fluctuations, including a figure of 200 % for construction and a 40 % annual rise in industry[8] but GINV movements remained within a relatively narrow range.

There is an additional problem with the interpretation of the overtime statistics. Contemporary legal stipulations limited overtime for manual workers to 8 hours per month. This could be increased in exceptional cases to 12 hours with the permission of the Minister of the industry concerned (Timár, 1988 p. 133). Assuming a 192-hour working month and an extreme situation where all manual workers are required to accept overtime, this stipulation limits the maximum possible increase of labour inputs to 6.25 % - hardly sufficient to absorb the impact of fluctuations in investment demand. The solution to this contradiction was that the relevant chapters of the *Labour Code* were not taken seriously. In the infamous year 1963, monthly overtime was almost 8 hours *on average* in the construction industry. One can only speculate about the size of the maximum values behind such an average. It is little wonder that this amount of overtime was considered extraordinary at the time and the press diligently followed up the story (*Figyelö*, 29 January and 11 March 1964).

It was found that the doubling of overtime in the construction sector was a direct consequence of the 1962/63 winter cold spells. After the first few months of 1963, the leadership of the *construction industry* was shocked by the magnitude of plan underfulfilment. All their hopes were vested in overtime. People were forced to work like mad. This weapon was indeed effective: the annual plan was finally fulfilled by 96 %.

The clear breach of earlier norms regulating overtime was not accepted by the central planning authorities. They launched their own inquiry, too. It was quickly established that the problem had started earlier. In the previous two years the winters had been unusually mild. Hence little preparation was made on the most important construction sites for the eventuality of a harsh winter. When the harsh winter did come in early 1963, construction firms were not in a position to provide work assignments to their workers. Since by that time performance-related wage schemes were widely employed in the sector, discontented workers voted with their feet. When spring set in with warm weather, there was already an acute shortage of manpower. This was the real reason for the very extensive use of overtime.

In *industry*, the 1963 overtime surge was less spectacular, although a 40 % annual rise does require some explanation. The weather seems to have played no role. The clue was the nationwide reorganisation campaign, which happened to occur just that year. This was one of the successive centralisation campaigns, focusing this time on the metallurgical and engineering branches. Very quickly medium-sized enterprises were amalgamated into large trusts, affecting an estimated one fourth of the industrial labour force. The accompanying uncertainties were detrimental to morale and discipline. Plan targets were in danger. Company managers asked for overtime and the branch ministries agreed. The eight largest engineering firms - all of them affected in the reorganisation - used twice as much overtime than stipulated in their plans, amounting to 40 % of total overtime approved and paid in the entire engineering branch. One breach in the dyke tends to increase the probability of further breaches elsewhere. In mining,

[8] For some reason these extreme outliers were left out of Bauer's table (here reproduced in Appendix table 1), although the necessary raw data were directly available from the statistical yearbook (SE/1962, p. 103, SE/1963, p. 93.). At my request, Professor Bauer kindly made an effort to reconstruct the reasons for this omission, but the only answer he could give me was that the 1963 industrial overtime figure had been "lost" somewhere in the process of editing and retyping the manuscript.

for instance, a 76 % rise was registered in the same year and the food industry did not lag far behind (40 %).

And what happened in 1964? In industry, overtime - which was already very high - went up by another 7 %, due to liberalization measures introduced on an experimental basis.[9] This runaway behaviour triggered an immediate reaction from the central planning authorities. As from the following year, the previous regime of monthly base-rate wage taxation was replaced by a system based on actual wage flows (*Figyelö*, 20 January 1965.), which meant a clear attack on the use of highly-paid overtime work. A glance at Appendix table 2 is enough to see the effectiveness of the method chosen. Overtime in 1965 fell substantially in both industry (22 %) and construction (14%). On the production side, these developments had no visible impact: in 1965 construction investment was on the rise, and the same happened with domestic machinery installation.

[9] As from 1 July 1964, enterprises belonging to the Ministry of Metallurgy and Engineering were permitted to decide for themselves on overtime. According to the official reasoning, similar measures in other branches of the economy had proved fruitful, so the experiment was expanded.

TABLE AP.3 Hungary: GINV and the evolution of labour market variables, 1950-1989

(Socialist sector)

(Annual percentage change)

	Investment	Construction investment	Changes in the construction sector			Machinery investment	Changes in industry			
			Employment	Manual workers' overtime	Per capita real wages	home-produced	Employment	Manual workers' overtime	Per capita real wages	Gross output
	(GINV)	(GINV-C)	(EMP-C)			(GINV-MD)	(EMPI)			(INDT)
	[1]	[2]	[3]	[4]	[5]	[6]	[7]	[8]	[9]	[10]
1951	38.0	50.5	31.0	31.9	-10.9	...	18.0	...	-11.6	29.0
1952	18.1	14.0	16.2	32.6	-10.5	...	16.9	...	-9.3	24.0
1953	0.6	-6.4	3.7	-60.7	9.4	...	11.9	...	6.2	11.9
1954	-29.3	-36.2	-23.7	2.3	17.7	...	4.6	...	15.6	1.1
1955	-8.6	-12.8	-2.7	-29.9	7.4	...	0.1	...	5.7	7.7
1956	1.9	1.9	7.1	40.7	8.4	...	1.6	...	7.7	-8.2
1957	-7.4	-5.9	-3.3	...	20.9	...	0.0	...	15.6	13.4
1958	25.0	19.4	1.6	...	-2.1	...	3.9	1.9	0.3	11.3
1959	40.8	27.6	12.7	16.9	5.5	27.9	5.2	15.3	4.4	11.1
1960	17.6	10.7	-1.2	4.1	0.3	14.5	6.6	-19.1	0.4	12.7
1961	-5.8	2.2	-2.8	-9.5	-0.2	-9.0	3.3	4.4	-0.4	11.0
1962	15.4	5.8	5.2	6.9	2.4	38.5	3.3	9.7	1.8	8.3
1963	12.9	6.8	3.2	208.7	6.2	11.9	3.8	39.9	4.0	7.1
1964	6.7	4.0	3.2	-42.5	0.3	2.1	3.4	7.1	1.5	9.1
1965	0.4	1.2	-2.5	-13.9	-0.2	4.9	0.5	-22.0	-0.6	4.8
1966	10.7	10.7	5.3	4.4	3.5	4.6	1.4	2.3	2.6	6.7
1967	20.6	17.9	8.3	6.7	5.0	19.0	3.2	9.6	2.0	8.8
1968	0.6	-14.6	11.2	-9.8	4.1	-1.8	4.4	11.7	2.1	4.8
1969	11.5	46.7	10.5	19.6	3.5	19.6	2.9	18.0	2.3	2.6
1970	16.7	11.6	6.1	65.3	6.5	11.7	0.5	32.3	3.8	8.5
1971	9.7	6.8	2.2	-27.0	0.0	7.5	-0.2	-16.2	1.3	6.9
1972	-1.6	0.0	-1.0	-8.4	0.8	-3.5	-0.8	-5.8	1.9	5.1
1973	3.6	3.0	-2.2	-0.3	3.9	8.1	1.3	1.5	5.4	7.0
1974	9.5	2.9	1.0	20.3	6.1	13.8	0.9	10.9	5.8	8.6
1975	14.4	10.4	1.6	7.8	3.1	17.0	-0.2	2.4	3.0	4.6
1976	-0.3	-1.4	-0.5	-6.8	-0.2	-0.6	-0.8	7.7	0.1	4.7
1977	14.3	14.3	-0.1	4.7	2.5	9.3	-0.2	3.7	3.4	6.6
1978	5.5	2.6	0.2	-1.0	2.9	7.9	-0.1	-1.7	3.2	4.9
1979	1.1	3.0	-1.8	-10.8	-4.2	4.7	-1.6	-5.8	-4.0	3.0
1980	-6.6	-4.1	-3.9	-9.1	-4.4	-9.6	-2.8	-4.4	-3.1	-2.2
1981	-6.4	-5.6	-3.7	-5.3	2.0	-2.4	-2.1	2.6	2.5	2.9
1982	-3.1	-5.8	-4.8	-5.5	0.3	0.9	-2.0	15.1	-0.6	2.4
1983	-5.1	-5.8	-3.6	-5.7	-1.3	0.2	-2.0	-6.9	-2.0	0.8
1984	-4.9	-6.6	-3.0	-3.6	-1.6	1.4	-0.4	-3.0	-0.8	2.7
1985	-2.1	-3.8	-1.8	11.2	0.7	1.5	-0.6	-0.2	2.4	0.7
1986	1.6	0.4	-2.9	-16.5	2.6	8.9	-0.7	-3.1	2.0	1.9
1987	11.0	8.5	-0.6	12.4	2.4	15.4	-2.5	-2.7	0.0	3.7
1988	-8.3	-5.7	-2.4	-23.1	-4.5	-9.1	-2.6	-11.4	-4.5	-
1989	3.9	2.2	-9.1	-24.0	2.0	-1.8	-1.7	-4.4	-0.1	-1.0

Notes:

[1] Current price data, deflated by the official GINV price index

[3] 1950-75: Employees on construction sites
1975-89: Employees in construction industry proper

[4] 1950-56: State sector only
1956: Jan-Sept. data on comparable basis
1958-60: State sector only
1960-70: Construction enterprises
1970-87: Enterprises in construction industry proper

[5], [9] Average nominal earnings deflated by CPI

[6] 1959,1960: Author's estimate

[8] 1957-67: State sector

[10] Gross output, deflated by price index for total industry

Sources: Own calculations based on official statistics.

TABLE AP.4 Hungary: GINV and the development of labour market variables, 1959-1969

(Socialist sector)

Coefficients of correlation (r)

	GINV	GINV-C	GINV-MD	EMPC	EMPI	Overtime (constr.)	Overtime (industry)	INDT	Real wage (industry)	Real wage (constr.)
GINV	1.00									
GINV-C	0.55	1.00								
GINV-MD	0.75*	0.51	1.00							
EMPC	0.55	0.40	0.43	1.00						
EMPI	0.47	0.05	0.23	0.20	1.00					
Overtime (construction)	0.18	0.09	0.16	0.02	0.12	1.00				
Overtime (industry)	0.23	0.22	0.20	0.54	0.13	0.68	1.00			
INDT	0.37	-0.11	0.09	-0.31	0.61	-0.10	-0.21	1.00		
Real wage (industry)	0.67	0.36	0.45	0.75*	0.25	0.55	0.79*	-0.09	1.00	
Real wage (construction)	0.60	0.30	0.41	0.76*	0.17	0.60	0.77*	-0.22	0.90*	1.00

Note: * denotes coefficients significant at the 1 % level.

Sources and further notes: See table A. 10.

TABLE AP.5 Hungary: GINV and the development of labour market variables, 1970-1989

(Socialist sector)

Coefficients of correlation (r)

	GINV	GINV-C	GINV-MD	EMPC	EMPI	Overtime (constr.)	Overtime (industry)	INDT	Real wage (industry)	Real wage (constr.)
GINV	1.00									
GINV-C	0.96*	1.00								
GINV-MD	0.86*	0.76*	1.00							
EMPC	0.60*	0.55*	0.56*	1.00						
EMPI	0.58*	0.47	0.60*	0.51	1.00					
Overtime (construction)	0.55*	0.45	0.52	0.57*	0.43	1.00				
Overtime (industry)	0.39	0.27	0.34	0.37	0.36	0.83*	1.00			
INDT	0.71*	0.64*	0.69*	0.78*	0.79*	0.53	0.45	1.00		
Real wage (industry)	0.59*	0.48	0.63*	0.34	0.82*	0.50	0.46	0.72*	1.00	
Real wage (construction)	0.71*	0.57*	0.72*	0.36	0.69*	0.63*	0.61*	0.69*	0.91*	1.00

Notes: * denotes coefficients significant at the 1 % level.

Sources and further notes: See table A. 10.

The Level-of-Analysis Trap. It is time, at this point to abandon the micro-investigation into the details of Hungarian economic history. Appendix table 3 contains a number of other extreme values for overtime peaks and troughs alike. Most of them, I suspect, are reflections of the various centrally orchestrated campaigns of the wage and labour policy authorities but it would go beyond the scope of the present study to attempt to determine exactly what happened and why.

Our attention should now be concentrated on a systematic analysis of the relevant time series covering the period 1959-1989. This will be done by calculating linear correlation coefficients (r) between series expressed in the form of annual percentage changes.

The results are presented in Appendix tables 4 and 5. An asterisk (*) is place next to the numbers denoting r values which are statistically significant at the 1 % level. In presenting the results, a relationship is labelled a close one, if $r > 0.7$. In the remaining (significant) cases, the link between two variables will be termed modest or weak.

In the period 1959-1969 - i.e. before the 1968 economic reform made any sizeable impact - there was no significant relationship at all between the two main sub-components of investment and labour market variables (see the framed part of the data in Appendix table 4). In practical terms this means that performance requirements for labour utilisation were astonishingly loose, despite ostensibly strict central control of wage and output norms. Both in industry and in the construction sector, workers were always capable of producing 10-20 % more or less in exchange for a given wage bill, depending on the circumstances of the time.[10]

It appears, however, that the Hungarian labour market became more inter-connected after the 1968 reform. In industry and the construction sector, real wages and overtime evolved in parallel but displayed little sensitivity to changes originating in fluctuations in investment demand. This behaviour can probably be explained by the continuously strong presence of central labour market interventions chiefly aimed at regulating the total nominal wage bill. The hands of the planners were tied. The primary objective was to maintain a certain balance on the consumer goods market. Supply on this market was influenced by a host of exogenous factors (terms-of-trade developments, harvests, debt service, etc.), while short term changes in demand were largely dependent on domestic wage developments. Hence, the planners' instrumental variable was the wage bill. However, given the institutional setup of the system, they could not use this variable unimpededly, as the employment component was sacrosanct.[11]

In the post-reform Hungarian economy, as the framed data in Appendix table 5 indicate, the relationship between investment activity and the state of the labour market became more perceptible: the coefficients of correlation are higher and statistically significant. It is difficult to say whether this change was due entirely to the reform or whether the exhaustion of the rural labour reserves which also happened around 1970, played the decisive role. To complicate

[10] These findings are in line with the results of earlier research. Székffy (1978) found that the correlation (r) between per capita nominal wage changes and the rate of productivity increase in industry was 0.22 during the period 1950-74.

[11] Beyond those presented, several other possibilities were tested, but none of them yielded significantly different results. The analysis of overtime variables was carried out on time series without outliers; allowance was made for the fact that statistically reported overtime dropped after 1981 due the appearance of the so-called "intra-enterprise working communities" (*vállalati gazdasági munkaközösség*), etc.

matters further, it should be recalled that the 1968 reform itself was conceived primarily as a policy response to this irreversible demographic situation.[12]

It is interesting to note that in both periods, the pair-wise correlation between the first variable, denoting total investment, and the six labour market indicators is, in most cases, stronger than the correlation between these labour market variables on the one hand and GINV-C and GINV-DM taken separately on the other. This is a very important finding. As seen earlier, Marrese arrived at the same conclusion. The analysis of macro-economic processes, if carried out at an excessively high level of aggregation, yields misleading results. Either it suggests the presence of close causal relationships, even though there are none (as in the pre-1970 situation), or it magnifies the apparent strength of the correlation (as after 1970). The variable GINV-MD shows no close correlation with any labour market variables except real wages in the second period.[13] In many cases, the relationship was not even statistically significant. The situation is similar with the other component of investment demand. GINV-C behaved similarly to the employment indicator of the construction industry. Surprisingly, the link between GINV-C on the one hand and the wage and overtime variables on the other remained very unstable in the post-reform period, too.

Finding the correct level of aggregation is a problem well-known in empirical sociology under the name *ecological fallacy*. For the purpose of our analysis, we would prefer to talk of the *level-of-analysis trap*, since in a certain sense there is a similarity between this phenomenon and the two types of traps discussed in Chapter 5. According to sociologists, an ecological fallacy may occur when inferring from macro-level to micro-level data or vice versa. The classic example is the interference from the correlation between illiteracy and percentage of blacks on the regional level in the United States to the correlation between illiteracy and race on the individual level. Using 1930 U.S. census data, sociologists computed the correlation between race at the individual and at the regional level. These correlations were 0.2 and 0.95 respectively - graphic confirmation that aggregate data misestimate individual level correlations. Similar issues appear in the analysis of voting behaviour.[14]

Like all categorizations, dichotomous ones especially are not in themselves constructive. They reflect, however, as in our case, the dimensions of the debate and provide a structure for measurement. Thus, as the reader might have felt already throughout the previous chapters, the distinction between the micro and macro range of analysis is always somewhat artificial. In reality it is more of a continuum than a dichotomy. What is called a micro- or macro-level depends not so much on an absolute position but rather on the investigator's standpoint - i.e. his choice of units of analysis.

After this short methodological detour into the domain of sociology, let us go back to our own terrain - the analysis of Hungarian investment behaviour.

[12] In technical terms, this was formulated as a necessary shift from extensive to intensive economic growth.

[13] The picture was no different when allowance was made for lagged effects.

[14] For further references see Firebaugh (1978), Falter (1978) or Brown (1982).

2. Maintenance - capital repair - investment

Developments in the 1980s brought a surprise to Hungarian planners and cycle specialists alike. It was hoped that administratively repressed investment demand, combined with slow but still positive growth in production and consumption (Chart 1) would bring improvements on the investment front. In this spirit, austerity had been imposed on investments for more than a decade but the well-known deficiencies of investment behaviour (poor quality, protracted construction work) remained. To understand this "mystery", a new element will have to be incorporated in our analysis.

So far, investment has been treated in this book in a very conventional way, as adding to the stock of capital goods. Both the SNA and the MPS identify gross investment with the purchase of new durable goods, and define durable goods as those having an expected useful life of more than one year. In other words, the definition of investments is logically linked to the definition of fixed assets. In reality, however, the distinction between expenditures on additions to and maintenance of these assets is not as precise as would be desirable from a theoretical point of view. It is quite obvious, for example, that painting, decorating or repairing of buildings may last several years, yet these expenditures (which can be very large in modern high-wage societies) are not classified as part of gross investments. Maintenance of capital generally demands products from industries also producing goods destined for new investments. This contradiction was underscored in a brilliant but rarely mentioned study of Judik and Nötel (1949) - well before the internationally accepted rules of national accounting entered into force.[15]

Very few observers in Hungary noticed that the impact of GINV cuts had been more than offset by the seemingly uncontrolled rise of maintenance costs (Chart 2). Viewed in this perspective, it is clear that aggregate demand for investment goods will not fall (relative to supply) just because accounting and statistical rules require a two- (or three-) column breakdown of these very similar types of expenditures. It is thus little wonder that between 1979-1989 no improvement occurred on investment goods market. To be more precise, the fact of rising maintenance expenditures was registered by practical men[16], but its consequences were never seriously considered by planners or theoretical economists.

In what follows, I will focus attention on reconstructing the entire picture. By means of longer time series, an attempt will be made to identify those shorter periods, lasting 1-3 years, when the confusion between investment and maintenance costs was particularly significant from the perspective of cycle analysis.

[15] Another very important aspect of the problem, on which a completely new growth theory can be built (Scott, 1989), is the fact that maintenance of capital goods, just like new investments, induces production of which the fruits cannot be consumed. Hence, it is perfectly sensible for analytical purposes, to lump maintenance and capital stock increases into one single category and to define investments as a residual - i.e. in terms of consumption forgone.

[16] Among the authors of several shorter studies and newspaper articles it is worth mentioning the names of Vargha (1986), Gegesy (1987), Pálfi (1988) and Sárkány (1988). More or less independently from each other, these authors all came to the conclusion that there was no separate market for investment goods on the one hand and for maintenance goods on the other.

CHART AP.1 Hungary: Allocation of GDP, 1979-1989

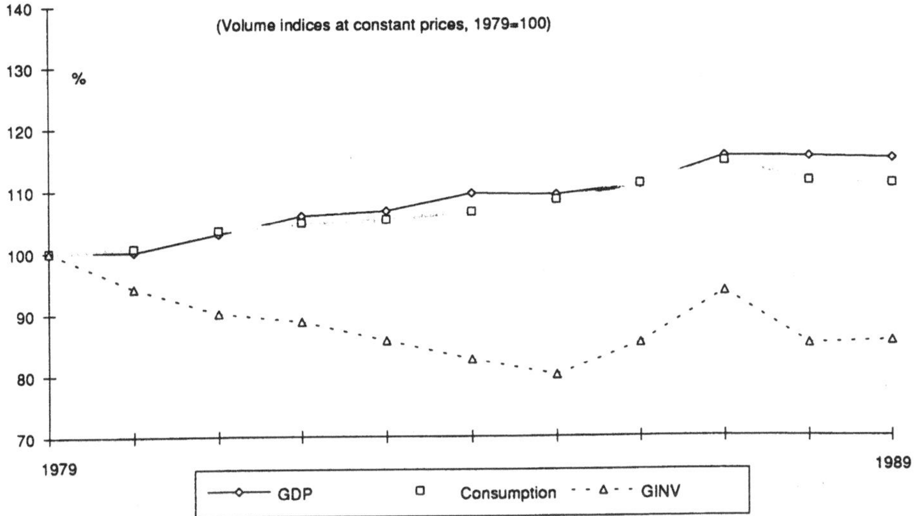

Source: ECE/DEAP Common Data Base

CHART AP.2 Hungary: GINV and maintenance costs, 1960-1989

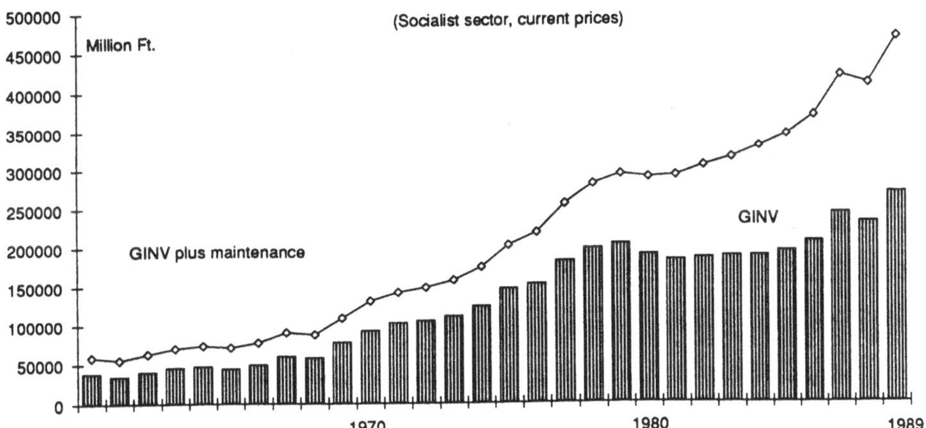

Source: See table AP.6

TABLE AP.6 Hungary: GINV and maintenance costs, 1950-1989

(Socialist sector, at current prices)

	Maintenance	Capital repairs a/	Reconstruction	GINV	Maintenance costs as % of GINV	Maintenance b/ (annual change)	GINV
	Mn Ft	Mn Ft	Mn Ft	Mn Ft	%	%	%
	[1] = [2]+[3]	[2]	[3]	[4]	[5]=[1]/[4]*100	[6]	[7]
1950	...	...	1143	9664	.	...	...
1951	...	...	1352	13127	.	18.3	35.8
1952	...	...	2251	15824	.	66.5	20.5
1953	...	...	3612	16741	.	60.5	5.8
1954	...	...	3248	11620	.	-10.1	-30.6
1955	...	...	4398	10892	.	35.4	-6.3
1956	...	...	4522	11284	.	2.8	3.6
1957	...	...	4879	10821	.	7.9	-4.1
1958	...	...	5665	13548	.	16.1	25.2
1959	...	...	10038	31708	.	.	.
1960	19885	8927	10958	38536	51.6	9.2	21.5
1961	19935	8957	10978	34787	57.3	0.3	-9.7
1962	22124	9877	12247	40147	55.1	11.0	15.4
1963	23675	10763	12912	45434	52.1	7.0	13.2
1964	25072	11573	13499	47592	52.7	5.9	4.7
1965	25872	12157	13715	44681	57.9	3.2	-6.1
1966	27649	...	...	49199	56.2	6.9	10.1
1967	30476	...	...	59662	51.1	10.2	21.3
1968	29107	...	...	57804	50.4	-4.5	-3.1
1969	31505	...	...	77532	40.6	8.2	34.1
1970	39095	...	...	91999	42.5	24.1	18.7
1971	39138	...	...	102866	38.0	0.1	11.8
1972	42764	...	...	105563	40.5	9.3	2.6
1973	46033	...	...	111616	41.2	7.6	5.7
1974	49851	...	...	124156	40.2	8.3	11.2
1975	55222	...	...	146522	37.7	10.8	18.0
1976	66128	...	...	152089	43.5	19.7	3.8
1977	73201	...	...	181493	40.3	10.7	19.3
1978	82096	...	...	197606	41.5	12.2	8.9
1979	88709	...	...	203957	43.5	8.1	3.2
1980	98766	...	...	189676	52.1	11.3	-7.0
1981	107892	...	...	182781	59.0	9.2	-3.6
1982	117520	...	...	185765	63.3	8.9	1.6
1983	126026	...	...	188148	67.0	7.2	1.3
1984	139987	...	...	188792	74.1	11.1	0.3
1985	150987	...	...	194128	77.8	7.9	2.8
1986	161221	...	...	207354	77.8	6.8	6.8
1987	175889	...	...	243605	72.2	9.1	17.5
1988	177465	...	...	231960	76.5	0.9	-4.8
1989	198066	...	...	269489	73.5	11.6	16.2

Note: a/ Calculated data
b/ In 1950-1958: reconstruction expenditure

Source: KSH (1967) p. 63; KSH (1979), p. 311, SÉ (various years)

The Method. The basic data are displayed in Appendix table 6. They cover, once again, the socialist sector only. What is more regrettable, however, is the lack of appropriate deflators for maintenance and reconstruction work. Thus, the analysis for maintenance (col.1), repair (col. 2), reconstruction (col. 3) and investments as such (col. 4) was carried out in current price terms.

The investigation tests a very simple hypothesis. By eliminating the trend effect, periods will be identified when expenditures on maintenance or investments are significantly different from zero. Then, a test is applied to find out whether these deviations are systematic in the sense that upward (downward) turns in one of them is a mere reflection of downward (upward) turns in the other.

Having experimented with different analytical functions, it appears that the best trend fit can be approximated by logarithmic functions. A single trend for the entire period is inadequate for the following two reasons.

(1) Since the underlying data are at current prices, the impact of abrupt price changes has to be taken into account. On 1 January 1959, there was a revision of wholesale prices throughout the Hungarian economy which resulted, on average, in a 100 % rise. To eliminate this effect, the periods before and after this date had to be treated separately.

(2) As noted above, the investment historical time series was broken in 1979. Hence a second trend was fitted for the period 1979-1989.[17]

The Results. The analysis yielded results which were not robust enough to pass statistical significance criteria. Our original model was built on the hypothesis that high values of GINV are *always* associated with low maintenance costs. This proved incorrect both for the entire period 1950-1987, as well as for the two selected sub-periods (1950-1965, 1968-1989).

Charts 3 and 4 suggest a plausible explanation. The assumed trade-off between investment and maintenance manifested itself only in certain years, not frequently enough to be felt in the intertemporal average. Correlation analysis, of course, is a method of reflecting comovements in time, exhibiting itself with considerable intensity throughout the entire test period. However, as the estimation results confirmed, it is not realistic to claim that every single above-average investment peak is the consequence of postponed or ill-registered maintenance. It seems that only the outliers can be explained by our initial hypothesis.

In the 1950-1965 period the deviation series behaved similarly for investments and maintenance alike. As Chart 3 shows, in the first sub-period there were only few years where the divergence between the two series was marked. This happened first in 1954-1955, when GINV cuts were implemented in a very drastic manner. Relative to 1953 (in the period of the "thaw") investments fell by 30 % in the first year and by another 6 % in the next (Appendix table 6). In 1954, maintenance expenditures seem to have been reduced as well but in 1955 they shot up by 30 %, as if enterprises had suddenly understood the new rules of the game. The

[17] The careful reader will certainly notice that figures displayed in Appendix table 6 contain a smaller break in 1968. This was related to the introduction of the *New Economic Mechanism.* The transition period in 1967/68 had resulted in a slight statistical confusion, because enterprises were allowed to record investments implemented in the early months of 1968, as a part of their 1967 activities (Gegesy, 1987). In the present computations, this problem was eliminated by means of averaging out the data for neighbouring years.

slackening of the investment process in 1964-1965 was induced by centrally orchestrated "austerity measures" in response to the deterioration in the balance-of-payments.[18] Maintenance expenditures were also affected by the cuts but not very significantly.

The period after 1968 was less homogenous than the earlier one. Until 1975, in an epoch when investments in absolute terms had risen steeply, maintenance expenditures fell well below the trend level in every year. Between 1976-1980 tendencies were rather blurred. This was a transitory period, perhaps. After 1981 the trade-off mechanism started to work with full force once again: when investments declined, maintenance expenditures remained above trend levels.

[18] Between 1959 and 1963 foreign indebtedness doubled (from $ 140mn to 350mn) and there was no improvement in 1964 either. In 1965, the level of western debt already surpassed the value of annual hard currency exports. The situation was particularly alarming as 80 per cent of the new debt was financed from short-term borrowing. (My estimates, based on figures reported in Berend T. (1983, pp. 416-418)).

CHART AP.3 Hungary: GINV and maintenance costs, 1950-1965

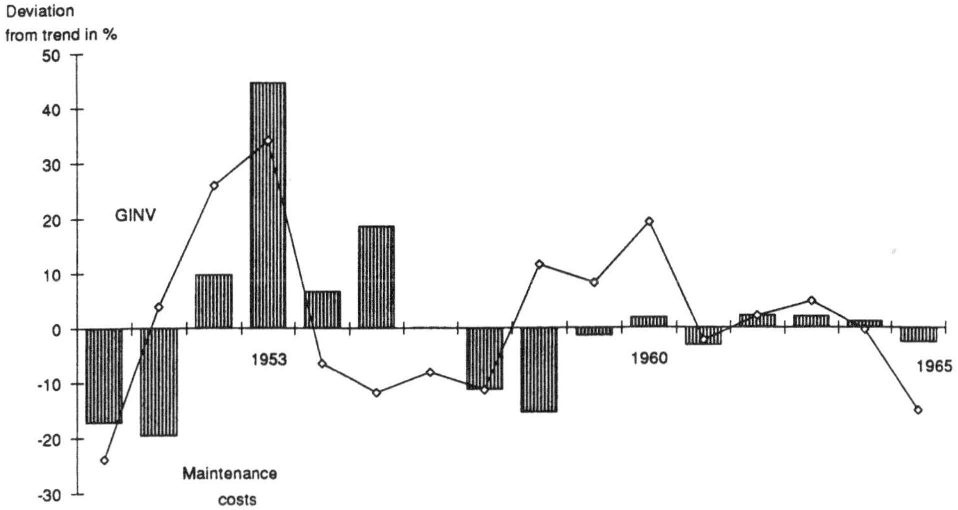

Source: Table AP.6

CHART AP.4 Hungary: GINV and maintenance costs, 1968-1989

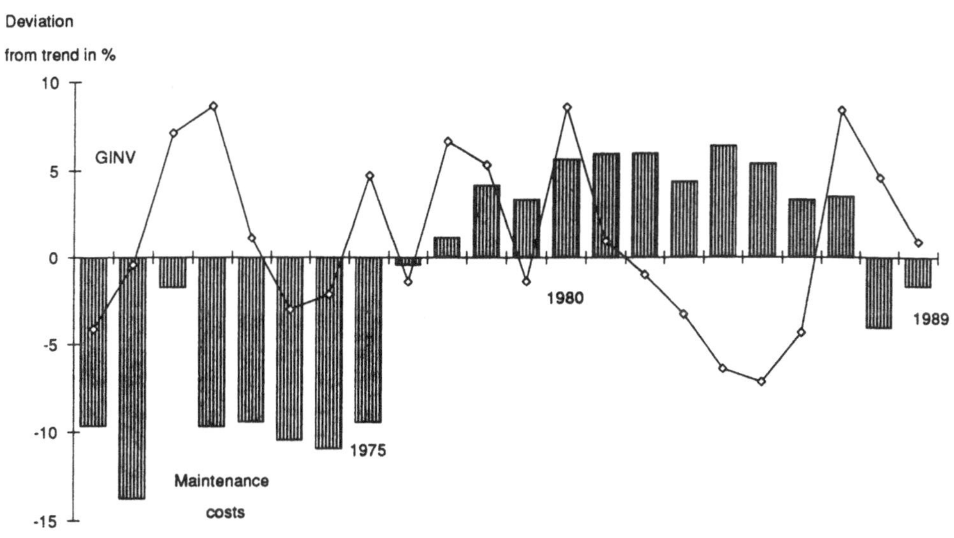

Source: Table AP.6

Enterprise Behaviour and Macro-economic Policy Making. Managers of socialist enterprises, as well as the centrally dispatched army of auditors, were fully aware of the practical difficulties of drawing a clear separation line between investment and maintenance expenditures. When machines were repaired or buildings were renovated, the replacement of old components by new and better ones was often the only practical and economically rational possibility. The centrally-set accounting rules also anticipated this problem by providing a list of examples to advise accountants.

In an imaginary world, it is possible that enterprise accountants could work out a sufficiently detailed (and centrally harmonized) list of examples to be applied in practice with a reasonable degree of consistency throughout the national economy. Alas, the real world is different. In state owned enterprises (SOEs), accounting is not an activity where honesty and professional integrity are the highest moral imperatives. It is, rather, an integral part of managers' survival strategy: bonus payments and promotion are linked to it. If top managers insisted, the accounting department of a typical SOE was always ready to shift part of investment expenditures under the heading of maintenance, or vice versa. Within certain limits this has always been possible and nobody from outside could prove that the accounts had been doctored.

This assumption begs a question: why were managers interested in such manipulation? And if they were, would it not be sufficient for the purpose of our analysis to simplify matters and have recourse to Nove's principle of "equal cheating"?[19] In the semi-monetized Hungarian economy, I believe, the principle of "equal cheating" cannot be applied. It should be recalled that from the very outset of the 1968 reform, enterprise taxation was primarily aimed at controlling the size of investment funds. Depending upon the short-term objectives of central planners, enterprise profits were taxed at different rates at different times while maintenance expenditures, which were treated as costs, remained immune to the impact of the short-term zigzags of fiscal regulation. Here are a few figures to illustrate the orders of magnitude. During the years 1968-1975 4 Forints of profits had to be earned for every Forint of investment. This ratio declined to Ft 2.50 in the period 1976-1980, and then rose again to 3 Forints between 1980-1986.[20] For this simple reason, the motivation to cheat was different from year to year; therefore it is very likely that the extent of exaggeration was also not the same in every year.

Let us now consider how this phenomenon was reflected in the aggregate statistics which served as the basis for planning and control of the Hungarian economy. In the first fifteen years of planning, SOEs were compelled to report repair, reconstruction and investment expenditures in a clearly separated manner. At the level of national aggregation, repairs were treated as costs and were omitted from macro-economic calculations of accumulation. Reconstruction and investment figures, by contrast, were closely monitored by the central planning and statistical authorities. In plan fulfilment reports and other planning documents the two categories were often mentioned separately but equally often only the combined value of the two was cited.

This practice, which was in line with both SNA recommendations and the practice of other CMEA countries, was followed until 1965. After that year the methodology changed in this respect. Enterprises were freed from the obligation to report maintenance and reconstruction costs separately. Consequently, the earlier three-level differentiation also contracted to two

[19] This "law" states that exaggerated reporting does not necessarily prevent meaningful economic analysis unless the extent of exaggeration changes (Nove 1977, p. 352).

[20] See Sárkány (1988) and the report of an expert meeting devoted to the subject of this chapter (*Figyelö*, 31 July 1986).

(investments and maintenance) in the system of national accounts. This was not a fortunate decision, since the earlier distinction between replacing a nut and bolt rather than the entire engine disappeared.

Why did this happen then? First of all, let us note that the decision was not initiated by the KSH. It was the Planning Office and the experts of the Ministry of Finance who insisted on the change. These bodies were led by their own logic. At that time economic reform was equated with decentralisation. The intention was to give more independence to enterprises and for this reason the earlier system of the compulsory build-up of "maintenance funds" was abolished.

The planning organs tried to learn from practice. In the pre-reformed Hungarian economy, investments were completely free of charge for enterprises. Investment funds were centrally allocated to them, while maintenance costs, as noted, formed a part of production costs. In this system, where cost-reduction was an important plan target, managers had a particularly strong interest in reporting even the most trivial maintenance expenditures as part of investment work. Undeserved bonuses and promotion were "earned" in this way, a phenomenon which annoyed the ministerial bureaucracy.

The consequences were important at the macro-level as well. As maintenance costs were hidden in investment expenditures, the rate of investment appeared to be unrealistically high and the corresponding capital-output ratios showed a serious decline, which was due partly to this very effect.[21]

As an unwanted consequence of the 1965 changes, which were partly aimed at eliminating a statistical artefact, another disturbing factor was built into the Hungarian investment statistics. Up to the present day, reported GINV figures are smaller than they should be according to the SNA methodology because of the exclusion of reconstruction expenditures. The current practice of mixing up maintenance with reconstruction at the enterprise level is most unfortunate, since this fact also precludes the systematic separation of the two phenomena at the macro-level.[22]

It is very difficult to quantify the magnitude of this type of distortion, because a good part of reconstruction work "which results in an addition to the size, power, capacity or functionability of the fixed asset in question" (KSH 1977, p. 22) still has to be registered as investment. In other words, the present practice of the KSH represents a half-way solution between the original idea of the Hungarian planners and the SNA recommendation with which the Hungarian statisticians have had an ongoing love affair.[23]

[21] I am grateful to Mr. J. Arvay (KSH), who was kind enough to shed some light on the motives for the changes described above.

[22] A quick look at column <2> in Appendix table 5 suggests that an approximate solution can be found by applying coefficients to estimate the missing data. When the new method was introduced, KSH published a retrospective time series for the period 1960-1965, thereby creating an alternative series for those early years according to the new methodology. A closer inspection of the data in cols. <2> and <3>, however, reveals that the ratio of the two series for the overlapping years is suspiciously stable (1: 1.2). This means - and Mr. J. Dudás (KSH) was kind enough to confirm this surmise - that we do not really possess two alternative data series. The first six figures in column <1> are already the result of retroactive estimates; hence they cannot be used as a basis for further extrapolation.

[23] In the relevant passages, the SNA suggests that "to identify the part of repair work that lengthens the expected life of the fixed assets or increases their productivity, and to transfer the expenditures on these major repairs to gross fixed capital formation." (UN 1986a, p. 136)

The other side of the coin is also interesting. The statisticians were ready to give in to the demand of the planners because the most important objective for those really involved in the discussions was the integrity of the national income calculation. From this point of view the 1965 changes did not matter at all. If, in the calculation of net accumulation, allowance is made for a part (or for the whole) of reconstruction works, a corresponding increase has to be applied in the calculation of depreciation. As long as macro-economic accounting and planning are carried out in the framework of national income calculations (which do not include depreciation) the whole issue was of secondary importance. The situation changed, of course, in the second half of the 1980s, when emphasis was shifted towards the GDP concept. Since the value of depreciation is included in GDP, the deviation from SNA methodology in the daily application of GINV calculations has become more and more embarrassing.

From the perspective of our narrower subject - the analysis of the investment process - the 1965 decision had another very important consequence. The accepted method, whereby maintenance and reconstruction expenditures were mixed together to a very great extent, has created a logically untenable situation for investment planning as well. I believe that this statement holds even if the Hungarian planners have themselves failed to realise it. The methodology deceived planners into thinking that they had control over investment demand. This was simply not true. Planners thought that the reported GINV figures could be equated with the volume of transactions on the investment good markets. But the improper and unreliable treatment of maintenance and reconstruction expenditures meant that the figure in their hands had a much smaller information content than they thought.

According to 1987 data only 58 Ft out of 100 Ft investment demand were embodied in GINV and the remaining 42 Ft were for maintenance work. It should be noted, however, that these figures reflected the prevailing proportions in the socialist sector only, as maintenance data were not readily available from households and the private sector. If allowance is made for the estimated amount of maintenance carried out in these two sectors, the 58 % share drops back to only 36 %.

* * *

In the classical system of direct planning - i.e. in the pre-1968 period - the methodological confusion concerning the treatment of maintenance, repair and construction did not cause too much trouble. This was so, first, because in those years the volume of such expenditures was relatively small (col. <5> in Appendix table 6). The second, more important reason was that in those years firms were kept on a short leash anyway. Both inputs and outputs were strictly planned and controlled in physical terms. Bricks remained bricks, imported machinery components remained imported components. It did not matter much what the accounting department did with the corresponding monetary flows.

3. Conclusions

The first part of Appendix I focused on testing the multiplier hypothesis in the context of investment cycle theory. It was shown that, contrary to widespread belief, there was no strong relationship between fluctuations in investment demand on the one hand and labour market developments on the other. It would go beyond the scope of the present book to investigate the presence of similar spill-over effects in other key variables - for example consumption, stock-building or hard currency imports. Such an inquiry, I suspect, would yield results similar to those presented above.[24] In a highly centralised (and politicised) system everything is potentially interlinked - which means, paradoxically, that pair-wise relationships between selected variables tend to be highly unstable over time.

The second part of the Appendix extended the analysis of the investment process, showing the difficulties arising from an outdated, artificial delineation between gross fixed investments on the one hand and capital repair and maintenance on the other. Once again, the complexities of the issue have been demonstrated only for Hungary but it is fairly obvious that the situation was very much the same in the other socialist countries.

[24] This suggestion has been corroborated by a recent study (Abel *et al.*, 1989). Analyzing the period 1960-1986, the authors found virtually no correlation (r) between the annual growth rates of GINV and the above-mentioned three variables. Using current price series for all variables, their results were as follows: 0.300, 0.180 and 0.362. None of these values are significant at the 5 % level.

APPENDIX II: BASIC DATA

TABLE SA. 1 Gross fixed investments (GINV) at comparable prices, 1949-1989

	Bulgaria	CSSR	GDR	Hungary	Poland	Romania	USSR	Yugoslavia
	(In millions of national currency units)							
1949	357	18335	3804	...	110695	...	12035	21681
1950	363	22020	4786	32170	151430	6371	14379	19089
1951	446	26664	6041	40084	169493	8720	16298	18790
1952	528	31820	7713	47773	201684	11466	17612	15600
1953	580	33288	9269	47162	233048	14517	19270	19300
1954	622	32710	9465	36160	247963	13130	22778	20870
1955	663	35016	10864	34197	256188	14740	25727	20372
1956	670	39552	13708	36578	269174	16887	29622	19757
1957	679	43047	14213	32524	288378	16594	33451	23566
1958	830	48368	16406	41950	316634	18407	38879	27105
1959	1255	57965	19898	57038	370390	21396	44031	31238
1960	1463	64859	21949	63312	393530	27958	47600	36340
1961	1471	69239	22190	61626	422257	32746	49562	41657
1962	1591	67228	22780	67972	463184	36960	51914	44960
1963	1814	59688	23104	77253	475384	39775	54528	49628
1964	1994	66305	25277	80009	497815	43749	59358	57177
1965	2141	71253	27556	81187	545038	47677	64200	50056
1966	2562	77997	29339	90103	590688	52378	68690	52791
1967	3166	80338	31955	107702	657588	61086	74285	58731
1968	3450	86869	35423	109503	715043	68205	80109	57933
1969	3484	95165	40930	118508	773679	72677	82798	61587
1970	3853	100672	43707	138506	804768	81118	92264	68478
1971	3919	106449	44447	153156	864191	89635	98826	72668
1972	4311	115910	46681	151513	1062923	98915	105777	74910
1973	4607	126302	50587	156432	1332885	107056	110628	77074
1974	4965	137837	53337	173554	1630393	121353	118354	84054
1975	5825	149251	55793	193493	1805120	139674	128479	92181
1976	5860	155811	59867	193522	1823616	151567	134003	99689
1977	6690	164685	63059	217066	1879891	169260	138638	109109
1978	6732	171424	64846	227530	1920031	196294	146614	120589
1979	6581	174488	65606	229270	1768128	204368	147584	128330
1980	7078	176977	65702	216754	1550900	210451	150853	120717
1981	7818	168754	67307	206641	1204300	195509	156442	108885
1982	8098	164932	63853	203421	1058200	189406	161939	102892
1983	8152	165840	63660	196427	1157300	194036	170987	92901
1984	8179	158874	60560	189189	1289700	205611	174278	83979
1985	8880	167482	62602	183422	1366600	208978	179464	80903
1986	9587	169891	65933	195335	1436297	211277	194396	83710
1987	10274	177418	71205	214557	1496621	208351	205452	79390
1988	10525	184640	76368	194987	1577439	203753	218218	74780
1989	10662	187638	77053	196000	1539580	200493	228442	75360

Bulgaria:	1982 price level	(1984-date: from published current price indices)
CSSR	1984 price level	
GDR	1985 price level	
Hungary	1981 price level	
Poland	1982 price level	
Romania	1977 price level	
USSR	1 January 1984 "smet" prices	
Yugoslavia	1972 price level	

Source: ECE/DEAP Common Data base and SG/ various years

TABLE SA. 2 Gross fixed investments: incomplete series, 1950-1989

(In millions of national currency units)

	Albania	China	Cuba	Ethiopia	Mongolia	Viet Nam
1950	309	...	...	...	41	...
1951	404	...	...	...	...	...
1952	554	...	...	...	...	...
1953	547	9159	...	...	...	...
1954	324	10268	...	...	...	...
1955	467	10524	...	...	124	...
1956	510	16084	...	...	...	...
1957	659	15123	...	...	...	...
1958	1005	27906	...	...	378	...
1959	1092	36802	...	...	511	...
1960	1087	41658	389	...	579	...
1961	1135	15606	...	...	847	...
1962	984	8728	572	...	930	...
1963	1037	11666	696	...	919	...
1964	1347	16589	772	...	760	...
1965	1650	21690	842	...	815	...
1966	1820	25480	935	...	846	...
1967	1707	18772	1032	...	1018	...
1968	1727	15157	916	527	1195	...
1969	2094	24692	817	533	1139	...
1970	2442	36808	800	513	1062	...
1971	2512	41731	953	554	1149	...
1972	...	41281	1068	603	1146	12808
1973	...	43812	1456	569	1236	...
1974	...	46319	1698	549	1596	...
1975	3265	54494	2304	580	1883	...
1976	...	52394	2588	578	2575	...
1977	...	54380	2766	606	3010	...
1978	...	66872	2624	545	3724	...
1979	...	69936	2606	698	2600	...
1980	3928	74590	2769	854	3104	15959
1981	4058	66751	3430	922	4289	14351
1982	4396	84531	3056	1082	4646	14409
1983	4556	95196	3493	1119	3924	18594
1984	4505	118518	4093	1570	4282	23226
1985	4107	168051	4396	1540	4634	24839
1986	4252	197950	4419	1563	4763	20559
1987	4351	229700	3901	1797	4555	16020
1988	4432	...	4136	1873	4538	16757
1989	4915	...	4583	1661	4807	16278

China, Cuba, Ethiopia, Mongolia : At current prices.

Albania: 1986 price level, socialist sector, presumably without agricultural cooperatives.

China: State sector

Vietnam: State sector at 1982 prices

Source: National and CMEA statistics; Albania, Mongolia: GDR stat. yearbooks for early years; Cuba: UN National Account yearbooks, Bettelheim, 1987 p. 248; Ethiopia: UN national account yearbooks, IMF and World Bank data.

TABLE SA. 3 CSSR, USSR: Alternative GINV time series

	Soviet Union				Czechoslovakia	
	Official data		CIA estimates			
	At 1 July 1955 prices Billion roubles	At 1 January 1984 prices Million roubles		1970 prices Billion roubles		At 1984 price level (Mn Kcs)
1929	7.6	1203.5	1950	19.0	1960	64859
1930	12.7	2011.1	1951	22.6	1961	68744
1931	18.4	2913.7	1952	22.7	1962	67246
1932	21.6	3420.5	1953	26.2	1963	61901
1933	18.0	2850.4	1954	28.1	1964	68796
1934	23.7	3753.0	1955	34.1	1965	71844
1935	27.8	4402.3	1956	38.8	1966	80976
1936	38.1	6033.3	1957	43.3	1967	78790
1937	33.8	5352.4	1958	48.1	1968	81845
1938	35.1	5558.3	1959	53.4	1969	91023
1939	40.8	6460.9	1960	56.2	1970	96173
1940	43.2	6841.0	1961	62.5	1971	103216
1941	37.4	5922.5	1962	65.1	1972	112128
1942	23.0	3642.2	1963	60.0	1973	122097
1943	23.1	3658.0	1964	74.0	1974	131832
1944	31.7	5019.9	1965	80.9	1975	141943
1945	39.2	6207.5	1966	81.6	1976	146918
1946	46.8	7411.0	1967	84.7	1977	157412
1947	50.8	8044.5	1968	90.2	1978	163334
1948	62.1	9833.9	1969	96.0	1979	158281
1949	76.0	12035.0	1970	108.2	1980	163755
			1971	113.4	1981	160130
			1972	118.2	1982	158417
			1973	129.1	1983	156841
			1974	137.6	1984	159488
			1975	140.6	1985	166265
			1976	151.8	1986	176053
			1977	159.5	1987	174340
			1978	165.5	1988	183401
			1979	168.3		
			1980	173.3		

Source: USSR: Table SA.1 and NKh/1956, p. 173; CIA (1982) Table A-6.
Czechoslovakia: Own calculations based on Nachtigal (1989) p. 221.

TABLE SA. 4 Investment ratios (IR), 1950-1989

	Bulgaria	CSSR	GDR	Hungary	Poland	Romania	USSR	Yugoslavia
				(Percentages)				
1950	20.6	22.7	15.8	25.1	17.4	17.7	24.9	32.3
1951	19.9	25.1	16.2	26.9	18.1	19.3	25.2	29.3
1952	22.3	27.0	17.7	32.8	20.3	23.3	24.5	28.5
1953	20.8	26.6	19.9	28.8	21.2	26.6	24.5	34.9
1954	21.6	25.2	18.4	23.1	20.4	23.0	25.8	31.8
1955	20.8	24.5	19.3	20.2	19.5	22.0	26.1	27.3
1956	20.8	26.3	23.2	24.4	19.1	27.1	27.0	28.0
1957	18.6	26.6	22.6	17.7	18.5	22.9	28.4	27.7
1958	21.3	27.7	23.9	21.6	19.2	24.6	29.4	31.4
1959	26.5	31.2	26.4	27.6	21.4	25.3	31.0	31.1
1960	28.9	32.3	27.7	27.9	21.8	29.8	31.1	33.7
1961	28.3	32.3	27.5	26.0	21.6	31.8	30.3	36.6
1962	28.7	30.9	27.5	27.1	23.2	34.3	30.0	38.3
1963	30.5	28.0	26.9	29.2	22.3	33.7	30.3	37.7
1964	30.5	31.0	28.1	29.0	21.8	33.2	30.2	39.0
1965	30.6	32.2	29.3	29.4	22.4	33.0	30.6	33.6
1966	33.0	32.3	29.7	30.1	22.6	33.0	30.3	32.9
1967	37.2	31.6	30.7	33.3	23.8	35.8	30.1	35.8
1968	38.2	31.8	32.4	32.2	23.8	37.4	30.0	34.1
1969	35.1	32.5	35.6	32.3	25.0	37.1	29.6	33.0
1970	36.2	32.5	36.0	36.0	24.7	38.7	30.2	34.8
1971	34.5	32.6	35.0	37.6	24.6	37.7	30.7	34.2
1972	35.2	33.6	34.8	35.0	27.3	37.8	31.6	33.9
1973	34.8	34.8	35.7	33.8	30.9	37.0	30.3	33.2
1974	34.9	35.8	35.4	35.4	34.2	37.3	30.8	33.4
1975	37.6	36.5	35.3	37.2	34.8	39.1	32.0	35.4
1976	35.5	36.6	36.6	36.1	32.9	38.1	31.5	36.8
1977	38.1	37.2	36.7	37.8	32.3	39.2	31.2	37.3
1978	36.3	37.2	36.4	38.1	32.0	42.3	31.4	38.7
1979	33.3	36.7	35.4	38.0	30.2	41.4	30.9	38.4
1980	33.9	36.2	33.9	36.2	28.2	41.5	30.4	35.3
1981	35.7	34.5	33.2	33.7	24.8	37.7	30.5	31.4
1982	35.4	33.7	30.7	32.3	23.1	35.6	30.4	29.6
1983	34.6	33.1	29.2	31.1	23.8	35.2	30.8	27.0
1984	33.2	30.6	26.3	29.2	25.1	34.6	30.5	24.0
1985	35.4	31.4	25.9	28.8	25.8	33.2	30.9	23.0
1986	36.3	31.0	26.1	30.4	25.8	31.3	32.8	23.0
1987	37.0	31.7	27.3	32.0	26.4	30.2	34.1	22.1
1988	37.1	32.3	28.5	29.3	26.5	28.9	34.7	21.2
1989	34.4	32.5	28.2	29.7	25.9	31.5	34.1	21.2

IR = (GINV/NMP)*100

Source: Own calculations, based on ECE/DEAP Common Data Base

TABLE SA.5 Gross fixed capital formation in the developed market economies, 1960-1989

	France	FRG	Italy	U.K.	Austria	Belgium	Denmark	Finland	Ireland	Netherlands	Norway	Sweden
	In million 1985 dollars at 1985 exchange rates											
1960	39557	73852	45417	40285	6168	7078	5358	6126	927	12635	5220	10091
1961	43857	78773	50669	44219	6943	7904	6104	6686	1075	13397	5865	10899
1962	47580	81892	55617	44522	7133	8398	6510	6722	1234	13851	6535	11590
1963	51764	83028	60110	45142	7379	8490	6353	6522	1382	14008	6782	12374
1964	57184	92488	56613	52616	7651	9662	7844	6918	1542	16691	7006	13310
1965	61181	96809	51853	55340	8047	10053	8212	7640	1696	17578	7482	13847
1966	65620	97987	54095	56752	8759	10748	8562	7942	1646	18990	7925	14479
1967	69577	91227	60443	61715	9109	11050	9022	7844	1753	20596	8858	15252
1968	73424	94506	66968	65580	9369	10884	9189	7437	1983	22895	8587	15351
1969	80153	103791	72160	65195	9829	11492	10273	8380	2347	22381	7851	16011
1970	83857	113542	74351	66842	10794	12507	10497	9424	2354	24068	9018	16532
1971	89940	120427	74476	68077	12283	12261	10701	9779	2561	24435	10709	16436
1972	95359	123643	75454	67927	13773	12614	11692	10418	2750	23875	10271	17121
1973	103434	123227	82059	72357	13821	13495	12097	11304	3195	24874	11672	17577
1974	104762	111411	83733	70603	14370	14493	11026	11699	2824	23878	12267	17044
1975	98005	105514	77593	69200	13658	14227	9660	12394	2750	22837	13729	17571
1976	101205	109295	77630	70359	14180	14765	11315	11301	3122	22340	15118	17897
1977	99366	113208	79061	69102	14902	14783	11038	10906	3249	24518	15669	17370
1978	101446	118513	79560	71185	14295	15171	11160	10151	3862	25136	13912	16182
1979	104630	127082	84103	73176	14797	14783	11111	10457	4388	24704	13221	16905
1980	107374	130614	91422	69243	15238	15456	9711	11547	4245	24473	13023	17489
1981	105346	124347	88540	62608	15028	13006	7844	11797	4556	21925	15357	16471
1982	103901	117809	83942	66001	13801	12748	8400	12321	4404	21033	13667	16422
1983	100197	121527	83164	69321	13722	12170	8556	12822	4008	21468	14462	16726
1984	97593	122484	86869	75229	14012	12391	9658	12550	3901	22585	16045	17732
1985	100754	122554	88106	78235	14713	12481	10871	12916	3611	24161	12671	19035
1986	105281	126568	89484	79700	15255	13048	12731	12918	3564	25938	15704	19159
1987	109600	129291	94645	87278	15689	13806	12251	13620	3431	26218	15374	20619
1988	118983	135884	101029	100206	16626	15652	11444	15051	3519	28628	15481	21942
1989	126055	145585	106210	104451	17535	17777	11472	17023	3941	29738	14738	24329

Note: a/ Private sector only.

Source: ECE/DEAP Common Data Base.

(continued)

	Switzerland	U.S. a/	Canada	Greece	Portugal	Spain	Turkey	Japan	Cyprus	Malta
1960	10369	254270	21180	2254	2009	9444	2379	54179	...	...
1961	12000	253364	21179	2436	2130	11133	2461	69252	...	...
1962	13226	274092	22025	2641	2153	12400	2627	77088	...	...
1963	14193	292304	23012	2786	2468	13814	2750	85125	...	...
1964	15352	312127	26050	3362	2580	15889	2830	99359	...	...
1965	14973	343923	28999	3792	2850	18529	2900	102550	...	...
1966	14849	355897	32113	3913	3346	20889	3543	116245	...	...
1967	14870	347747	32009	3852	3540	22142	3770	136801	...	...
1968	15327	373002	32167	4674	3210	24231	4276	164000	...	...
1969	16238	387492	33906	5545	3498	26605	4549	194411	...	...
1970	17688	375619	34020	5469	3901	27390	5164	227191	...	...
1971	19431	402183	36692	6234	4284	26596	4908	236611	...	...
1972	20399	446456	38277	7196	4863	30810	5633	260312	...	...
1973	20990	483786	42076	7746	5327	35222	6374	293214	...	...
1974	20097	450783	44870	5766	4956	37563	7055	265374	...	...
1975	17369	398560	47477	5778	4396	36099	8799	262137	...	...
1976	15544	434080	49670	6172	4432	35383	10359	269130	249	167
1977	15795	495257	50704	6652	4964	35300	10765	279802	389	179
1978	16759	543555	52277	7050	5272	34474	9692	303709	488	173
1979	17613	563680	56739	7671	5201	32931	9345	319705	590	192
1980	19360	519406	62465	7175	5645	33372	8410	319815	621	194
1981	19825	524940	69825	6636	5956	32286	8553	329880	581	227
1982	19326	474730	62152	6509	6091	32448	8849	332535	603	260
1983	20115	513570	61707	6423	5656	31623	9114	331676	590	302
1984	20950	599802	63024	6060	4673	29791	9162	347958	717	281
1985	22059	631800	68984	6374	4507	31026	10693	368177	661	269
1986	23799	638039	73267	5976	4997	34125	11870	389707	614	246
1987	25568	650214	80823	5507	5750	39112	12530	430292	642	321
1988	27342	686337	89052	5992	6610	44667	12380	484343	682	341
1989	28977	697405	93097	6507	7106	50583	12281	537348	...	...

BIBLIOGRAPHY

Abbreviations and short description of frequently used sources:

AER = *American Economic Review*
AO = *Acta Oeconomica* (Hungarian academic journal in English)
CES = *Comparative Economic Studies*
CUP = Cambridge University Press
EB = *Economic Bulletin for Europe* (Annual survey, prepared by the United Nations Economic Commission for Europe)
EEE = *Eastern European Economics* (Journal of translations, published in Armonk (N.Y.))
EMM = *Ekonomika i matematicheskie metody* (Soviet academic journal)
EP = *Economics of Planning*
ESA = *Economic Survey of Asia and the Far East 19..* (Annual survey prepared by the United Nations Economic Commission for Asia and the Far East
ESE = *Economic Survey of Europe in 19..* (Annual survey, prepared by the United Nations Economic Commission for Europe
ET = *Economic Thought* (Series of the Institute of Economics of the Bulgarian Academy of Sciences in English)
Fi = *Figyelö* (Hungarian economic weekly)
Ga = *Gazdaság* (Hungarian academic journal)
GP = *Gospodarka Planowa* (Polish academic journal)
IM = *Ikonomicheska Mis'l* (Bulgarian academic journal)
JCE = *Journal of Comparative Economics*
JEC = U.S. Congress Joint Economic Committee
JPE = *Journal of Political Economy*
KJK = Közgazdasági és Jogi Könyvkiadó
KSZ = *Közgazdasági Szemle* (Hungarian academic journal)
MTA KTI = Magyar Tudományos Akadémia Közgazdaságtudományi Intézete (Institute of Economics of the Hungarian Academy of Sciences)
NBER= National Bureau of Economic Research
OUP = Oxford University Press
PSZ = *Pénzügyi Szemle* (Hungarian academic journal)
RC = *Revue d'études comparatives Est-Ouest*
RES = *The Review of Economic Statistics*
SE = ANSSSR *Seriya ekonomicheskaya* (Soviet academic journal)
SS = *Soviet Studies*
St = *Studies* (Series of the Institute of Economics of the Hungarian Academy of Sciences in English)
SSZ = *Statisztikai Szemle* (Hungarian academic journal)
VE = *Voprosy ekonomiki* (Soviet academic journal)
SEEFT= *Soviet and East European Foreign Trade* (Journal of translations, published in Armonk (N.Y.))
UN ECE= United Nations Economic Commission for Europe

Abel, I. - A. Chikán *et al.* (1989): "A készletek a makroökonómiai folyamatokban", in: Chikán *et al.* (1989) pp. 13-91.

Adam, J. (1989): *Economic Reforms in the Soviet Union and Eastern Europe since the 1960s*, London: Macmillan Press.

Aftalion, A. (1909): "La réalité des surproduction générales", *Revue d'économie politique*, No. 3.
----- (1927): "The Theory of Economic Cycles Based on the Capitalistic Technique of Production", *RES*, pp. 165-170.

Antal, L. - É. Várhegyi (1987): *Tökeáramlás Magyarországon* (Capital movements in Hungary), Budapest: KJK.

Antonov, V. (1987): "Nyakoi characteristiki na structurnite promeni v ikonomikata: prisposobimost i tsiklichnost v promyshlennosta" (On the characterization of economic structural change: adaptivity and the cyclical pattern of industrial productivity), *IM*, No. 5.

Arvay, J. (1973): *Nemzeti termelés, nemzeti jövedelem, nemzeti vagyon - Magyarország népgazdasági mérlegrendszere* (National product, national income, national wealth - The system of national accounts in Hungary), Budapest: KJK.

Ashton, B. - K. Hill *et al.* (1984): "Famine in China, 1958-1961", *Population and Development Review*, No. 4.

Avramov, R. (1986): "Typology of Business Cycles - Principles and Methods of Analysis", *ET*, pp. 135-151.
----- (1990a): "Tsiklichnosta v bylgarskata ikonomika: vnishni sokove i btreshni faktori" (The cyclical rhythm of Bulgarian economy: External shocks and internal factors), *IM*, No. 2, pp. 13-29.
----- (1990b): "Cycles in the Bulgarian economy: Theoretical and methodological foundations of the analysis", *ET*, pp. 25-37.

Bajt, A. (1969): "Fluctuations and Trends in Growth Rates in Socialist Countries", *Ekonomska Analiza*, No. 3-4,
----- (1971): "Investment Cycles in European Socialist Economies: A Review Article", *Journal of Economic Literature*, No. 1, pp. 53-63.
----- (1989): "Transformation of Investment Cycles into Business Cycles", in: Frateschi (1989a) pp. 1-20.
----- (1991): "Irrelevance of the Soft Budget Constraint for the Shortage Phenomenon", *EP*, No. 1, pp. 1-12.

Baran, P. A. (1952): "National Economic Planning", in: Haley (ed.) *A Survey of Contemporary Economics*, Vol. II., Homewood, Ill.: Richard D. Irwin. pp. 355-403.

Barancsi, É. - A. Gyulavári (1983): *Eröforrás-tartalékok a gazdaságban - A KSH adatszolgáltatási rendszere alapján* (Input slacks in the economy - Using the CSO data base), Budapest: Management GM.

Barát, M. - F. Gegesy (1981): "A folyamatban lévö beruházások néhány jellemzöje" (Certain characteristics of current investment projects), *Ga*, No. 3, pp. 43-53.

Barta, I. (1980): "Gondolatok a beruházások és a gazdasági fejlödés összefüggéseiröl" (Some thoughts on the investments and economic development), *Ga*, No. 4, pp. 59-72.

Bauer, T. (1977): *A beruházási volumen a közvetlen tervgazdálkodásban* (The volume of investment in the system of directive planning), Budapest: MTA KTI (Mimeo).
----- (1978): "Investment Cycles in Planned Economies", *AO*, No. 3, pp. 243-260.
----- (1981): *Tervgazdaság, beruházás, ciklusok* (Central planning, investment, cycles), Budapest: KJK.
----- (1988): "From Cycles to Crisis? Recent Development in East European Planned Economies and the Theory of Investment Cycles", *WIIW Forschungsberichte*, No. 136,

Bencze, L. (1990): "Farkas Mihály hadserege - A "legfontosabb" beruházások" (The army of Mihály Farkas - The most important investment projects), *Magyar Nemzet*, 12 February

Berend, I. (1972): "A beruházások népgazdasági tervezéséröl" (Planning of investments at macroeconomic level), *KSZ*, No. 10, pp. 1167-1186.
----- (1974): "Long-range Development Policy - Interrelations Between Economic Development and Capital Intensity", *AO*, No. 3-4, pp. 339-361.
----- (1983): "The Renewal Cycle of Fixed Assets under the Conditions of the 1980s in Hungary", *AO*, No. 3-4, pp. 401-412.

Berend, T. I. (1983): *Gazdasági útkeresés, 1956-1965 - A szocialista gazdaság magyarországi modelljének történetéhez* (Searching for a new path, 1956-1965 - The history of the Hungarian model of a socialist economy), Budapest: Magvetö Könyvkiadó.
----- (1988): *A magyar gazdasági reform útja* (The road of the Hungarian economic reform), Budapest: KJK.

Bergson, A. (1951): "Comment on Haberler (1949)", in: NBER (1951) pp. 387-396.

Berliner, J. S. (1956): "A Problem in Soviet Business Administration", in: Berliner (1988) pp. 47-60.
----- (1971): "Bureaucratic Conservatism and Creativity in the Soviet Economy", in: Berliner (1988) pp. 188-211.
----- (1988) (ed.) *Soviet Industry from Stalin to Gorbachev - Essays on Management and Innovation*, Ithaca: Cornell University Press.

Bernstein, A. H. (1989): *Soviet Defense Spending: The Spartan Analogy*, Santa Monica: Rand.

Bettelheim, C. (1987): "Les grands cycles de l'économie cubaine, 1959-1985", in: Chavance (1987a) pp. 241-262.

Birman, I. I. (1981): *Secret Incomes of the Soviet State Budget*, The Hague: Martinus Nijhoff Publishers.
----- (1988): "The Imbalance of the Soviet Economy", *SS*, No. 2, pp. 210-221.
----- (1989): "Rosefilde and My Cumulative Disequilibrium Hypothesis: A Comment", *SS*, No. 1, pp. 141-148.
----- (1990): "The Budget Gap, Excess Money and Reform", *Communist Economies*, No. 1, pp. 25-46.

Bogár, L. (1986): "A nagy "M" rejtélye" (The secret of the "M), *Fi*, 15 May
----- (1989): *Kitörési kísérleteink* (Hungarian attempts to break through), Budapest: KJK.

Boot, P. (1984): "Industrial Cycles in the German Democratic Republic and Professor Wiles' Thesis", *The ACES Bulletin*, No. 1, pp. 1-26.

Borosznói, V. - S. Puskás *et al.* (1978): "A beruházások ingadozása a mezögazdaságban" (Fluctuations of investments in agriculture), *KSZ*, No. 12, pp. 1466-1475.

Box, G. E. P. - G. M. Jenkins (1976): *Time Series Analysis, Forecasting and Control* (2nd ed.), San Francisco: Holden-Day.

Brabant, J. M. van (ed.) (1990): *Economic Reforms in Centrally Planned Economies and Their Impact on the Global Economy*, New York: United Nations.

Brada, J. (1986): "The Variability of Crop Production in Private and Socialized Agriculture: Evidence from Eastern Europe", *JPE*, No. 3. pp. 545-563.

Brainard, L. J. (1974): "A Model of Cyclical Fluctuations Under Socialism", *Journal of Economic Issues*, No. 1, pp. 67-81.

Breton, A. - R. Wintrobe (1986): "The bureaucracy of murder revisited", *JPE*, No. 5, pp. 905-926.

Bródy, A. (1956): "A hóvégi hajrá és gazdasági mechanizmusunk" (The end-of-month rush and our economic mechanism), *KSZ*, No. 7-8, pp. 870-883.
----- (1969a): "Cycles and Equilibrium", *European Economic Review*, No. 2, pp. 307-313.
----- (1969b): "The Rate of Economic Growth in Hungary, 1924-1965", in: Bronfenbrenner (1969) pp. 312-327.
----- (1972): "Zur Feinstruktur der Investitionszyklen" (Manuscript), Budapest.
----- (1978): "A Linearised Model of the Cycle", *AO*, No. 3, pp. 261-267.
----- (1980): *Ciklus és szabályozás - Kísérlet a klasszikus piac- és cikluselmélet matematikai modelljének megfogalmazására* (Cycle and control - An attempt of constructing the mathematical model of the classical market and business cycle theory), Budapest: KJK.
----- (1983a): "About Investment Cycles and Their Attenuation", *AO*, No. 1-2, pp. 37-51.
----- (1983b): *Lassuló idö* (The slowing time), Budapest: KJK.
----- (1989): "A kormányzás ára" (The price of governing), *Népszabadság*, 8 December
----- (1990): "Tünödés egy indulatos röpirat kapcsán" (Reflections on an emotional pamphlet), *Valóság*, No. 3, pp. 11-15.

----- (1991): "Defence of the realm", *AO*, No. 1-2, pp. 167-176.

Bronfenbrenner, M. (ed.) (1969): *Is the Business Cycle Obsolete?*, London: John Wiley & Sons.

Brown, C. (1982): "The Nazi Vote: A National Ecological Study", *The American Political Science Review*, pp. 285-302.

Bunce, V. (1980): "The Political Consumption Cycle: A Comparative Analysis", *SS*, No. 2, pp. 280-290.

Burns, A. F. - W. C. Mitchell (1946): *Measuring Business Cycles*, New York: NBER.

Castoriadis, C. (1981): *Devant la guerre*, Paris: Fayard.

Charemza, W. - G. Miroslaw (1988): *Plans and Disequilibria - Empirical Investigation for Poland*, Amsterdam: North-Holland.

Chavance, B. (ed.) (1987a): *Régulation, cycles et crises dans les économies socialistes*, Paris: ÉHESS.
----- (1987b): "Fluctuations et cycles économiques en Chine", in: Chavance (1987a) pp. 263-284.

Chelinski, R. (1964): "Etapowy charakter rozwóju gospodarczego w Polsce Ludowej" (Stagewise development in Poland), *Ekonomista*, No. 5, pp. 1032-1061.

Chikán, A. (ed.) (1988): *Eröforrás-tartalékok a vállalati gazdálkodásban* (Input slacks of enterprises), Budapest: KJK.
----- (ed.) (1989): *Készletek, ciklusok, gazdasági irányítás* (Inventories, cycles and economic control), Budapest: KJK.

Christin, E. D. - N. C. Short (1991): "Testing a Planners' Reaction Function Using Disequilibrium Model Excess Demand Indicators: The Case of Poland", *JCE*, pp. 122-131.

Chung, J. S. (1983): "Economic Planning in North Korea", in: Scalapino, R. A. - J. Kim (eds.) *North Korea Today - Strategic and Domestic Issues*, Berkeley: Institute of East Asian Studies, etc.

CIA (Central Intelligence Agency) (1982): *USSR: Measures of Economic Growth and Development, 1950-1980* in JEC, USSR: Measures of Economic Growth and Development, 1950-1980, Washington: U.S. Government Printing Office.
----- (1989): *Handbook of Economic Statistics 1989*, CIA.

Cobeljic, N. - R. Stojanovic (1961): "Prilog proucavanju investicionih ciklusa u socijalistickoj privredi" (Contribution to the theory of investment cycles in a socialist economy), *Ekonomist*, No. 4, pp. 487-511.
----- (1969): *The Theory of Investment Cycles in a Socialist Economy*, White Plains, NY: International Arts and Sciences Press.

Cohn, S. H. (1973): "Economic Burden of Defence Expenditures" JEC, *Soviet Economic Prospects for the Seventies*, Washington: U.S. Government Printing Office. pp. 147-175.

Comisso, E. (1986): "Introduction: state structures, political processes, and collective choice in CMEA states", *International Organisation*, No. 2, pp. 195-238.

Crane, K. (1988): "Military Spending in Czechoslovakia, Hungary and Poland", *JCE*, pp. 521-545.

Cuddy, J. D. A. - P. A. Della Valle (1978): "Measuring the Instability of Time Series Data", *Oxford Bulletin of Economics and Statistics*, No. Feb. pp. 79-85.

Czechowski, T. (1957): *Cyklicznosc procesu reprodukcji prostej* (Cycles in a system of simple reproduction), Warsaw.

Dahlstedt, R. (1979): "Cyclical Fluctuation under Central Planning: An Inquiry into the Nature and Causes of Cyclical Fluctuation in the Soviet Economy", *EP*, No. 1, pp. 1-17.
----- (1980): *Cyclical Fluctuation under Central Planning: An Inquiry into the Nature and Causes of Cyclical Fluctuation in the Soviet Economy*, Helsinki: The Helsinki School of Economics.

Dallago, B. (1987): "Les interprétations des fluctuations et des cycles dans les économies de type soviétique", in: Chavance (1987a) pp. 17-44.

Dickey, D. A. - W. A. Fuller (1979): "Distribution of the Estimators for Autoregressive Time Series with a Unit Root", *Journal of the American Statistical Association*, No. June, pp. 427-431.

Dimitrov, A. (1980): "Za inertsionnostta v ekonomikata" (On inertia in the economy), *EM*, No. 8, pp. 41-52.
----- (1987): "Za periodichnosta v ikonomikata" (On periodicity in the economy), *Ikonomika, matematichesko modelirovaniye v dneistvo* Sofia: Bulgarian Academy of Sciences. pp. 56-71.

Dobb, M. (1939): "A Note on Saving and Investment in a Socialist Economy", in: Dobb (1955) *On Economic Theory and Socialism*, London: Routledge & Kegan Paul.

Drechsler, L. (1983): *A gazdasági eredmények mérésének problémái* (The problem of measuring economic results), Budapest: Országos Tervhivatal Tervgazdasági Intézete (Mimeo).

Dyba, K. - T. Jezek (1990): "A központi tervezés tapasztalatai Csehszlovákiában" (Lessons from central planning in Czechoslovakia), *Gazdasági Fórum*, No. 1, pp. 95-104.

Dyker, D. A. (1983): *The Process of Investment in the Soviet Union*, Cambridge: CUP.
----- (1988): "Restructuring and "Radical Reform" - The Articulation of Investment Demand", in: S. J. Linz - Moskoff W. (1988) *Reorganization and Reform in the Soviet Union*, M.E. Sharpe, Inc.

Dziewulski, P. - A. Maciejewski (1980): "Nierównomiernosc inwestowania a ekspansja inwestycyjna" (Unbalanced investments and the expansion of investments), *GP*, No. 4, pp. 218-223.

Eckstein, A. (1960): "A Comment (on Professor Bendix's paper)", in: G. Grossman (ed.) *Value and Plan - Economic calculation and organisation in Eastern Europe*, Berkeley: University of California Press. pp. 262-266.
----- (1968): "Economic Fluctuations in Communist China's Domestic Development", in: Ho, Ping-ti. - T. Tsou (eds.) *China's Heritage and the Communist Political System*, Chicago: The University of Chicago Press. pp. 691-729.

Edvardsen, K. (1965): "Selection of Investment Projects from Given Aims for Economic Policy", *EP*, No. 1-2, pp. 10-28.

Ellman, M. (1989): *Socialist Planning* (2nd edition), Cambridge: CUP.

Eucken, W. (1950): *The Foundation of Economics - History and Theory in the Analysis of Economic Reality*, London: William Hodge and Company Limited.

Falter, J. W. (1978): "Theoretical and methodological problems of multilevel analysis reconsidered", *Social Science Information*, No. 6, pp. 841-870.

Faltsman, V. K. (1991): "Dinamika natsinalnogo bogatstvo SSSR" (The dynamics of national wealth of the USSR), *EMM*, No. 2, pp. 242-257.
----- (1989): "Statistika perestroyki i perestroyka statistiki" (Statistics of *perestroika* and restructuring of statistics), *SE*, No. 4, pp. 32-44.
----- - Ozhegov A. (1983): "Vybytie osnovnykh fondov: investitsionnye vozmozhnosti i ogranicheniia" (The Retirement of Fixed Capital: Investment Opportunities and Limitations), *VE*, No. 6, pp. 56-66.

Fazekas, K. (1988): "Munkaerőtartalékok", in: Chikán (1988) pp. 75-121.

Fekete, J. (1990): ""Coup" as a Method of Management - Crisis Management Methods in Hungary in the Eighties", *AO*, No. 1-2, pp. 55-72.

Fink, G. - J. Sláma (1976): "Le probleme du renouvellement du capital fixe dans quelques pays socialistes", *RC*, No. 4, pp. 113-139.

Firebauch, G. (1978): "A Rule for Inferring Individual-Level Relationships fro Aggregate Data", *American Sociological Review*, No. August, pp. 557-572.

Frateschi, C. (ed.) (1989a): *Fluctuations and Cycles in Socialist Economies*, Aldershot: Avebury.
----- (1989b): "Macroeconomic Stability and Cycles in Czechoslovakia", in: Frateschi (1989a) pp. 21-47.

Frickey, E. (1934): "The Problem of Secular Trend", *RES*, pp. 199-206.

Frisch, R. (1933): "Propagation Problems and Impulse Problems in Dynamic Economics", in : *Economic Essays in Honour of Gustav Cassel*, London: George Allen and Unwin Ltd. pp. 171-205.
----- (1967): "Investment Starting vs. Investment Sinking", *EP*, No. 3, pp. 219-231.

Friss, I. (1966): "Berend T. Iván könyvéröl" (On a book of Mr. Berend, I. T.), *KSZ*, No. 1, pp. 98-105.

Gács, J. - M. Lackó (1973): "A Study of Planning Behaviour on the National-Economic Level - An attempt at analysing a few correlations based on Hungarian data", *EP*, No. 1-2, pp. 91-119.

Garamvölgyi, I. (1988a): "Mi télen nyaralunk?" (Holidays in winter?), *Fi*, 4 February
----- (1988b): "Év végén minden kapható" (Year-end sales), *Fi*, 18 February

Gegesy, F. (1987): *A központi szándékok érvényesülése a beruházási folyamatokban* (The impact of central intentions in the investment process), (Manuscript), Budapest.

Gleitze, B. (1975): "Die Produktionswirtschaft der DDR im Wettbewerb mit der Westlichen Industriewelt", *Wirtschaft und Gesellschaft im Mitteldeutschland*, pp. 13-64.

Goldmann, J. (1964): "Fluctuations and Trend in The Rate of Economic Growth in Some Socialist Countries", *EP*, No. 2, pp. 88-98.
----- (1965): "Short- and Long-term Variations in the Growth Rate and the Model of Functioning of a Socialist Economy", *Czechoslovak Economic Papers*, No. 5, pp. 35-46.
----- (1973): *Od nestability k stabilite ekonomického rustu v CSSR* (From unbalanced towards balanced economic growth in Czechoslovakia), Praha: Ekonomicky ústav CSAV (Mimeo).
----- - J. Flek (1967): "Vlnovity pohyb v tempu rustu a cyklus v dynamice zásob" (Fluctuation of economic growth and the inventory cycle), *Plánované hospodárství*, No. 9,
----- - K. Kouba (1969): *Economic Growth in Czechoslovakia*, White Plains - Prague: IASP-Academia.

Gordon, R. A. (1961): *Business Fluctuations* (2nd edition), New York: Harper and Row, Publishers.

Granick, D. (1987): *Job Rights in the Soviet Union: Their Consequences*, Cambridge: CUP.

Green, D. W. (1977): "The Use of Econometric Methods in the Analysis of Centrally Planned Economies: The SRI-WEFA Experience", *JCE*, pp. 259-275.
----- (1978): "Capital Formation in the USSR, 1959-1974: An Econometric Investigation of Bureaucratic Intervention in the Process of Capital Construction", *RES*, No. 1, pp. 39-46.

Gregory, P. R. (1990): *Restructuring the Soviet Economic Bureaucracy*, Cambridge: CUP.

Griliches, Z. (1986): "Economic Data Issues", in: Z. Griliches - M. D. Intrilligator (ed.) *Handbook of Econometrics*, Amsterdam: North Holland. pp. 1466-1514.

Grosfeld, I. (1984): "Fluctuations du taux de croissance de l'investissement dans les économies à planification centralisée", *RC*, No. 3, pp. 105-124.
----- (1986): "Endogenous Planners and the Investment Cycle in the Centrally Planned Economies", *CES*, No. 1, pp. 42-53.
----- (1987): "Modelling Planners' Investment Behaviour: Poland, 1956-1981", *JCE*, pp. 180-191.

Gruszczynski, M. - G. W. Kolodko (1975): "Regularnosc wahan tempa wzrostu gospodarczego" (The regularity of fluctuations in the rate of economic growth), *GP*, No. 7-8, pp. 421-429.

Haberler, G. (1951): "Business Cycles in a Planned Economy", in: NBER (1951) pp. 375-387.

Hajdú, O. (1986): "A beruházások koncentrációjának vizsgálata" (The concentration of investment projects), *SSZ*, No. 3, pp. 234-260.

Hanson, P. (1978): "Mieczkowski on Consumption and Politics. A Comment", *SS*, No. 4, pp. 553-556.

Harvey, A. C. (1990): *Forecasting, structural time series models and the Kalman filter*, Cambridge: CUP.

Havas, P. (1975): "A beruházások kivitelezési ideje rövidítésének néhány kérdése" (Some questions concerning the shortening of completion of investment projects), *PSZ*, No. 7, pp. 548-557.

Henschel, G. (1990): "Zur kritischen Analyse der Entwicklung des Planungssystems in der DDR", *Wirtschaftswissenschaft*, No. 5, pp. 670-683.

Hicks, J. (1965): *Capital and Growth*, Oxford: Clarendon Press.

Hildebrandt, G. G. (ed.) (1985): *Rand Conference on Models of the Soviet Economy*, Santa Monica: Rand.
----- (1991): *Models of the Military Sector in the Soviet Economy*, Santa Monica: Rand.
----- - P. B. Staugaard (1991): *The Changing Soviet Priority Economy: Modelling the Conflict Between Gold and the Sword*, Santa Monica: Rand

Hoch, R. - B. Martos *et al.* (1965): "Planning the rate of increase in consumption", *EP*, No. 3, pp. 19-29.

Horvat, B. (1975): "Short-Run Instability and Long-Run Trends in The Yugoslav Economy's Development", *EEE*, No. 1, pp. 3-31.

Hough, J. F. (1985): "Debates About the Postwar World", in: S. J. Linz (ed.) *The Impact of World War II on the Soviet Union*, Totowa, N. J.: Rowman and Allanheld Publishers. pp. 253-280.

Hutchings, R. (1971): *Seasonal Influences in Soviet Industry*, Oxford: OUP.

----- (1976): "Recent Trends of Seasonality in Soviet Industry and Foreign Trade", *Jahrbuch der Wirtschaft Osteuropas*, pp. 247-285.

Ickes, B. W. (1986): "Cyclical Fluctuations in Centrally Planned Economies: A Critique of the Literature", *SS*, No. 1, pp. 36-52.
----- (1989): "Cyclical Fluctuations in Centrally Planned Economies: Some Cross Country Considerations", in: Frateschi (1989a) pp. 105-129.
----- (1990): "Do Socialist Countries Suffer a Common Business Cycle ?", *RES*, No. 3, pp. 397-405.

Janacek, K. - V. Klaus (1970): "Uvod do zkoumaní inflace v ceskoslovenské ekonomice - emprická cast" (An introduction into the investigation of inflation in the Czechoslovak economy - empirical part), *Politická ekonomie*, No. 4, pp. 289-312.

Jánosi, A. - G. Kepecs *et al.* (1980): "A nagyberuházások költségütemezésének vizsgálata" (Cost scheduling of large investment projects), *SSZ*, No. 3, pp. 261-275.
----- - G. Pál (1983): "Az 1970-es évek 150 beruházásának költségütemezése" (Cost scheduling of 150 investment projects in the 1970s), *SSZ*, No. 3, pp. 244-260.

Judik, J. - R. Nötel (1949): "Statistical Investigation of Capital Formation", *Schweizerische Zeitschrift für Volkswirtschaft und Statistik*, No. 2, pp. 145-164.

Kalecki, M. (1954): *Theory of Economic Dynamics - An Essay on Cyclical and Long-Run Changes in Capitalist Economy*, London: George Allen and Unwin Ltd.

Kaser, M. C.- E. A. Radice (eds.) (1985): *The Economic History of Eastern Europe 1919-1975*, Vol. I., Oxford: Clarendon Press.
----- - A. Schnytzer (1977): "Albania - A Uniquely Socialist Economy", in: JEC, *East European Economies Post Helsinki*, Washington: U.S. Government Printing Office.

Kemme, D. M. (1989): "The Chronic Shortage Model of Centrally Planned Economies", *SS*, No. 3, pp. 345-364.

Kendall, M. G. - A. Stuart (1966): *The Advanced Theory of Statistics*, London: Charles Griffin and Company Limited.

Kennan, G. F. (1962): *Russia and the West Under Lenin and Stalin*, New York: New American Library.

Keynes, J. M. (1936): *The General Theory of Employment, Interest and Money*, Cambridge: CUP [1973].

Khanin, G. (1988): "Ekonomichesky rost: alternativnaya ocenka" (Economic growth - an alternative assessment), *Kommunist*, No. 17, pp. 83-90.

Khudokormov, G. N. (1967): *Political Economy of Socialism*, Moscow: Progress Publishers.

Klacek, J. *et al.* (1989): *Makroeknomická analyza a prognostické scénáre* (Macroeconomic analysis and prognostic scenarios), Praha: Ekonomicky Ustav CSAV.

Klaus, V. (1985): "Rozestavenost investicní vystaby, model i empirická analyza" (Unfinished constructions, model and empirical analysis), *Finance a úvér*, No. 3, pp. 152-162.
----- (1988) "Socialist Economies, Economic Reforms and Economists: Reflections of a Czechoslovak Economist." Paper presented at the conference *Alternative Models of Socialist Economic Systems*, Györ (Hungary), 18-22 March 1988.
----- - T. Jezek (1989): "The Czechoslovak Economy (The evolutionary approach)", *Financial Times*, 13 December

Kliszko, A. (1967): "Próba weryfikacji hipotezy wystepowania ogolnego cyklu inwestycyjnego w polsce ludowej" (An attempt to verify the hypothesis of a general investment cycle in Poland), *GP*, No. 7, pp. 8-15.

Kohn, M. J. - R. E. Leggett (1986): "A Look at Soviet Capital Retirement Statistics: Unravelling Some Mysteries?", *CES*, No. 2, pp. 21-36.

Kolodko, G. W. (1979): "Fazy wrostu gospodarczego w Polsce" (Phasis of economic growth in Poland), *GP*, No. 3, pp. 137-143.
----- (1986): "Economic Growth Cycles in the Centrally Planned Economies - A Hypothesis of the "Long Cycle", *University of Illinois BEBR Faculty Working Paper*, No. 1280,
----- (1987): "Development Goals and Economic Macroproportions", *EEE*, No. 3, pp. 72-85.

Kontorovich, V. (1989): "Inflation in the Soviet Investment and Capital Stock", *SS*, No. 2, pp. 319-329.

Kornai, J. (1980): *Economics of Shortage*, Amsterdam: North-Holland.
----- (1982): *Growth, Shortage and Efficiency - A Macrodynamic Model of the Socialist Economy*, Oxford: Basil Blackwell.
----- (1984): *Bürokratikus és piaci koordináció* (Bureaucratic and market coordination), Budapest: Akadémiai Kiadó.
----- (1985): "On the Explanatory Theory of Shortage: Comments on Two Articles by K. A. Soós", *AO*, pp. 145-162.
----- (1990): *The Road to A Free Economy -Shifting from a Socialist System - The Example of Hungary*, New York and London: W.W. Norton and Company.

Kotowicz-Jawor, J. (1979): "Presja inwestycyjna w rozwoju gospodarczym" (Investment pressure in economic development), *GP*, No. 3, pp. 144-148.

Kovács, J. - T. Tarján (1988): "Cycle and Replacement", *AO*, No. 3-4, pp. 325-340.
----- - I. Virág (1981): "Periodic versus Continuous Growth", *AO*, No. 1-2, pp. 41-51.

Központi Statisztikai Hivatal (1966): *Ipari adattár* (Vol. I) (Compendium of industrial data), Budapest: KSH.
----- (1967): *Beruházási adattár, 1950-1966* (Compendium of investment data, 1950-1966), Budapest: KSH.

----- (1973): *Beruházási adattár, 1950-1971* (Compendium of investment data, 1950-1971), Budapest: KSH.
----- (1977): *Beruházásstatisztika* (Investment statistics), Budapest: KSH.
----- (1979): *Beruházási adattár, 1950-1977* (Compendium of investment data, 1950-1977), Budapest: KSH.
----- (1983): *A statisztikai fogalmak meghatározásának jegyzéke* (A list of statistical definitions), Budapest: KSH.
----- (1990): *A gazdaság fejlödésének föbb mutatói 1988* (Main indicators of economic development in 1988), Budapest: KSH.

Krasovskii, V. P. (1967) Problemy ekonomiki kapitalnych vlozhenii (Economic problems of capital formation), Moscow: Ekonomika.

----- (ed.) (1978): *Faktor vremeny v planovoi ekonomike* (The time factor in the planned economy), Moscow: Ekonomika.

----- (1979) "Investitsionnaia politika i rekonstruktsia", *Ekonomika i organizatsiia promyshlennogo proizvodstva*, No. 4. pp. 79-61.

Kravis, I. B. *et al.* (1975): *A System of International Comparisons of Gross Product and Purchasing Power*, Baltimore: World Bank and The Johns Hopkins University Press.
----- *et al.* (1982): *World Product and Income - International Comparisons of Real Gross Product*, Baltimore: The Johns Hopkins University Press.

Kupka, V. (1983): *Investice A Ekonomycky Rust v CSSR* (Investment and economic growth in the CSSR), Academia Praha.

Kyn, O. - W. Schrettl (1979): "Growth Cycles in Centrally Planned Economies: An Empirical Test", in: O. Kyn - W. Schrettl *et al.* (ed.) *On the Stability of Contemporary Economic Systems*, Göttingen: Vandenhoeck und Ruprecht. pp. 109-132.

Lackó, M. (1980): "Cumulating and Easing of Tensions (A simple model of the cyclical development of investments in Hungary)", *AO*, No. 3-4, pp. 357-377.
----- (1986): *Feszültségek és normák szerepe a beruházás szabályozásában Magyarországon, 1961-1980* (The role of strains and norms in the Hungarian investment process, 1961-1980), Budapest: MTA KTI (Mimeo).
----- (1990): "The Role of Tensions and Norms in Investment Control", *St*, No. 33,

Lafay, J.-D. (1981): "Empirical Analysis of Politico-economic Interaction in East European Countries", *SS*, No. 3, pp. 386-400.

Laki, M. (1980): "End-year Rush-Work in Hungarian Industry and Foreign Trade", *AO*, No. 1-2, pp. 37-65.

Lange, O. R. (1943): *Working Principles of the Soviet Economy*, New York: Russian Economic Institute.
----- (1971): *Political Economy* (vol. 2), Oxford: Pergamon Press.

----- (1969): *Theory of Reproduction and Accumulation*, Warsaw:
----- (1978): *Introduction to Econometrics* (4th edition), Oxford: Pergamon Press

Levine, H. S. (1969): "Comment on Nove", in: Bronfenbrenner (1969) pp. 303-311.

Lippi, M. - L. Reichlin (1991): "Trend-cycle decompositions and measures of persistence: Does time aggregation matter?", *The Economic Journal*, No. March, pp. 314-323.

Lissowska, M. (1987): "Les fluctuations de l'investissement et de la productivité des facteurs en Pologne et en Hongrie", in: Chavance (1987a) pp. 123-144.

Liu, S. C. (1958): "Report on the Work of the Central Committee of the Communist Party of China to the Second Session of the Eighth National Congress" (quoted in Eckstein (1968)

Liu, T.-C. (1959): "Structural Changes in the Economy of the Chinese Mainland, 1933 to 1952-1957", *AER*, No. 2, pp. 84-93.

Major, I. (1983): "The Years 1978-1981 and the "Long Stages" in the Development of the Hungarian Economy", *AO*, No. 3-4, pp. 381-400.

Malinvaud, E. (1969): *Méthodes statistiques de l'économetrie* (2nd edition), Paris: Dunod.

Marrese, M. (1977): *Hungarian investment fluctuations: A theoretical and econometric study of hierarchical decision-making* (PhD thesis), Graduate Faculty of the University of Pennsylvania.
----- (1981): "The Bureaucratic Response to Economic Fluctuation: An Econometric Investigation of Hungarian Investment Policies", *Journal of Policy Modelling*, No. 2, pp. 221-243.

McCauley, M. - S. Carter (eds.) (1986): *Leadership and Succession in the Soviet Union*, Houndmills: Macmillan.

McFarlane, B. (1984): "Political Crisis and East European Economic Reforms", in: P. G. Lewis (ed.) *Eastern Europe: Political Crisis and Legitimation*, London: Croom Helm. pp. 176-199.

Mieczkowski, B. (1978): "The Relationship Between Changes in Consumption and Politics in Poland", *SS*, No. 2, pp. 262-269.

Mihályi, P. (1983): "Das ungarische Model", *Ost-Europa Wirtschaft*, No. 2. pp. 138-146.
----- (1987): "La synchronisation des fluctuations de l'investissement en Europe de l'Est, 1950-1985", in: Chavance (1987a) pp. 197-220.
----- (1988a): "Common Patterns and Particularities in East European Investment Cycles", *SS*, No. 3, pp. 444-459.
----- (1988b): "Cycle or Shocks: East European Investments, 1950-1985", *EP*, No. 1-2, pp. 41-56.
----- (1989a): "A beruházási ciklusok 'anyagi alapjáról'" (On the "material foundation" of investment cycles), *KSZ*, No. 7-8, pp. 951-962.
----- (1989b): "A beruházások mérésének csapdái" (Traps of measuring investments), *SSZ*, No. 7, pp. 653-662.

----- (1989c): "Common Patterns and Particularities in East European Investment Cycles", in: Frateschi (1989a) pp. 84-104.

Minc, B. (1962): "Problem nierównomiernosci wzrostu w gospodarce socjalistycznej" (Problem of the non-uniform growth in the socialist economy), *Ekonomista*, No. 3, pp. 499-508.

Montias, J. M. (1962): *Central Planning in Poland*, New Haven: Yale University Press.
----- (1967): *Economic Development in Communist Rumania*, Cambridge: The M.I.T. Press.
----- (1976): *The Structure of Economic Systems*, New Haven: Yale University Press.

Moorsteen, R. - R. P. Powell (1966): *The Soviet Capital Stock, 1928-1962, Homewood*, Illin: Richard D. Irwin, Inc.

Morgenstern, O. (1965): *On the Accuracy of Economic Observations* (2nd edition), Princeton: Princeton University Press.

Nachtigal, V. (1989): *Príspevek k problematice kvantifikace agregátu hruby domácí produkt za CSSR* (Contribution to the problem of quantifying GDP for the CSSR), Praha: Ekonomicky Ustav, CSAV.

Narkiewicz, O. A. (1986): *Eastern Europe, 1968-1984*, London and Sydney: Croom Helm.

NBER (1951): *Conference on Business Cycles*, New York: NBER.

Nelson, C. R. (1985): "Macroeconomic time series, business cycles, and macroeconomic policies (A Comment)", *Carnegie-Rochester Conference Series on Public Policy*, pp. 55-60.
----- - H. Kang (1981): "Spurious Periodicity in Inappropriately Detrended Time Series", *Econometrica*, No. May,
----- - C. I. Plosser (1982): "Trends and Random Walks in Economic Time Series: Some Evidence and Implications", *Journal of Monetary Economics*, pp. 139-162.

Neményi, I. (1975): *A magyar beruházási politika 30 éve* (Thirty years of Hungarian investment policy), Budapest:KJK.

Notkin, A. I. (1961): *Tempy i proportsii sotsialisticheskogo vosproizvodstva* (The rates and proportions of socialist reproduction), Moscow:

Nove, A. (1960): "Some Observations on Professor Olivera's Article", *Kyklos*, pp. 256-260.
----- (1969): "Cyclical Fluctuations under Socialism" in : Bronfenbrenner (1969) pp. 287-302.
----- (1977): *The Soviet Economic System*, London: George Allen and Unwin Ltd.
----- (1989): "The Investment Process in the USSR", *Berichte des Bundesinstitutes für ostwissenschaftliche und internationale Studien*, No. 53,

Nuti, D. M. (1985): "Political and economic fluctuations in the socialist system", *European Institute Working Paper*, No. 156,

Nutter, G. W. (1962): *Growth of Industrial Production in the Soviet Union*, Princeton:

OECD (1987): *Purchasing Power Parities and Real Expenditures 1985*, Paris: OECD.

Olivera, J. H. G. (1960): "Cyclical Economic Growth Under Collectivism", *Kyklos*, pp. 229-255.

Ortona, G. (1987): "Régulation et fluctuations cycliques de l'investissement en U.R.S.S.", *RC*, No. 2, pp. 92-113.
----- (1989): "A Model of Political Business Cycle in a Soviet-type Economy", in: Frateschi (1989a) pp. 130-146.

Pacsi, Z. (1979): "A megvalósítási idö alakulása és szerepe a beruházásokban" (Lead times in investments and their significance), *PSZ*, No. 8-9, pp. 628-638.

Pálfi, J. (1989): "Kapacitástartalékok", in: Chikán (1989) pp. 40-74.

Paraskewopoulos, S. (1985): *Konjunkturkriesen im Sozialismus*, Stuttgart, N.Y.: Gustav Fischer Verlag.

Petö, I. - S. Szakács (1985): *A hazai gazdaság négy évtizedének története, 1945-1985. I. - Az újjáépítés és a tervutasításos irányítás idöszaka* (The history of four decades in the Hungarian economy, 1945-1985 Vol.I. - The period of reconstruction and direct planning), Budapest: KJK.

Pindyck, R. S. - D. L. Rubinfeld (1981): *Econometric Models and Economic Forecasts* (2nd edition), Auckland: McGraw-Hill International Book Company.

Pitzer, J. S. - A. P. Baukol (1991): "Recent GNP and productivity trends", *Soviet Economy*, No. Jan-March, pp. 46-82.

Plosser, C. I. (1989): "Understanding Real Business Cycles", *Journal of Economic Perspectives*, No. 3, pp. 51-77.

Podkaminer, L. (1985): "Investment Cycles in Centrally Planned Economies: An Explanation Invoking Consumer Market Disequilibrium and Labour Shortage.", *AO*, No. 1-2, pp. 133-144.
----- (1989): "Theory of investment cycles in the centrally planned economies. An economic reinterpretation", *WIIW Forschungsberichte*, No. 158.

Popper, K. R. (1965): *Conjectures and Refutations: The Growth of Scientific Knowledge*, New York: Harper & Row Publishers.

Portes, R. (1969) "A Comment on Bródy (1969)", in: Bronfenbrenner (1969) pp. 328-331.

Przybylski, P. (1991): *Tatort Politbüro - Die Akte Honecker*, Berlin: Rowohlt.

Rappaport, P. - L. Reichlin (1989): "Segmented trends and non-stationary time series", *The Economic Journal*, pp. 168-177.

Roland, G. (1987a): "Investment Growth Fluctuations in the Soviet Union: An Econometric Analysis", *JCE*, pp. 196-206.

----- (1987b): "Régulation et fluctuations cycliques de l'investissement en U.R.S.S.", *RC*, No. 2, pp. 93-113.

Röpke, W. (1936): "Socialism, Planning, and the Business Cycle", *JPE*, No. 3, pp. 318-338.

Rosefielde, S. (1990): "Soviet Defence Spending: The Contribution of the New Accountancy", *SS*, No. 1, pp. 59-80.

Rostowski, J. - P. Auerbach (1986): "Storming Cycles and Economic Systems", *JCE*, pp. 293-312.
----- (1988): "Intra-year Fluctuations in Production and Sales: East and West", in: P. J. D. Wiles (1988) pp. 82-111.

Sabov, Z. (1983): *Zyklische wirtschaftliche Aktivitätschwankungen in Sozialistischen Planwirtschaften - Eine systematisierung ihrer Ursachen anhand der vorhandenen Erklärungsversuche*, Berlin: Verlag Duncker & Humblot.

Salvini, G. (1989): "Economic Fluctuations in China", in: Frateschi (1989a) pp. 48-60.

Sanders, A. J. K. (1987): *Mongolia - Politics, Economics and Society*, London: Frances Pinter & Lynne Rienner.

Sapir, J. (1987): "Cycles économiques et relations entre l'investissement, l'emploi et la productivité dans le cas de l'URSS: un modele", in: Chavance (1987a) pp. 159-182.
----- (1989): *Les fluctuations économiques en URSS, 1941-1985*, Paris: Éditions de l'ÉHESS.

Sárkány, P. (1988): "A "címkézett" forintok problémái" (The problems of "earmarked" forints), *Ga*, No. 3, pp. 82-89.

Sawyer, M. C. (1985): "The Economics of Michal Kalecki", *EEE*, No. 3-4,

Scott, M. F. (1989): *A New View of Economic Growth*, Oxford: Clarendon Press.

Screpanti, E. (1985): "A model of the political economic cycle in centrally planned economies", *European University Institute Working Paper*, No. 201.

Selyunin, V. (1989): A Profound Reform or the Revenge of the Bureaucracy, *Problems of Economics*, March.
----- (1989): "Dangers from Delaying Economic Reform", *Socialisticheskaya Industriya*, 6 April

Shabad, T. (1979): "The BAM, Project of the Century", in: JEC, *Soviet Economy in a Time of Change*, Vol. I., Washington: U.S. Government Printing Office, pp. 164-176.

Shapkarev, P. (1979): *Proizvostvenijat ritm v narodnoto stopanstvo na NRB* (The productive rhythm of the Bulgarian economy), Sofia: Nauka i izkoustvo.

Shimakura, T. (1982): "Cycles in the Chinese Economy and their Politicio-Economic Implications", *The Developing Economies*, No. 4, pp. 374-389.

Simon, A. (1981): "A magyarországi beruházások ciklusainak egy modellje" (A model of Hungarian investment cycles), *KSZ*, No. 3,

Simonovits, A. (1987a): "Investment Cycles: A New Interpretation of an Old Model", *AO*, No. 1-2, pp. 155-164.
----- (1987b): "A stop-go beruházási ciklus" (Stop-go investment cycles), *KSZ*, No. 9, pp. 1027-1034.
----- (1989): "Hidden Investment Cycles in Socialist Economies", *Scandinavian Journal of Economics*, No. 3, pp. 583-597.
----- (1990): *Ciklus és stagnálás - A szocialista gazdaság makroökonómiai modellcsaládja* (Cycle and stagnation - A family of macro-models for the socialist economy), Budapest: MTA KTI (Mimeo).
----- (1991a): "Investment Limit Cycles in a Socialist Economy", *EP*, No. 1, pp. 27-46.
----- (1991b): "Investments, Starts, and Cycles in Socialist Economies: A Mathematical Model", *JCE*, No. 3, pp. 460-475.

Slutzky, E. (1937): "Summation of Random Causes as the Source of Cyclic Processes", *Econometrica*, pp. 105-146.

Smyshliaeva, L. (1983): "Sovershenstvovanie vosproizvodstvennoi struktury kapital'nykh lozhenii" (Improving the structure of reproduction of capital investment), *VE*, No. 9, pp. 25-35.

Soós, K. A. (1976): "Causes of Investment Fluctuations in the Hungarian Economy", *EEE*, No. 2, pp. 25-36.
----- (1978): "Some General Problems of the Hungarian Investment System", *AO*, No. 3, pp. 223-242.
----- (1983a): "The Problem of Time Lags in the Short-Term Control of Macroeconomic Processes", *AO*, No. 3-4, pp. 369-380.
----- (1983b): *Gazdasági reformok és rövid távú makroökonómiai szabályozás* (Economic reforms and short term macroeconomic control), Budapest: MTA KTI (Mimeo).
----- (1984): "A Propos the Explanation of Shortage Phenomena: Volume of Demand and Structural Inelasticity", *AO*, pp. 305-320.
----- (1985): "A Rejoinder", *AO*, pp. 163-167.
----- (1986): *Terv, kampány, pénz - Szabályozás és konjunktúraciklusok Magyarországon és Jugoszláviában* (Plan, campaign, money - Control and business cycles in Hungary and Yugoslavia), Budapest: KJK.
----- (1987): "Informal Pressures, Mobilization, and Campaigns in the Management of Centrally Planned Economies", *EP*, No. 1, pp. 39-48.
----- (1988): "A pénz szerepe a szocialista gazdaságok ciklusainak leszálló ágában" (The role of money in the downward phase of cycles in socialist economies), *Tervgazdasági Fórum*, No. 1, pp. 19-33.
----- (1989) "Regular Investment Cycles or Irregular Investment Fluctuations under Central Planning?", in: Frateschi (1989a) pp. 61-83.

Spenser, H. (1914): *Principles of Sociology*, New York: Appleton and Co.

Stalin, J. V. (1925): *Works*, (Vol. 7), Moscow: Foreign Languages Publishing House [1954].

Staller, G. J. (1964): "Fluctuations in Economic Activity: Planned and Free-Market Economies, 1950-1960", *AER*, No. 6, pp. 385-394.

Stankiewicz, T. (1991): "Investment Under Socialism", *Communist Economies*, No. 2, pp. 123-138.

Stark, A. (1980): *A szocialista tervgazdálkodás nemzetközi gyakorlata* (The international experience of socialist planning), Budapest: KJK.

Suba-Varga, J. (1986): ""Foreign Trade Constraint" and Cyclical Development", *AO*, No. 3-4, pp. 251-270.
----- (1987): "Foreign Trade Constraint in the Socialist Economy - The case of Hungary", *St*, pp. 31.
----- (1988): "The «Foreign Trade Limitation» and Cyclical Growth", *SEEFT*, No. Fall, pp. 6-30.

Summers, J. A. (1990): "The Macroeconomic Correlates of Investment Growth in the Soviet Union", *SS*, No. 4, pp. 795-809.
----- (1991a): "An Empirical Analysis of Industrial Investment Fluctuations in the Soviet Union: 1962-1988", *CES*, No.
----- (1991b): "Investment Under Socialism: A Comparative Study of the USSR and Poland", *Communist Economies and Economic Transformation*, No. 2, pp. 235-250.
1, pp. 103-128.

Sutela, P. (1988): "Soviet Investments and the Decline of Economic Growth", *Nordic Journal of Soviet & East European Studies*, No. 2, pp. 99-115.

Szabó, J. (1988): "Review of "A. K. Soós: Terv, kampány, pénz", *AO*, No. 3-4, pp. 388-395.

Szakolczai, G. - G. Bagdy *et al.* (1987): "The Dependence of the Hungarian Economy on the World Economy: Facts and Consequences", *SEEFT*, No. 1, pp. 54-88.

Székffy, K. (1978): "Relations Between Wages and Productivity in the Hungarian Industry Between 1950-1974", *AO*, No. 1-2, pp. 73-89.

Tarján, T. (1988): Beruházási ciklusok és ráfordítási megoszlások (Investment cycles and cost structures), (Manuscript), Budapest.
----- - G. Tényi (1976): "Kísérlet a beruházási folyamat modellezésére" (Experiment for Modelling the Investment Procedure), *Szigma*, No. 1-2, pp. 11-24.

Tényi, G. (1976): *Beruházási egyenetlenségek a magyar népgazdaságban* (Unevenness of investments in the Hungarian economy, Budapest: MTA KTI (Mimeo).

Timár, J. (1988): *Idö és szabadidö* (Time and leisure time), Budapest: KJK.

Tsygichko, A. N. - T. N. Nikolaeva (1989): "Noviy podchod k otsenke srednih srokov prodolzhityelnosty storitelstva predpriyatiya i obiektov" (A new approach in estimating the average construction time of enterprises), *SE*, No. 4, pp. 65-75.

Ungvárszki, A. (1986): *GazdaságPOLITIKAI ciklusok Magyarországon 1946-1986* (Economico--Political Cycles in Hungary (1946-1986), Budapest: MTA KTI (Mimeo).
----- (1989): *GazdaságPolitikai ciklusok Magyarországon* (1948-1988), Budapest: KJK.

United Nations (1977): *Comparison of the System of National Accounts and the System of Balances of the National Economy*, New York: UN.
----- (1986): *National Accounts Statistics: Main Aggregates and Detailed Tables, 1983*, New York: UN.
----- (1989a): *National Accounts Statistics: Main Aggregates and Detailed Tables, 1986*, New York: UN.
----- (1989b): *Basic Methodological Principles Governing the Compilation of the System of Statistical Balances of the National Economy* (Vol I. and II.), New York: UN.
----- - Commissions of the European Communities (1987): *World Comparisons of Purchasing Power and Real Product for 1980*, New York: UN.

UN ECE (1955): "The Economy of Hungary, 1950 to 1954", *EB*, No. 2, pp. 85-110.
----- (1956): "The Planning and Finance of Investment in the Soviet Union and Eastern Europe", *ESE* in 1955, pp. 198-247, A1-A6, Geneva: UN.
----- (1966): "A Fifteen-year Review of Investment and Output in Eastern Europe and the Soviet Union", *EB*, No. 1. pp. 31-64.
----- (1987): "Aspects of Capital Formation in Manufacturing Industry", *ESE* in 1986-1987, pp. 72-101.

United Nations Economic Commission for Asia and the Far East (1958): *ESA 1957*, Bangkok: UN.

United Nations Library (1972): *Catalogue of Periodicals, Annuals and Special Series Currently Received at the United Nations Library*, Geneva: UN.

U.S. Department of Commerce, Bureau of the Census (1975): *Historical Statistics of the United States*, Washington, D.C.: U.S. Department of Commerce.

Vajda, M. (1989): *Orosz szocializmus Közép-Európában* (Russian socialism in Central Europe), Budapest: Századvég Kiadó.

Vargha, J. (1986): "Beruházni vagy fenntartani?" (Investment or maintenance?), *Fi*, 17 July

Vesselinov, R. (1991): "Trends and regularities in the economic development of Bulgaria", *Bulgarian Quarterly*, No. 2, pp. 85-100.

Vincentz, V. (1980): "Planungszyklen: Eine Untersuchung des Planungs- und Produktionsverhaltens in sozialistischen Wirtschaften", *Working Papers* No. 67., München: Osteuropa-Institut.

Virén, M. (1985): *Some Aspects of Economic Growth in Western Europe and North America* (Manuscript), Geneva.

Westfall, G. (1986): *Bibliography of Official Statistical Yearbooks and Bulletins*, Alexandria, VA: Chadwyck-Healey Inc.

Wiles, P. J. D. (1962): *The Political Economy of Communism*, Cambridge, Ma: Harvard University Press.
----- (1968): *Communist International Economics*, Oxford: Basil Blackwell.
----- (1982): "Are There Any Communist Economic Cycles?", *The ACES Bulletin*, No. 2, pp. 1-20.
----- (ed.) (1988): *The Soviet Economy on the Brink of Reform* (Essays in Honor of Alec Nove), Boston: Unwin Hyman.

Will, G. (1987): "Vietnam 1975-1979: Vom Krieg zu Krieg", *Mitteilungen des Institutes für Asienkunde* (Hamburg), No. 156.

Willett, T. D. (ed.) (1988): *Political Business Cycles*, Durham: Duke University Press.

Winiecki, J. (1982): "Investment Cycles and an Excess Demand Inflation in Planned Economies: Sources and Processes", *AO*, No. 1-2, pp. 147-160.
----- (1986): "Distorted Macroeconomics of Central Planning", *Banca Nazionale Del Lavoro Quarterly Review*, No. 157, pp. 197-223.
----- (1988): *The Distorted World of Soviet-Type Economies*, London: Routledge.

Zala, J. (1968): "1958-1697: The Economic Trends of a Decade", *AO*, pp. 133-144.

Zhuravlev, S. N. (1987): "Tsykli obnovleniya osnovnych fondov" (Fixed assets cycles), *EMM*, No. 4, pp. 618-633.

INDEX

International Studies in Economics and Econometrics

1. T. Harder: *Introduction to Mathematical Models in Market and Opinion Research.* With Practical Applications, Computing Procedures, and Estimates of Computing Requirements. Translated from German. 1969 ISBN 90-277-0096-6
2. A.R.G. Heesterman: *Forecasting Models for National Economic Planning.* 2nd rev. and ext. ed. 1972 ISBN 90-277-0224-1
3. A.R.G. Heesterman: *Allocation Models and Their Use in Economic Planning.* 1971 ISBN 90-277-0182-2
4. M. Durdağ: *Some Problems of Development Financing.* A Case Study of the Turkish First Five-Year Plan (1963-1967). 1973 ISBN 90-277-0267-5
5. J.M. Blin: *Patterns and Configurations in Economic Science.* 1973 ISBN 90-277-0203-7
6. A.H.Q.M. Merkies: *Selection of Models by Forecasting Intervals.* Translated from Dutch. 1973 ISBN 90-277-0342-6
7. H.C. Bos, M. Sanders and C. Secchi: *Private Foreign Investment in Developing Countries.* A Quantitative Study on the Evaluation of the Macro-Economic Effects. 1974 ISBN Hb 90-277-0410-4; Pb 90-277-0439-2
8. R. Frisch: *Economic Planning Studies.* A Collection of Essays. Selected, introduced and edited by Frank Long, with a Preface by Jan Tinbergen. 1976 ISBN Hb 90-277-0245-4; Pb 90-277-1194-1
9. K.L. Gupta and M. A. Islam: *Foreign Capital, Savings and Growth.* An International Cross-Section Study. 1983 ISBN 90-277-1449-5
10. C.A. van Bochove: *Imports and Economic Growth.* 1982 ISBN 90-247-3052-X
11. O. Bjerkholt and E. Offerdal (eds.): *Macroeconomic Prospects for a Small Oil Exporting Country.* 1985 ISBN 90-247-3183-6
12. D. Weiserbs (ed.): *Industrial Investment in Europe.* Economic Theory and Measurement. 1985 ISBN 90-247-3270-0
13. J.-M. Graf von der Schulenburg and G. Skogh (eds.): *Law and Economics & The Economics of Legal Regulation.* 1986 ISBN 90-247-3377-4
14. S. Pejovich (ed.): *Socialism: Institutional, Philosophical and Economic Issues.* 1987 ISBN 90-247-3487-8
15. R. Heijmans and H. Neudecker (eds.): *The Practice of Econometrics.* Studies on Demand, Forecasting, Money and Income. In Honor of Jan Salomon Cramer. 1987 ISBN 90-247-3502-5
16. A. Steinherr and D. Weiserbs (eds.): *Employment and Growth.* Issues for the 1980s. In Honor of Albert Kervyn de Lettenhove. 1987 ISBN 90-247-3514-9
17. M.J. Holler (ed.): *The Logic of Multiparty Systems.* 1987 ISBN 90-247-3515-7

18. J.M. van Brabant: *Regional Price Formation in Eastern Europe.* Theory and Practice of Trade Pricing. 1987 ISBN 90-247-3540-8
See also below under Volume 23
19. A.M. Wesselman: *The Population-Sample Decomposition Method.* A Distribution-Free Estimation Technique for Minimum Distance Parameters. 1987 ISBN 90-247-3603-X
20. P. Coffey (ed.): *Main Economic Policy Areas of the EEC - Toward 1992.* The Challenge to the Community's Economic Policies when the 'Real' Common Market is Created by the End of 1992. 3rd rev.ed., 1990 ISBN 0-7923-0810-7
21. A. Breton, G. Galeotti, P. Salmon and R. Wintrobe (eds.): *The Competitive State.* Villa Colombella Papers on Competitive Politics. 1991 ISBN 0-7923-0835-2
22. S. Pejovich: *The Economics of Property Rights.* Towards a Theory of Comparative Systems. 1990 ISBN 0-7923-0878-6
23. J.M. van Brabant: *Remaking Eastern Europe.* On the Political Economy of Transition. 1990 ISBN 0-7923-0955-3
24. J.M. van Brabant: *Privatizing Eastern Europe.* The Role of Markets and Ownership in the Transition. 1992 ISBN 0-7923-1861-7
25. J.M. van Brabant: *Integrating Eastern Europe into the Global Economy.* Convertibility through a Payments Union. 1991 ISBN 0-7923-1352-6
26. G.W. Kołodko, D. Gotz-Kozierkiewicz and E. Skrzeszewska-Paczek: *Hyperinflation and Stabilization in Postsocialist Economies.* 1991 ISBN 0-7923-9179-9
27. P. Mihályi: *Socialist Investment Cycles.* Analysis in Retrospect. 1992 ISBN 0-7923-1973-7

KLUWER ACADEMIC PUBLISHERS – DORDRECHT / BOSTON / LONDON